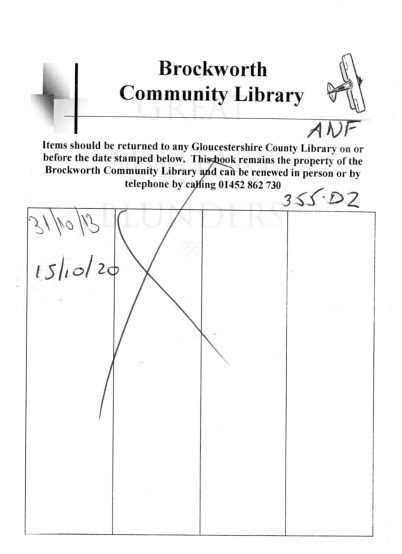

# GREAT MILITARY BLUNDERS

## GEOFFREY REGAN

This edition published by PAST TIMES, Oxford, England.

First published in 2000 by Channel 4 Books
This edition published 2000 by Channel 4 Books
an imprint of Macmillan Publishers Ltd
25 Eccleston Place London SW1W 9NF
Basingstoke and Oxford

www.macmillan.co.uk

Associated companies throughout the world.

ISBN 0 7522 1898 0

9 8 7 6 5 4 3 2 1

A CIP catalogue record for this book is available from
the British Library.

Designed by Dan Newman/Perfect Bound Design
Colour reproduction by Aylesbury Studios Ltd, Kent
Printed by New Interlitho, Spa, Milan

This book accompanies the television series *Great Military Blunders*
made by Darlow Smithson for Channel 4.
Executive Producer: David Darlow

PAST TIMES®

# DEDICATION

For Andy May

# ACKNOWLEDGEMENTS

To say that this book is a joint effort is an understatement. Over 200 experts contributed to the television programme and I was allowed to use the transcripts of their interviews for this book. As a result I had a veritable mountain of material from which to choose, literally a pile of historical wisdom of biblical proportions which drowned my own puny efforts as Pharaoh's army in the Red Sea (an early blunder).

Although I have written extensively on the subject of military blunders myself – probably a million words of my own – there were times in this project when I felt like a very greedy 'Little Jack Horner' sitting in the corner and pulling out plums by some of the legends of the profession, like Richard Holmes, Max Hastings, Martin Middlebrook and . . . my pen is petrified with embarrassment and does not know when to stop. Thank you all, ladies and gentlemen, for helping with the programme and with the book.

Thanks also go to Charlie Carman, Emma Tait and Kate Aaron at Channel 4 Books for tolerating my 'blunderbuss' approach to writing.

I would also like to thank the good folk at Darlow Smithson who helped flavour me as 'meat in the sandwich' displayed in the canteens of two different worlds: one, as Series Consultant for a television documentary series and second, as an author in the world of book publishing. Particular thanks go to David Darlow and John Smithson for taking up the idea of 'blunders' in the first place and next to the four directors, Kate English, Peter Bate, Jeremy Lovering and Heenan Bhatti who translated an idea into the reality of a successful television series.

My thanks go in addition to the members of the four teams who worked on the programmes, including Tim Altman, Erika Dodd, Dominic Sutherland, Kate Shepherd, Emma Jessop, Frederic Casella and Helen Britton. Coping with the demands of an insatiable author was handled with supreme diplomacy by Maxine Carlisle and by her assistants Madeline Eaton, Jane Macaulay and Alison Moody. Finally, I cannot miss the opportunity to thank the indefatigable Daphne Walsh who typed thousands of pages of transcript and as a result could make a fair case for being Series Consultant for any future series of *Military Blunders*.

# CONTENTS

# INTRODUCTION

✄

In an age where selection for military command is more careful and scientific than ever before, where hi-tech weapons have allegedly given soldiers far greater precision in target selection, and where professional training has made the average soldier far more efficient, it is frightening to find that military blunders occur as frequently as ever. Ironically, it is in the field of 'friendly fire' that the graph rises most rapidly, and in the infliction of unintended civilian casualties by smart weapons and precision bombing. 'Smart', 'precision' and 'clinical' are the modern buzz words, but they are merely words with no greater guarantee of helping soldiers do their jobs properly than the orders previously barked at them by their NCOs. Today one would hardly expect to encounter senior command officers who believed they were pregnant with elephants or who could not rise from their beds because they believed their legs had turned to glass. Nor would one find officers who were too fat, old, myopic, rheumatic or decrepit to ride their horses, as was not uncommon in the past. While such a parade of freaks, blimps and noodles might once have filled a book of blunders to the amusement of the uninitiated and the despair of the professionals, they do so no more. Today they have been replaced by managers, penpushers and specialists in everything but handling soldiers and their weapons. Promotion by weight, length of teeth, notoriety and bribery has long since gone, but there are now far too many chiefs and not enough Indians, in the opinion of Colonel David Hackworth:

*The number of people that are back in the rear has consistently grown larger and larger, and so America is in a position today where they have more colonels than they have machine gunners; they have more computer operators than they have anti-tank warriors. If America were to go to war, they would find themselves having to gum the enemy to death because it's virtually toothless, because it's got this great huge logistics tail.*

In the first chapter of the book we examine the problem that the 'Peter Principle' has brought to the military profession, namely unfitness to command as a result of over-promotion. Professor John Potter has described what happens in battle when stress levels overcome a commander:

*One of the first signs of somebody getting under pressure and not managing effectively in a situation is when they lose the ability to handle the big picture. They focus on little details; they lose emotional contact with the reality of what's happening at the front line, and almost work in a world of their own.*

The most famous example of this happened to the French Marshal Achille Bazaine at the Battle of Vionville in 1870. Bazaine, a man promoted to supreme command through his renowned courage in the lower ranks, could not cope with the burden of responsibility, left his staff and went AWOL for an hour, leaving the whole army without direction. When found by his staff officers, he was quietly siting a field gun and commanding its crew. Professor Potter records a more modern example:

*I can recall a very senior officer who was managing a terrorist situation, and the demands grew and the pressure came on that commander, and all he could do was to concentrate on tidying his desk.*

The second chapter examines the problems of military planning, which attempts to place an inflexible order on what is essentially a chaotic activity: war. Major-General Julian Thompson experienced an example of the friction of war that would have taxed a lesser man.

*I can remember, for example, in the Falklands War planning to do a move by helicopter, and the helicopters were being brought in a ship called the* Atlantic Conveyor. *I was sitting in my command post putting the final touches to the plan when a man thrust his head through the flap and said: 'Atlantic Conveyor's gone to the bottom taking all the helicopters with her.' So it was tear it up and start again.*

The outcome was the phrase beloved of British tabloids - 'yomping'. The British 'yomped' to Port Stanley. Flexibility won the day.

The third chapter covers painting the wrong picture by underestimating the enemy, often a product of ethnocentrism and much associated with colonial warfare. The following chapter looks at the way in which hubris on the part of great commanders can undermine their efficiency and often wreck what had hitherto been a glittering career. Julian Thompson reflects on the dangers of too much ego on the part of such senior officers:

*I think the worst thing that you can ever do is imagine that the whole thing's been laid on for your benefit and that this is going to give you a step up into some higher rank. What you actually should be thinking about is the people you command and how you're going to defeat the enemy, and not be worrying about how you're going to present yourself.*

War may be the continuation of politics by other means, as the German military strategist Clausewitz tells us, but once a military solution is undertaken, the politicians must take a back seat and leave the operation to the experts. In the twentieth century there have been more meddling ministers, backseat drivers and sawdust Caesars than ever before, and at a time when the conduct of war has become more complex. As a result, blunders on a hitherto undreamed-of scale have flowed from the minds of such pseudo-soldiers as Winston Churchill, Adolf Hitler, Benito Mussolini and Margaret Thatcher.

In the final chapter, we see that military technology has offered warriors false gods, and the opportunities for new forms of military incompetence. We see that unjustified belief in the effectiveness of a piece of technology, as with the Patriot missile in the Gulf War and the precision-bombing campaign in Kosovo, can result in avoidable disasters. In other cases, technology emboldens a commander into taking risks he otherwise would shun, as with the first-day assault on the Somme in 1916, which resulted from a presumed successful artillery bombardment. The unexpected side effects of military technology are examined in the use of the herbicide Agent Orange in Vietnam.

# CHAPTER ONE

# UNFIT TO LEAD

## THE 'PETER PRINCIPLE'

What is it about the military profession that attracts men, and increasingly women, as mankind enters a new millennium? Professor John Potter of Exeter University offers a suggestion:

*Why is it that people want to become generals, why do people want to become senior military officers or indeed why do people want to enlist in organisations where there is a real risk of dying? I think there are many reasons. Certainly in the past family influences were very strong, if your father or your grandfather was in a regiment then socially and in family terms I suspect there's quite a bit of pressure for you to follow in their footsteps. As a child the early socialization, as we call it, would have introduced you to the feeling that that was the natural thing to do, so that's a predictable reason why people want to go into the military, want to become senior officers. But what about those people who join the military when they don't have a family background? What are their personality characteristics? What is it that they're looking for? Well I suspect in many cases there is an image that's been created — whether it's created by the media, by films, by books or whatever — but I suspect a lot of people are attracted by the image and for many people the reality is not the same as the image. However, in terms of personality it's going to be those individuals who like to operate within a fairly clear-cut structure. Now there's been a lot of talk over the years that we have the so-called authoritarian personality that is attracted to the military, I suspect that may have been the case in the past.*

Psychologist Norman Dixon has memorably demonstrated in his *On the Psychology of Military Incompetence*, how the 'Peter Principle' has operated within the military profession, so that all too often promotion to high military command has gone to men unsuited to it. For, as John Potter shows, the military profession is an unforgiving one compared with any other.

*Compared to most human situations, senior military people have a tremendous responsibility to bear. For example in most organizations, in most ways that human beings work together, it's unlikely that you're going to be ordering your subordinates, the people you work with, your colleagues, to a possible death, yet this is the situation that the military leader faces. So how does the military leader come to terms with that; maybe they use denial, maybe they refuse to actually admit that anyone is going to get killed or injured.*

As Norman Dixon has shown, many worthy middle-rank officers have been elevated above their levels of competence and this has resulted in many cases of military incompetence, particularly in the last two centuries. Physical courage in battle frequently led to promotion during the past in spite of the Duke of Wellington's famous condemnation of 'gallant officers.' Too many British generals got to the top on the back of a Victoria Cross earned in some colonial skirmish where youthful impetuosity was mistaken for military capacity. Such commanders continued to do in high command what they knew best and what served them so well – acting rather than thinking and flinging lives away in re-enactments of the Charge of the Light Brigade on battlefields from New Zealand to Canada.

Major-General Julian Thompson believes that the 'Peter Principle' continues to operate even today, in a world of scientific selection procedures:

*I'm absolutely positive that people do get promoted sometimes several levels above their capability, either because they proved themselves absolutely first class in a previous situation, where they haven't been tested and, therefore they're promoted, or because they've rumbled the system, if you like. They have done terribly well, say, at staff college or in some staff job, working for someone who is able to give them a leg up the tree and they've not actually been tested.*

Promotion in the US army can result from all the wrong reasons in terms of efficiency in combat as Julian Thompson also relates:

*The ticket-punching business I think is appalling. One saw it, of course, particularly in Vietnam with the Americans where they did a*

△ General Buller encounters eccentric British general Sir Charles Warren taking his morning bath to entertain the troops before the battle of Spion Kop.

*year, under a year sometimes, as commanding officer in order to have their ticket punched, so that they could move on up the ladder. I think its totally reprehensible. I have come across people who are commanders who I know were ticket-punching and couldn't wait to get out of the job they were in, in case they made a nonsense of it and it was going to ruin their careers.*

In this chapter we will examine military leaders who, for one reason or another, proved to be unsuited to high command. Although united by failure or disaster these generals and admirals possessed different personalities, abilities and career experiences. Their responses to military disaster illustrate, additionally, the essential difference between military incompetence and military errors, between blunders and setbacks. The ability to learn from mistakes is essential if a military career is to be successful. To err is human, to continue to err is incompetent.

# TWILIGHT OF THE 'GOD OF BATTLES'

⚔

Rarely can a career as successful as that of General Sir Redvers Buller, VC, commander-in-chief of the British army in the Second Boer War, have disintegrated with such startling rapidity. This 'veritable God of battles', as a contemporary called him, revealed himself to an astonished British public to have feet of clay. Defeat after defeat at the hands of untrained Boer farmers and farmboys during the Second Boer War attended his efforts and he was eventually recalled with his reputation so tarnished that even his own soldiers, who had loved him as few commanders had ever been loved by their men, cruelly dubbed him 'Sir Reverse Buller'. How could it have happened? How could a man whose career as a junior officer had been a model for others to follow fail so completely?

Redvers Henry Buller was born in 1839, the second son of a niece of the Duke of Norfolk and a wealthy Devonshire squire. His father was a shy but conscientious man, who was much loved by his tenants, and Redvers was brought up in an atmosphere of loving piety, becoming so attached to his mother that her influence was to stay with him throughout his life. Indeed, as Norman Dixon has pointed out, when he became commander of an army in South Africa in 1899 he took on traits of his internalized mother and became over-protective to his men. In common with many Victorian gentleman of his age his schooling was attended with as much violence to his person as attention to his intellectual needs. Even at the tender age of seven he suffered beatings at school from a teacher who brought a whip to class with him. Redvers was, on one occasion, 'thrashed within an inch of his life' for running down a nearby street ringing all the doorbells. Moving on to Harrow at the age of thirteen Redvers promptly ran into trouble with the authorities again, this time for painting several masters' doors red. He was transferred to Eton, where his studies continued, though without much effecting his intellectual development. By the time he left Eton's hallowed halls he was a large, clumsy, red-faced country boy, without any of the intellectual skills necessary to make him a 'thinking soldier' on the French or German models. Although he possessed no great intelligence, Redvers had a powerful and obstinate nature. On one occasion, after cutting his leg so badly that a surgeon wanted to amputate it, he resolutely refused to allow the operation to take place, even at the risk of his life.

The death of his mother, when he was only sixteen, was a major formative event in his life. Redvers was devoted to her as both his ideal of womanhood and the authority figure he needed, and he carried her photograph everywhere with him. In 1855 she was taken so ill at Exeter railway station that she could not be moved and a bed was set up for her in a waiting room. For three days Redvers sat by her bedside, hoping against hope that his mere presence could hold death at bay, but in vain. When her death was followed, just six months later, by that of his beloved sister Julia, Redvers suffered a loneliness that could find no remedy in civilian life. In searching for a new mother, like so many other lost souls, he found the regular army with its tight regimental system offering him a refuge. In 1858 Buller bought a commission in the 60th Rifles.

His introduction to army life was hardly auspicious. The nineteenth-century officer corps was filled with snobs who found Redvers an unsophisticated and obstinate country clodhopper. But he was not the sort of man to take kindly to ridicule, being quicker with his fists than with his tongue, and those who met him in his early days in the army remember his sharp, little eyes and his furious temper. In arguments Redvers was obstinate and obtuse, rarely matching the logic of his opponents but outstaying them by sheer doggedness. Enormously strong, he proved time after time that what he lacked in intelligence he made up for with physical force. Serving in Canada as a captain, Buller once rescued two of the regimental hounds from snowdrifts by placing a dog under each arm and snowshoeing his way to safety. On another occasion he saw two exhausted troopers struggling under the weight of an enormous basket of provisions. Buller simply hoisted the basket onto his own shoulders and marched off without another word.

During the Red River campaign in Canada in 1870, Redvers served under his longtime friend and mentor Sir Garnet Wolseley, who was much impressed by not only his strength but the way he identified with the men under his command, winning their respect and cooperation. Buller's simplicity and directness was appreciated by all his men. As a fellow officer wrote, his men realized that 'his interests were identical with their own, that there was no barrier of class distinction between them, that he could do everything better than they could'. And above all, behind the tough even ferocious exterior of the man, there was a very tender heart.

Buller had so impressed Wolseley that his career now advanced by leaps and bounds. The general took him as his intelligence officer on the Ashanti Campaign in 1873 and from then on Buller was firmly wedded to the circle of officers – 'The Ashanti Ring' – which surrounded Sir Garnet Wolseley. The following year Redvers inherited his father's estate, on the death of his elder brother, and became a wealthy man. In 1878 he went to South Africa as commander of a unit of Light Horse and fought with great distinction in both the Kaffir and the Zulu Wars. His reckless courage in the terrible events of the latter war made him a household name in Britain. In the fighting around Inhlobana Mountain, Redvers rescued two wounded soldiers from the advancing Zulu impi, rode out again and brought in a riderless officer and then, not content with that, charged out into the ranks of the Zulus to rescue a wounded lieutenant. For his valour he was awarded the Victoria Cross, earning the title 'the Bayard of South Africa'. In battle his huge figure terrified the Zulus, who thought him a devil or an evil spirit, as he charged them, reins held in his teeth, revolver in one hand and a Zulu knobkerry (warclub) in the other. His eccentricities won him the affection of all his men: parading around camp in shirtsleeves and carpet slippers – hardly the model of a nineteenth-century British officer.

On his return to Britain, though still only a colonel, he was feted as much as the army commanders. Invited to Balmoral by Queen Victoria, he won the admiration of his monarch as easily as he had won that of his men. The queen wrote of him that he was 'a grand soldier, who has shown an amount of bravery and power of indefatigable work hardly to be surpassed'. On returning to his home town of Crediton, the townspeople unharnessed the horses and dragged his carriage through the streets to his home. Few Roman commanders had returned to a greater triumph. Yet the British people can hardly be blamed for not asking questions about Buller's suitability for higher command. In military circles he was viewed as 'the coming man' in whom the British nation could feel confident in entrusting its safety. Yet apart from his popularity with the men, his physical strength and his courage, Redvers had not been asked to apply his mind to commanding an army in battle. He had not been asked to think, he had been content to do – and he had done very well, so far.

In 1885, during the expedition to relieve General Gordon at Khartoum, Buller found himself in command of the Desert Column, on the death of Sir Herbert Stewart. For the first time he faced the problems of acting on his own initiative. With nobody to lean on, Buller lost his swagger and became tentative. In spite of his physical strength and force of character, Buller concealed a soft and passive nature when confronted with the need to make decisions involving the lives of his men. He was a prisoner of a deep, underlying uncertainty both about his masculinity and his ability to

A romanticized view of the battle of Spion Kop in 1900. The British had few opportunities for fighting at close quarters as the Boers relied on superior marksmanship to defeat their professional opponents.

◁ The truth of Spion Kop. Faulty generalship by Buller and Warren left British troops trapped beneath Boer positions and unable to entrench because of the rocky terrain and the lack of shovels.

command. Advised by Wolseley to attack the Mahdist town of Metemmeh he seemed to lose his nerve and ordered a withdrawal after a week of indecision. A more thorough scrutiny of Buller's performance in this minor campaign might have saved the British army much suffering fifteen years later. What is apparent now is just how much Buller's abilities had been overestimated. In fact Buller was aware of his own limitations: he was an executive officer not a director. As he wrote, the job that suited him best was:

*...one that involved all the responsibilities of execution without those of invention and preliminary organization. I never have credited myself with much ability on the inventive side; all mine, if I have any, is on the executive side, and possibly if I have a strong point it is resource, which is a great help in organization.*

But if Buller knew himself others continued to exaggerate his military abilities; Gladstone said that Joshua 'couldn't hold a candle to Redvers Buller as a leader of men', while Viscount Esher commented, 'Buller is said to be the best man in the British Army.'

Between 1886 and 1899 Buller lived upon a reputation that he had done little to warrant. In a Europe dominated by Prussian and French military thinkers, Buller was a pygmy, whose reputation had been won in colonial wars, against poorly armed savages, where his kind of daring had been enough. But against European opponents, armed with modern rifles and artillery he had no experience and no clear understanding of the issues involved. Traditional views of the superiority of the British footsoldier, fighting with a bayonet, would prove a catastrophic philosophy for use in future European warfare. Professor Ian Beckett of the University of Luton explains the difficulties Buller faced as he rose in the military profession:

*There is a difference between command and leadership. Leadership tends to be interpreted as the actions of junior officers. Command is where the senior officers take over, so there's a distinction between command and leadership. Buller is a great leader of men, it doesn't make him a great commander. The problem I think is that Buller is not a good butcher because he doesn't like casualties which is you know an understandable and in many respects an admirable trait, but one which in war doesn't necessarily enable you to get the job done. He's also not a good butcher because he doesn't sack people.*

Twelve years of deskwork ravaged the powerful figure of Redvers Buller, turning him into the kind of blimp – with

walrus moustache, double-chin and red face – beloved of cartoonists. He dined too well – his appetite was as legendary as his courage – and his predilection for champagne was notorious. In South Africa he had a specially constructed cast-iron kitchen which was dragged laboriously along in company with his wagons of champagne wherever his duties took him. Buller became obese through over-eating. Under stress he suffered from a psychosomatic disorder: eating as an oral gratification of his need to identify with his mother.

In 1899 his best days were behind him and yet his greatest challenge lay ahead. In the military manoeuvres of that year, held at Aldershot, Buller, who had not commanded troops for twelve years, made such a mess of things that the whole matter had to be hushed up. His conduct of the manoeuvres was comically inept: no trenches were dug for fear of damaging the countryside, no man was allowed to dive for cover lest he damage his uniform, and the soldiers – for simplicity's sake – eventually had to resort to volley firing at each other in the open and at ranges of less than three hundred feet. To cap it all, the manoeuvres could only take place between 9am and 5pm so that they did not interfere with the officers' social diaries. At one moment Buller ordered his troops to make a full frontal assault against a powerful defensive position, forgetting that the men had just completed a 14-mile route march and were too exhausted to attack anybody. Most of them were thoroughly winded, and sat down to take a rest. Not surprisingly the manoeuvres had to be abandoned as a fiasco.

This did no good to Buller's self-confidence. He had simply had it confirmed in the most embarrassing way that although he held the seniority for command he did not have the ability that went with it. He knew it and anybody watching the Aldershot fiasco should have known it as well. His appointment to command in the Second Boer War, Britain's first major war for half a century, was as unkind as Lord Auckland's decision to appoint a sick cripple, suffering from rheumatoid arthritis, in the shape of sixty-year old General William Elphinstone to force the Kyber Pass and subdue Afghanistan in 1840. At first Buller modestly refused the command but, reminded of his duty, accepted with the comment, 'I will do my best.'

What surprised observers in 1899 was the way in which Buller seemed to have changed. The man who had an actual lust for battle, had lost that vital spark. The 'God of Battle' was now in his dotage; a harmless, dithering old man; a figure of fun to his enemies. In place of the Spartan life of a junior officer, came such 'gigantic meals of rich fare, washed down by quantities of Veuve Cliquot that the wagon-train of food and champagne which followed him on active service became a byword in the Army'. Buller was past his sell-by date as Ian Beckett describes:

△ Sir Redvers Buller, nicknamed the 'God of Battles' in his prime, ended his career with the sobriquet 'Sir Reverse Buller'.

*He was not the right man to command a large army and in fact he did not want the job at all. It is clear from the very beginning that he disliked that assignment. I mean he said that in effect he didn't want to go. There's this extraordinary episode when just three days after he lands in Cape Town, he actually writes a letter to his brother, Tremayne, where he sets out in advance of any operations a kind of defence of his position, almost in a sense that he expected to fail. Now that's not the best basis on which you begin a campaign. He'd always said himself*

*that he would have much preferred to have been chief of staff to somebody, Wolseley or maybe even Evelyn Wood. He wasn't comfortable with a supreme command. The larger picture of the war was something that I think was beyond Buller's capability. He's a likeable man, there are many aspects of his character which are quite endearing, but he probably wasn't the man to command in South Africa.*

On his arrival in South Africa, Buller planned to relieve the besieged towns of Ladysmith, Kimberley and Mafeking. Within a week his forces had suffered three disastrous defeats. At Colenso, Buller had controlled the battle himself and had, in between sandwiches, overseen a farce during which the British artillery had spent hours bombarding an empty landscape before abandoning their guns on an open plain. Next a British brigade had been drilled in full view of the enemy before advancing in parade-ground order straight into massed rifle fire from entrenched Boers. Finally, the British had charged straight into the swollen River Tugela and dozens of men were drowned. The lucky ones were dragged out by the Boers and made prisoners. With 8,000 of his men uncommitted, Buller spent the remainder of the battle sending small parties of volunteers on suicidal missions to save the guns. Seven Victoria Crosses were awarded, almost all posthumously.

Overwhelmed by his experiences at Colenso, Buller abrogated his responsibilities becoming 'umpire at manoeuvres' by handing over command at the battle of Spion Kop to one of the maddest men ever to fill the rank of British general – Sir Charles Warren – ex-police commissioner and the man who had failed to trap Jack the Ripper. Warren was both eccentric and incompetent, and Buller knew this when he entrusted an army of 25,000 men to his command. For no apparent reason Buller agreed with Warren's decision to capture Spion Kop. At night 2,000 men with just twenty shovels climbed the steep hillside, watched by at least 20,000 redundant British soldiers. In the darkness the assault troops believed they had reached the top but at first light they found they were overlooked by Boer positions on three sides. With no communication with the men on the hill Buller and Warren did nothing while their men were mown down by the Boers, suffering nearly 1,200 casualties to the Boers' 198. Buller's letter to his wife summed up the British war effort so far under his command; 'We were fighting all last week, but old Warren is a duffer and lost me a good chance.'

Buller was a good-hearted soul but he lacked the killer touch, particularly when it came to his incompetent generals. When Lord Roberts took over it was as much a relief for him as for his country. The 'Peter Principle' had exacted a heavy price in British lives for over-promoting a brave but essentially kind English gentleman, more at home on his estates in Devon than on the battlefields of South Africa.

# GOERING'S FLIGHT OF FANCY

A German historian has observed that at the start of the Second World War Germany possessed 'the Navy of Imperial Germany, the Army of eighteenth-century Prussia and the Air Force of National Socialism'. It is a shrewd analysis of how Germany lost the war yet for former American Ambassador to Luxembourg John Dollibois, who met the Nazi leaders before their trials at Nuremburg in 1945, it does not go far enough. For him the problems of the *Luftwaffe* went far deeper, and were inextricably linked with the personality of its leader, Hermann Goering. John Dollibois maintains from his personal contacts with the Reichsmarschal, that Goering:

> *. . was a clown. I was curious from the psychological standpoint with the dressing up in a Roman toga which he did or dressing up in the Reichsmarshal's uniform of course, the equivalent of a seven-star general, the highest military rank in the history of the world. He wore jewellery, he collected emeralds and they weren't just modest rings, he had a ruby and an emerald and a diamond ring that were fabulous. He had one particular emerald which was about an inch in length and half an inch wide, the biggest emerald I had ever seen and probably the biggest in existence and his decorations were not silver or gold, they were platinum. His* Pour le Merité*, the highest military award which he received for his bravery during World War One was diamond encrusted; his watches were solid gold, encrusted with jewellery and all of that was part of his show and he had to wear that along with his Reichsmarshal's uniform.*

Goering's vanity was legendary. He often tried to brief his air staff during stag hunts and dictated letters between shots. According to one biographer, 'Among the dark Satanic forests of pine, beech and oak, Goering felt like a Teutonic knight of old. He would carry a spear' and be dressed in 'red

△ Goering inspecting German troops in 1939. He wore the uniform of a seven-star general, a rank higher than any commander in history.

top boots of Russian leather with golden spurs, in floor length coats like a French emperor, in silk blouses with puffy sleeves.'

While Hitler lived an almost puritan lifestyle, often claiming to be inspired by the hardships of camp life experienced by Prussian king Frederick the Great, the sybaritic Goering seemed to ape the Roman emperor Heliogabalus in his love of fantastic excess. While his deputy, Edward Milch, tried to organize a modern and efficient air force, he was thwarted at every step by the theatricality of the Reichsmarschal, who held command through political contacts rather than any military capability, as Dr Hörst Boog, Senior Director of Research in Military History for the Federal German Armed Forces, shows:

*I already said that Goering was a military leader because he just led a squadron in World War One and his rise later on was a political rise and the* Luftwaffe *was always considered the Nazi* Luftwaffe *because Goering was considered to be a politician. Although he had a military rank he was considered to be a politician you know.*

The battle honours of Hermann Goering read like a contents

list in a book of military blunders. His cancellation of plans for the German four-engined bomber during the 1930s robbed the *Luftwaffe* of the chance to destroy London in 1940 and Soviet industry behind the Urals in 1941. Both were potentially war-winning operations. In May 1940 his promise to Hitler to destroy the British forces in the Dunkirk pocket with air power alone allowed the Royal Navy to evacuate a third of a million Allied troops, without which the pressure on Churchill to make peace may have proved irresistible. At the start of the Battle of Britain Goering's failure to concentrate his attacks on the British radar stations resulted in defeat for the *Luftwaffe*.

*It was a very strange relationship between Hitler and Goering. In the later years of the war when the* Luftwaffe *just faded Hitler shouted at him and said 'the* Luftwaffe *isn't worth anything' in the presence of other generals and Goering as Highest General wept. 'You are lazy,' he said to Goering, 'you are lazy you know, this is why the* Luftwaffe *isn't worth anything.' Nevertheless at other times Hitler said, 'When there is a crisis you can rely on Goering. He is the iron man.' So he kept him for this and for propagandistic reasons. Hitler had also a sort of sentimental relation to his old henchman.*

Hermann Goering was never a serious military commander, he had too many personal deficiencies for that. Although he was undoubtedly intelligent he could not take war seriously enough because it interfered with his love of culture and the arts. Fate provided him with immense wealth and the power to pillage the museums and galleries of Europe but fate exacted a high price: namely that he must spend time at war which he hated and in which he experienced continual failure as well as having to report to a boss who terrified him and brought on his neuralgic pains.

Professor Eric Zilmmer of Drexel University felt that Goering's biggest flaw was his narcissistic personality that interfered with everything he did. He allowed his feelings to cloud his decisions and over-personalized situations. Professor Zilmmer adds:

*Goering was quite careless about how he connected details; we call that in psychology an under-incorporative style. We call this somebody an under-incorporator and this is Hermann Goering in his essence, somebody who does not take all available information into account in coming to a decision. Hermann Goering, as somebody who was care less in making a decision impulsively based on emotions, may also be more influenced by his environment and maybe also somebody who's more influenced by others because he's not putting everything together on his own – he needs somebody else to do it so he's quite vulnerable to somebody like a strong Führer.*

If the German defeat at Stalingrad was one of history's decisive battles, Hitler's decision to rely on Goering's *Luftwaffe* to supply the trapped Sixth Army of General Paulus was one of history's great mistakes. Historians must face the difficult question of why the Fuhrer allowed himself – again – to be misled by 'Goering's frivolous assurances' as von Manstein has described them. Joel Hayward, of Massey University, New Zealand, reports the words of Edward Milch, Goering's deputy:

*Deceit plus incompetence equals one Reichsmarschal. I guessed it already, but now I get proof of it, it makes me want to throw up all over again.*

On 19 November 1942, Hitler's brief holiday at Berchtesgarden was disturbed by the start of Operation Uranus, the immense Soviet counter-offensive northwest of Stalingrad, which threatened to encircle the German 6th Army. Faced with imminent catastrophe Hitler turned to his best general, von Manstein, and

△ General Paulus, commander of the German 6th Army. Instead of fighting his way out of Stalingrad he relied on Goering's promise of a *Luftwaffe* airlift to supply his troops. He was finally forced to surrender to the Russians.

ordered him to organize a relief operation to break the developing Soviet stranglehold on the Sixth Army. In the meantime, Hitler turned to the *Luftwaffe* and examined the possibilities of supplying General Paulus from the air until von Manstein could relieve him. Incredibly, when Goering was summoned to HQ he told Hitler he was 'too busy' at Karinhall, his country estate, and sent Jeschonnck, his chief of staff, instead. This decision was to have immense consequences.

Hitler explained to Jeschonnek that he expected the Soviet ring around General Paulus to close within hours rather than days and that the von Manstein relief operation would take some time to fight its way through to Stalingrad. In the meantime, therefore, he asked if the *Luftwaffe* could keep the Sixth Army supplied. Jeschonnek knew that his chief, Goering, never admitted to the Fuhrer's face that there was anything he or his *Luftwaffe* could not do. It was asking a lot of Goering's deputy to tell the truth when his commander had risen so high on lies alone. Jeschonnek presumably reasoned that the airlift would be a temporary operation anyway and that soon von Manstein would break the Soviet offensive as he had so often in the past. In time, he probably thought, the *Wehrmacht* would bale out the *Luftwaffe*, and the truth need never be told. But what was the truth?

Jeschonnek, eager to please the Fuhrer and pressed for an immediate response, told Hitler that he believed the *Luftwaffe* could repeat their success of the previous year when they had airlifted supplies to 100,000 men trapped in the Demyansk pocket and kept them supplied for several months. But com-

◁ Narcissus in full regalia. Goering loved to dress up but the inner man continually failed to match the uniform he wore.
△ Dunkirk in 1940. The British Navy rescued a third of a million British and French troops from under the noses of the Germans. They had relied on Goering's promise that the *Luftwaffe* would destroy the British on the beaches.

parisons with Stalingrad were far-fetched. In the Demyansk operation 500 Ju-52s had dropped 300 tons of supplies per day against a negligible Soviet fighter threat. Now, the task was to supply nearly three times as many men with at least 750 tons of supplies against a new and powerful Soviet fighter force and with a minimal force of Ju-52s. It was sheer madness as Jeschonnek must have known. Yet he also knew that Hitler would accept no answer which would have necessitated the break-out by the 6th Army and the loss of Stalingrad, with all its propaganda value. Assured by Jeschonnek Hitler contacted the 6th Army and informed them that an airlift was being organized and that they should hold fast to their positions. A breakout was to be out of the question.

Goering now discovered the consequences of his earlier 'too busy' reply to the Fuhrer. As soon as he arrived at Berchtesgarden Hitler asked him bluntly, 'Listen here, Goering.

If the *Luftwaffe* cannot carry this through, then the 6th Army is lost.' Goering replied, '*Mein Führer*, we'll do the job.' However, Jeschonnek had got his sums wrong and he told Goering that he wanted to admit as much to Hitler but Goering would not let him. It was far too late for that. Instead Goering telephoned the Fuhrer and insisted that he need have no fears – the *Luftwaffe* would save the 6th Army.

Goering now found himself at odds with senior army officers who refused to accept that he could save the 6th Army by an airlift alone. Most formidable of his opponents was the army chief of staff, General Zeitzler. On 23 November Hitler listened to the arguments of the protagonists. Zeitzler presented a rigorous proof, based on statistics assembled by his staff, that the *Luftwaffe* could not save Paulus and that the 6th Army must try to break out on its own:

*Allowing for all the stocks at present with the 6th Army, allowing for absolute minimum needs and the taking of all possible emergency measures, the Sixth Army will require delivery of 300 tons per day. But since not every day is suitable for flying, as I myself learned at the front last winter, this means that about 500 tons will have to be carried to the 6th Army on each and every flying day if the irreducable minimum average is to be maintained.*

△ The Ju–52, workhorse of the *Luftwaffe*. Shortages of these transport plans made a nonsense of Goering's promise to support the German 6th Army in Stalingrad.

Goering's response, 'I can do that', far from being based on the research of his staff officers was now in absolute defiance of the opinion of his chief of staff, Jeschonnek. The exasperated Zeitzler exploded. '*Mein Führer!* That is a lie!' Hitler calmly replied, 'The Reichsmarschal has made his report to me, which I have no choice but to believe.' Professor Zilmmer explains the consequences of Goering's lie:

*Now you and I, if we were charged with the biggest military airlift in the history of war would immediately consult with our people that we work with and with weather experts. We would consult maps of the state of the 6th Army, we would find out what the forces of the Red Air Force were. He did none of that, in fact there was incredible opposition to this idea, he knew about this opposition. They calculated that to supply 250,000 men it would require 700 tons to be dropped daily. That's unheard of, what they just did then was just rationalize it. Okay, let's make it 500. He said, I can do 500; he neglected the fact that he did not have enough planes. Initially the idea was that it was a temporary airlift and then it became a permanent airlift to keep the German forces in Russia for all of the winter. Okay, there's two ways to go about this, one is you get all the facts and then you make a decision. Goering, astonishingly after having made the decision took his train, Asia, to Paris for four days to collect more art for his collection. That just shows you how little patience he has in reviewing facts and how this is all clouded by him, he thinks art is more important than preparing for this airlift. The other way to go about this is more intuitively which is, gee, this seems like a bad idea, there's a winter, there's a lot of people, maybe it's better for the 6th Army to break out, Hermann Goering's problem solving*

*capabilities were not well defined. Most military leaders have a strategy for how they go about solving problems but most of the time he would just do whatever would advance Hermann Goering the most, and in this situation it was best for Hermann Goering to say it is possible, because his stock had already slipped in the early forties because of all of the mistakes that he had made regarding the airforce. So the way he went about this, which is utterly surprising, is he did not consult with individuals who were experts. He ignored facts that were presented to him, he did not consult with his local military experts, in this case Von Richthofen who was in charge of Luftwaffe 4. He would have told him, gee, we only have about, you know, fifty planes and it would require eighth-grade arithmetic to figure out that you could only drop 35 tons a day in this scenario. None of these things were thought through and as we all know now this turned into an incredible disaster. Only 6,000 Germans returned home.*

Most of Hitler's generals believed that the 6th Army's only hope was to break out and try to link up with von Manstein's rescue column. To stay at Stalingrad and depend upon Goering's flippant promises was to court certain disaster. Yet, for perhaps the fourth or fifth time in the war Hitler allowed his deputy to have his way, with disastrous effects for Germany. Jeschonnek may have made the initial miscalculation, partly through stupidity and partly through fear of the Fuhrer, but once he had realised his mistake he had wanted to put it right. Goering stopped him. Jeschonnek's blunder became Goering's crime and 250,000 German troops were condemned to captivity and eventual death in Soviet camps. Having convinced Hitler that he could do the impossible, Goering simply set off for a shopping trip to the Parisian art galleries in his private train. According to historian Samuel W. Mitcham, 'It was the major turning point of the war.'

# NOT MAKING WAVES

Military blunders do not come any bigger or more dramatic than the one perpetrated by Admiral Sir George Tryon, commander of the British Mediterranean fleet, on 22 June 1893 as he was cruising off the coast of Lebanon. To order a manoeuvre that sinks the fleet flagship from under your own feet takes some beating.

The eleven ironclad battleships of the Mediterranean fleet were cruising in two divisions, one headed by Tryon in the *Victoria* and the other by his second-in-command, Rear-Admiral Albert Markham, in the *Camperdown*. It was a hot, drowsy day and Tryon decided to get everybody on their toes by issuing an order for the two columns to reverse direction by turning inwards just six cables – 1,200 yards – apart. As soon as he issued the order the officers around him felt alarm. Six cables was not enough room for the ironclads to safely pass each other, eight was the minimum. There would be a danger of collision. But who dared tell a man of Admiral Tryon's reputation that he had got his sums wrong? Surely that responsibility must be left to his second-in-command, Rear-Admiral Markham. If Markham followed orders and carried out the turn there would be a collision between the *Victoria* and the *Camperdown*. In the event, Markham did not remonstrate with Tryon, followed orders and his ship rammed the *Victoria*, sending her to the bottom with the loss of 357 lives, including that of Sir George Tryon. The naval tradition of the captain going down with his ship did not usually apply to admirals but, in this case, Tryon seemed to have his own agenda, as Professor John Potter indicates:

> *It's interesting to think why Tryon actually did go down with the ship. My suspicion is that he just could not believe what had happened. It's almost that third stage if you like of the stress reaction. It's almost the freeze response, that he was in denial, he just couldn't believe that this dreadful mistake had happened. He probably couldn't live with the consequences unconsciously at least and*

so maybe he was just frozen there, made the decision, that was the honourable way out.

But who was really to blame? Tryon, for giving a bad order? Or Markham, for following an order he knew to be wrong Personalities played their part as naval historian Dr Andrew Gordon shows:

*George Tryon was respected and feared, he was one of the most intimidating and capable officers in the Royal Navy at the time. He was very large, well over six feet, overweight, with a full beard and by one account he had a way of making his eyes seem to merge into one in the centre of his forehead especially if you were in trouble. His mind was a cascade of ideas and concepts and he had very little time for anyone who stood in his way. He had performed brilliantly in the 1888 annual manoeuvres when he'd made complete fools of the main Channel fleet and the admirals leading it and that really buoyed up his reputation and got him I suspect the command of the Mediterranean in 1891.*

It was supremely ironical that Tryon, innovator and possessor of the 'Nelson-touch', should succumb to his second-in-command, Rear-Admiral Albert Markham, prime representative of the 'Peter Principle' in naval leadership selection as Andrew Gordon relates.

*Albert Markham was an anxious, moralizing, authoritarian, very strict disciplinarian, typical Victorian officer. He didn't really enjoy the Navy, he was very dutiful, he did it, he had to belong to the Navy for financial reasons. He was very much in the chivalrous, muscular, Christian mode of obedience and duty and honour and he was, compared with Tryon, almost a two-dimensional character, the kind of Victorian template of the typical Victorian, what the Victorians desired in their officers. Ultimately he let the navy down by failing to disobey an order which even he saw to be impossible and that's his condemnation.*

Sometimes, however, a commander can be too good for his own good as Andrew Gordon demonstrates.

*There was a conflict of course in Tryon's agenda in trying to teach his juniors to interpret the situation and use their initiative and Tryon's formidable, overbearing presence which actually deterred his juniors from*

# BLACK&WHITE.

A WEEKLY ILLUSTRATED RECORD AND REVIEW, WITH WHICH IS INCORPORATED "THE PICTORIAL WORLD"

No. 127—Vol. VI. [Registered at the G.P.O. as a Newspaper]     SATURDAY, JULY 8, 1893     [Price Sixpence By Post 6½d]

THE "VICTORIA" DISASTER—THE LAST MOMENTS OF ADMIRAL SIR GEORGE TRYON

△ Sir George Tryon going down with his ship. It was not his duty as admiral to do so but after his mistaken order it must have seemed the easier option.
▷ A French engraving of the loss of HMS *Victoria*. It was in order to keep pace with the French navy that Tryon stressed the importance of initiative to his subordinates – something Rear Admiral Albert Markham obviously failed to appreciate.

*doing exactly that. It helped him to some extent but ultimately it was to hinder him as we shall see.*

War is for warriors. Peace for managers, trainers, planners and oddjob men. Markham was one of life's peacetime servicemen. For a century the Royal Navy had ruled the waves unchallenged. It was getting soft and Tryon knew that. Markham did

not know that and was frightened when Tryon tried to prove it to him. He lost his sense of security and, when confronted with a choice of following bad orders or challenging authority he chose what he had been brought up to do – to obey without question. As Andrew Gordon explains:

*It's a condemnation not just of Markham but also in a sense of what is liable to happen in peacetime, in career hierarchies in the armed forces. In a sense he epitomizes what had gone wrong with the tactical doctrine of the reliance on signalling, reliance on authority, always having permission, always having to have orders. But it's possible to argue and I think Tryon saw this quite clearly. A peacetime navy or peacetime armed forces tends to reward people for qualities that are not necessarily the same as the warrior qualities needed to succeed in combat and Markham was an example of somebody whose peacetime attributes were exceptional: he was a very strict officer, he was very punctilious, he was very correct, he was always very good at looking after his men, he was very good at polishing and painting and supervising the ship's performance.*

◁ Admiral Sir George Tryon, whose powerful, patrician stare terrified his subordinates and rendered them unable to challenge the mistaken order that led to the loss of HMS *Victoria*.
▽ The last moments of HMS *Victoria*, rammed and sunk by HMS *Camperdown* commanded by Rear Admiral Markham in the Mediterranean in 1893.

# PRISTINA – STARTING WORLD WAR THREE

The ill-managed Nato campaign in Kosovo almost achieved, in a matter of weeks, what the Cold War managed to avoid for nearly fifty years. As well as destroying the Chinese embassy through clinical incompetence (American Tomahawk missiles flew off target on many occasions, some even into neighbouring Balkan countries, as we will see in Chapter 6) Nato came close to bringing about fighting between British and Russian troops, an event with potentially catastrophic consequences for the whole world. The fact that the Nato commander-in-chief actually ordered his troops into action against the Russians and was defied by the commander on the ground shows that, even as the new millennium dawns, mankind has still to justify its designation as *homo sapiens*. America's most decorated soldier and one of her shrewdest military commentators, Colonel David Hackworth, was hardly surprised at the direction Nato's strategy took, in view of the leadership of Nato Supreme Commander, General Wesley Clark.

*What happened was there was a Russian parachute brigade located in Bosnia who sent a reconnaissance element through Bosnia, through Serbia, into Kosovo with a mission of securing the airfield and General Clark got wind of it. Here we are in a situation with satellites, with high-tech intelligence ability and with all of this, it took this convoy about twenty-four hours to arrive there and General Clark didn't know it until the last minute, so that tells me how good all this high-tech stuff is. The Russians occupied the airstrip which was going to be a principal player in the occupation of Kosovo. General Clark ordered General Jackson, the British commander, to push the Russians off the airfield and secure it and he was going to do that by sending in British heliborne troops, paratroopers and SAS to go in by helicopter and play king of the mountain, grab the terrain before the Russians got there or if they were already there to secure it. He ordered General*

△ Four-star general, Wesley Clark. His decision to seize Pristina airport might have plunged Nato into a war with Russia.
▷ The political general? Sir Michael Jackson referred Wesley Clark's order to his political bosses, a reminder of the political nature of Nato in 2000.

*Jackson to do this. General Jackson refused his order and he refused his order with the comment, 'I'm not going to be responsible for starting World War Three.' Now this was a lieutenant general telling a four-star general basically to get stuffed, he wasn't going to do it and was he right, absolutely! There's a time that a commander has to be insubordinate to do his job and his mission comes first and I'm certainly very thankful that General Jackson stood tall and did the right thing. The Soviets had thousands of intercontinental missiles with nuclear tips ready to be pointed at jolly old London Town and Washington DC and so on and it could have created a holocaust, and we have to remember within Russia there's still a lot of hardliners who*

*would like nothing better and it would make their day if they could press that little red button.*

When interviewed for *Great Military Blunders* General Wesley Clark was not eager to go into details of his Pristina stand-off with General Jackson. In his view all the details had not yet come out and certainly the matter had been taken out of military hands and was settled at political level. Nevertheless, the similarities between the Pristina incident and the overruling of General Douglas MacArthur in Korea by President Truman (see Chapter 4) cannot be overlooked. Military overreaction was the danger in Korea, with MacArthur threatening to bring about war with China or even the Soviet Union. In Kosovo, the Russian action may have been one of political desperation resulting from frustration at being cut out of a settlement with her ally, Serbia, by Nato's direct military action. On the other hand, and far more dangerously, the Russian military response may have resulted from the action of a maverick general. In the event of fighting between outnumbered Russian forces and Nato troops it is inconceivable that Russia's political leadership could have allowed her troops to be defeated and humiliated by the West. An escalation in the fighting would have been followed by an inevitable Russian fallback on her missile capacity. In that event General Clark's decision to fight for the prize of Pristina airport would have been considered one of the least appropriate responses in military history. In the event, the Russians were satisfied with their consolation prize through the wisdom of British general, Sir Michael Jackson.

When asked why Pristina airport was worth risking war for, General Clark replied:

First because Pristina airfield was a key to further re-enforcement by Russian air-landed forces in a way that could have been disruptive, and secondly because control of Pristina airfield was something that had been sought by Russian forces who broke their agreements with the stabilization force in Bosnia and came out, and they shouldn't have been rewarded for breaking their commitments.

Clark has come in for much media criticism for what some consider his failure of judgement over the Pristina incident. For Colonel David Hackworth, Clark was not sufficiently a master of his profession to be given such power and authority. For Hackworth, the promotion of General Wesley Clark is evidence of what is wrong with the American system today.

*When I look at the weaknesses of the American promotion system, General Clark to me is evidence of a system that is totally ruptured. Here is a man with thirty-three years service who has only seven and a half years in command; the rest of the time he was going to staff colleges, working in the White House, going to get advanced degrees, teaching at the military academy, everything but learning his trade. So*

△ The Russian seizure of Pristina airport was the most dangerous military situation between Nato and Russia since the Cuban Missile Crisis. General Clark's reaction could have been disastrous.

*here's a man that doesn't know his trade. He may know it superficially, but the problem is he's extremely arrogant – that comes probably from his high intelligence – and he doesn't view people as people but as numbers, as an organization. He's very power mad, he is the four-star and he's not going to accept any insubordination from anyone; and that kind of commander who doesn't have the experience to really lead is probably employing that kind of arrogance because of his own lack of confidence. I am very thankful that we had people like Jackson that probably had more command experience when he reached the rank of major, which in the military is rather insignificant, but more practical experience of leading soldiers, fighting soldiers when he was a major than General Clark had as a four-star general. General Wesley Clark, soon to be out of Nato, wasn't a very successful general basically because he didn't understand what his job was, he wasn't a professional. He's very bright and would make a wonderful ambassador somewhere but he's the wrong man for war.*

# CHAPTER TWO

# PLANNING

## THE ANSWER'S A PIECE OF STRING

The evolution of military planning was a natural consequence of the division between leadership and management in warfare. Until the nineteenth century, commanders tended to be either kings or noblemen who led by heroic example. As the scale and complexity of warfare grew, heroes like Boleslav the Brave, Albert the Bear and Henry the Lion needed professional advisers, and so staff officers became a feature of the command structure.

Planning developed along three lines: contingency, campaign and crisis planning. In contingency planning, planners need to look into the future and, in the words of Professor Richard Holmes, 'plan to meet a variety of circumstances that you cannot predict when you're making the plan. Such plans are like a series of recipes that you have to produce without being quite sure what the ingredients are going to be or exactly who's coming to dinner.' Richard Holmes says that in campaign planning military planners 'concentrate on the plan to meet the major political problem at that particular time', as the Germans did with the Schlieffen Plan. But sometimes plans can become so big and so essential to the politics of a country that they become like the tail that wagged the dog. And

△ Planning the defence of the English Channel during the Second World War. The coastal artillery operations room was situated in the dungeons of Dover Castle.

as time passes and the political environment changes, they become outdated, inappropriate or overtaken by events. Then it is that, like the Schlieffen Plan, planning can be literally damaging to national welfare. Crisis planning is inevitably the most difficult kind of military planning, as it is aimed to meet a crisis that breaks with little or no warning and for which no contingency plan exists. Possibly time and resources are inadequate to the task and, as a result, crisis planning is very risky.

Planners can be left with redder faces than eighteenth-century English parsons. In 1805 the Austrian general Weyrother arranged to rendezvous with his Russian allies under General Kutuzov on the River Danube only to discover, when the Russians arrived ten days late, that while he made his plans according to the Gregorian calendar the Russians were still using the antiquated Julian version. In one part of the French Maginot Line in May 1940, as the Germans struck, French troops could not occupy their forts because the officer who held the keys was away on leave and had taken them with him. Probably the Duke of Wellington had the answer when he admitted, 'my plans are made of string, and when they break I just tie the knots and go on again'.

# OPERATION FULLER
# AND THE CHANNEL DASH

✂

'Don't panic! Don't panic! Captain Mainwaring, the Germans are in the Channel.'
Walmington-on-Sea, alerted by Corporal Jones's strident alarms, awoke to the news
that a German fleet was offshore, just passing the novelty-rock emporium. Fraser, eyes
rolling in the early-morning light, Pike, complete with woolly scarf and jelly babies, and Godfrey,
lavatory flushing behind him as he shuffled up, donned their helmets and levelled their rifles at the
mist drifting in from the sea. All was well. Old England was safe in their hands. 'Who do you think
you are kidding, Mr Hitler?' The music rang out... But Britain was still asleep. It was 12 February
1942. The Germans were in the Channel and Mr Hitler wasn't kidding.

The Channel Dash, the name for the escape of the German battle cruisers *Scharnhorst* and
*Gneisenau* from Brest and their journey along the entire length of the English Channel and, finally,
through the Strait of Dover, was probably the most humiliating moment of the entire Second
World War for Great Britain. Irrelevant in terms of the outcome of the war, it stood instead as the
supreme indictment of the conduct of the war by Winston Churchill's government and by the British
service chiefs. So much smug amateurism was apparent that it seemed to represent the kind of incompetence in high places that had allowed Britain to drift unarmed into the war in the first place.

Yet the sacrifice of six Swordfish torpedo bombers led by Lieutenant-Commander Eugene
Esmonde was to become in the eyes of many – even, curiously enough, the Germans – a symbol of
noble sacrifice that redeemed the disgraceful incompetence of the day. As so often in the past, the
courage of ordinary British servicemen would be used to offset the incompetence of Britain's leaders.

With the story of Esmonde's sacrifice in his briefcase, and a recommendation for a posthumous
VC in his mind, Winston Churchill now had something that he could take to his new ally, President
Roosevelt of the United States. Roosevelt had been both shocked and embarrassed when he heard

of the ease with which the Germans thumbed their nose at history and breached the Strait of Dover. The Germans had joined the Japanese in demonstrating that Britain no longer ruled the waves. Even worse, if that were possible, the RAF, which had won the Battle of Britain, had demonstrated such staggering incompetence that one must have feared for the nation's survival had a second Battle of Britain occurred in 1942 with men like Trafford Leigh Mallory now in almost total charge of the situation. While Churchill must have felt the shame personally, he must have thanked the Almighty for Esmonde's sacrifice. The newspapers would not be able to resist such a story, and while they gloried in the heroism of the Swordfish aircrew they would not be able to pelt the politicians and the service chiefs with the mud they so thoroughly deserved.

The meticulous planning and operation of Operation Cerberus by the Germans stood in almost laughable contrast to the farcical Operation Fuller that the British offered as their answer to the greatest threat to naval security since the Spanish Armada. One doubts that Elizabethan sea dogs would have locked their plans in a safe and then gone on leave with the key, as happened to the intelligence officer at Biggin Hill, the most vital fighter station in southern England. Top-secret Operation Fuller was known apparently only to those at the top who, for their own reasons – school ties and golf clubs included – had not passed the details down the chain of command to those who had to do the fighting. In one shocking example – one among simply hundreds on the day – the Beaufort pilots who arrived at Coltishall in Norfolk from Scotland did not know the details of Fuller. The controller at Coltishall had found out about the German break-out on the old-boy network but was under strict instructions not to pass it on to anybody, including the aircrew of the torpedo bombers. As a result, the Beauforts took off with orders to look for a German merchant convoy. To the astonishment of the pilots, they found themselves – tactically unprepared – flying over a German fleet that included two battleships.

Apart from Adolf Galland, the German fighter ace who masterminded the German air umbrella over the *Scharnhorst* and *Gneisenau*, the man who emerged with the most credit from 12 February 1942 was another Adolf: Hitler himself. Yet again the Führer had overruled his service chiefs and backed a hunch. As far as he was concerned, the two battleships were doing no good in the French harbour of Brest, attracting British bombers like a honeypot. Soon the British would get lucky and sink them. The ships must come back to Germany, where they could

△ Master-planner of Operation Cerberus, Colonel Adolf Galland (but not with Cerberus). Galland's air umbrella protected the *Scharnhorst* and *Gneisenau*, during their famous Channel Dash in 1942.

be put to good use in Norwegian waters. They must run the gauntlet of the shorter Channel route, and they must come in daylight because the British would assume they would come by night. Hitler had always had great respect for the British Empire, but it was of the British Empire of the sixteenth and seventeenth centuries that he was thinking, the Empire that had been built by people like Drake and Clive, and he felt that the British men of the twentieth century were not made of the same stuff. Hitler believed that just as the French army had collapsed in humiliation in 1940, with a severe push the old British lion would be revealed for what it was – basically stuffed with sawdust. Hitler reassured his anxious admirals that the British would react slowly at first and would then panic. Where his own commanders were afraid of the ghosts of Britain's great past, Hitler saw only the weakness of her present. As Hitler said:

'You will find that this operation will turn out to be our most spectacular naval success of the war.'

The Germans planned their dash for the night of 11/12 February 1942. The two battleships and the heavy cruiser *Prinz Eugen* would maintain a cruising speed of 28 knots down the Channel and aim to pass through the Strait of Dover in daylight. It was a daring and dangerous decision. To cover the fleet in the Channel, the *Luftwaffe* would provide 280 fighters, rotating so that there would never be fewer than thirty overhead at any one time. If the RAF occasionally broke through the *Luftwaffe's* umbrella, as might be expected, the heavy ships were supported by destroyers and E-boats (fast torpedo boats), which would put up such a defensive fire that no British planes would survive.

Although British naval and air staff had studied the likelihood of a German break-out and prepared contingency plans, they were all designated top secret and locked away. The entire plan was called Operation Fuller and the codename Fuller was to be used as soon as it became apparent that the German ships had come out. It was imperative, therefore, that everybody knew the significance of Fuller and what they were to do if they heard the codeword. In fact, hardly anyone knew what Fuller meant. It was an intelligence cock-up of the most staggering kind.

The responsibility for stopping the *Scharnhorst* and *Gneisenau* was like a hot potato continually passed around between the service chiefs: the Navy's Sir Dudley Pound, the RAF's Sir Trafford Leigh Mallory and Coastal Command's Sir Philip Joubert. Nobody wanted to be left holding it when the music stopped. Pound had already said that he was unprepared to use any major units of the Home Fleet in the Channel. Still smarting from the loss of the *Repulse* and the *Prince of Wales* to

△ German battlecruiser *Scharnhorst* at sea. The escape of the *Scharnhorst* and her sister ship, *Gneisenau*, through the English Channel was one of the most humiliating episodes for Britain in the entire war.
▷ First Sea Lord Sir Dudley Pound. Illness and incompetence meant that Pound was unable to give the Navy the leadership it needed in 1942.

Japanese air attack off Singapore, he was not willing to lose to the *Luftwaffe* another battleship in the narrow seaways of the Channel. Instead, he made the token gestures of calling up six motor torpedo boats (MTBs) and six old destroyers to block the German fleet. At Manston six Swordfish torpedo planes of the Fleet Air Arm – capable of just 90 miles per hour and widely referred to as 'Stringbags' – would also be thrown into action against the Germans. Pound later described the Admiralty's efforts: 'We have scraped together all that is at present available.'

RAF Bomber Command was prepared to fill the skies with hundreds of its heaviest planes, but first it would need prior warning that Operation Fuller had begun. Such heavy bombers, however, would have virtually no chance of hitting high-speed warships and would undoubtedly succumb to the heavy anti-aircraft defences of the German ships and to Galland's air umbrella of the latest and best German fighters.

The best British option rested with Sir Philip Joubert. He had at his disposal the most modern British torpedo bombers, the Beauforts. Unfortunately, he had these located in Cornwall and in Scotland. If the German ships managed to break out of Brest undetected and to enter the Channel, the Beauforts would probably miss them and the main British attempt would be left to Esmonde at Manston with his six Swordfish.

It has – tediously – been said that 'bad luck and bad play are closely allied'. In the case of the British war effort on 12 February 1942, it is sometimes difficult to tell one from the other. The two German battleships escaped from Brest under a smokescreen provided by a British bombing raid on the harbour. The British submarine that patrolled the entrance to the harbour had, just an hour before, gone off station to recharge her batteries. Three Hudson reconnaissance aircraft that patrolled the entrance to the Channel successively developed minor faults – blown fuse, damp plug, and so on – and had to abort their missions when any one of them would have been enough to give early warning of the approaching German armada. Of three squadrons of Beauforts, one (of fourteen planes) was stationed at Leuchars in Fife. Joubert at Coastal Command had ordered this squadron south to Coltishall, but the planes were held up by heavy snow.

Captain Mainwaring slept on. Private Pike sucked his thumb. Sergeant Wilson woke up, remembered where he was and tiptoed to his own bed. The German battleships sailed on, undetected by the British defences or by Walmington-on-Sea. Dawn broke. Britain's fate now rested in the hands of Spitfire fighters operating on the 'Jim Crow' reconnaissance sweeps. Surprisingly, they had not been told what Fuller meant, nor even had the air controllers at Uxbridge, responsible for scrambling fighters across southern England. Knowledge of the secret of eternal youth was more easily obtained on 12 February than the details of Operation Fuller. The two 'Jim Crow' Spitfires missed the German fleet in heavy cloud, but by the time they returned to base to report 'All clear', radar blips were showing swarms of German planes and possibly some large warships. The penny was beginning to drop, but its descent, from senior to junior minds, seemed to defy the law of gravity. Everyone had to be so sure that it seemed better to let the German ships escape if they could not be identified positively as the Scharnhorst and Gneisenau. Perhaps they were previously unknown ships of similar design? Better not risk making a mistake.

The initial identification of the Scharnhorst was made by a sergeant – of all people: better wait until an officer could confirm what the man said. They could be fishing boats, insisted a bright spark at Uxbridge. After all, many fishing boats resemble 30,000-ton battleships!

Adolf Galland, in fact, intercepted the British reports of the sighting of the German battleships before even the British did. He at least was convinced. However, although three senior RAF officers and a sergeant had seen the ships, it still took nearly an hour to produce a response. At last, nearly twelve hours after they set sail from Brest, the German fleet had been spotted at sea. Britain was gathering herself for action, but very slowly. Captain Mainwaring was still eating his breakfast. At Manston, the six Swordfish bombers under Lieutenant-Commander Esmonde were placed in readiness for their mission impossible. The Cabinet Office was also informed, and Churchill was baying for blood. In a dozen airfields, fighter pilots waited for the order to scramble, while the pilots who were to escort the Swordfish torpedo bombers rushed about asking everyone who passed what they were supposed to do and what was the target. Some people said it was the Scharnhorst while others said it was a German convoy. Nobody seemed to know the truth.

Meanwhile, the German armada steamed on. It had already travelled unchallenged up much of the Channel, and aboard the Scharnhorst Helmut Backhaus was ecstatic. He was going home:

*Yes, the first time, you know, we were very glad, and I tell you every seaman cried, 'Hooray, hooray, we're going back home', then half an hour later we were singing. But this was very dangerous because this is under the English coast. You know what might happen now. But we go for one hour and the second hour, nothing happened, and then nearly Dover...*

All Operation Fuller could offer at this stage was to contest the narrowest point, the Strait of Dover, with Swordfish torpedo bombers in daylight. The supposition had been that if the Germans came they would aim to pass Dover at night, and the British had planned a combined naval/air attack by torpedo-firing destroyers and by the Swordfish. At night it was

△ During Operation Fuller. One could be excused for thinking these groundcrew had never seen a torpedo before as a Fairey Swordfish waits to be fitted.

believed the 'Stringbags' might have some chance of success. However, with daylight replacing darkness in the German plans it meant that the Swordfish would have no chance against the dozens of fast German fighters – Me 109s and Focke-Wulf 190s – travelling as an air umbrella over the battleships. Furthermore, the German ships had been fitted with extra anti-aircraft guns, and the flak defences of the ships would be truly formidable. It is not stretching the definition of the word to say that in daylight the Swordfish attack was suicidal. Esmonde and his aircrew were flying on what later in the war would be called a kamikaze mission.

At Dover, Admiral Ramsay rang Sir Dudley Pound in Whitehall, pleading with him not to send the six Swordfish alone against the German ships. But Pound coldly responded: 'The Navy will attack the enemy whenever and wherever he is to be found.' This, of course, is the same Dudley Pound who refused to commit any of the Home Fleet against the Germans

in the Channel. Esmonde and his men had been chosen as a blood sacrifice to atone for the blunders of Operation Fuller. In despair, Ramsay put down the phone. Pound had refused to relieve him of the awful responsibility he felt. He contacted Tom Gleave at Manston and asked him to tell Esmonde that the German battleships were approaching Dover. The rest was up to him, as Esmonde well knew. Five wings of Spitfires from Biggin Hill and Hornchurch were due to escort the six Swordfish, but in the appalling confusion that ensued only ten of the expected sixty Spitfires arrived at Manston. Esmonde could wait no longer if he was to intercept the German ships. As Esmonde left Manston, Gleave commented:

*Although his mouth twitched automatically into the semblance of a grin and his arm lifted in a vague salute, he barely recognized me. He knew what he was going into, but it was his duty. His face was tense and white. It was the face of a man already dead. It shocked me as nothing has ever done since.*

The six Swordfish and their ten escorts flew into an absolute maelstrom of German fire. While the 'Stringbags' went down to just 50 feet to facilitate the launching of their torpedoes, they flew through a thick sea mist, with the waves flinging spray into their faces in their open cockpits. Above them the Spitfires were overwhelmed by packs of German fighters and by the flak from the guns on the destroyers and E-boats. Helmut Backhaus described his experiences:

*At Dover we get hell on earth, you know, shooting. The Gneisenau was behind us. She shoot, you know, and the Prinz Eugen too. It was like an inferno, and then we passed slowly by Dover and then we're still thinking about what happens now. Somebody saw some planes...a slow one, it was a Swordfish, but we didn't know that, and then every gun that we had was shooting at the Swordfish, an aeroplane that carried only one torpedo but very slow, so we could shoot them down.*

As the Swordfish drew nearer the German fleet they encountered twin dangers, from German fighters as well as from the heavy anti-aircraft fire from the ships below them. Edgar Lee, an observer in 825 Squadron, describes his thoughts:

*Eight minutes out from the coast we had our first attack. They were mostly 109s in the first attack, and they shot us up a bit. The fighters did their best to keep them off us, but of course the fighters had terrible difficulty in remaining in close contact with us because of our low speed.*

▽ Air Marshall Trafford Leigh Mallory, brother of the lost Everest climber. By 1942 he was too 'fussy' for high command. His performance during Operation Fuller symbolized much that was wrong with the British war effort.

△ Germany's latest fighter in 1942, the Focke-Wulf 190, saw service during the Channel Dash and gave the Germans temporary air superiority.

*I mean, Spitfires don't like flying at 90 knots if they can help it, and so they were having problems weaving backwards and forwards across us to try and keep somewhere in touch, but they drove off that first attack.*

*A few minutes later many more German fighters came in, including Focke-Wulf 190s, and they began to do quite a lot of damage. My air gunner, Johnson, was killed in the second attack, and I tried to move his body with the idea of perhaps climbing over and crawling into the aft cockpit and manning the gun, but the aircraft was being thrown around so much in avoiding action and I couldn't move Johnson anyway. He was jammed, and so I decided the best thing to do was to stay in my cockpit, the centre cockpit, and try and tell Brian Rose, the pilot, which way to turn when the aircraft came in because when a fighter comes in behind you, I mean, he's got to line up on you, and you just have to guess when he's going to open fire, and then you instruct the pilot to turn port or starboard and hope that you manage to miss what's coming, if you're lucky, and this of course went on I suppose for what must be fifteen or twenty minutes while we approached the ships. And as we approached the screen, because the German destroyer screen was about three miles out from the main body, between them and the British coast not only did we have the aircraft attack – and I must say the German pilots showed great bravery in continuing to attack even in the face of their own anti-aircraft fire from the ships – but we came under fire from everything the destroyers had. And of course one must remember that the Germans were anticipating a lot of air attack, and so all the ships had been equipped with extra guns, extra Bofors and machine guns for close-range work.*

Here Edgar Lee describes his plane's attack on the *Prinz Eugen*:

*We crossed the destroyer screen and came under intense fire from the destroyers and also from the German fighters. By that time the whole aircraft was shredded. Fortunately, the Swordfish is fabric-covered and so a lot of the stuff just flew right through and out the other side. Unfortunately, a cannon shell injured Brian, must have probably hit the main bulkhead behind, between he and I, and he caught the full blast of it. How I managed to escape without getting bits and pieces in me I don't know to this day, but immediately then, although the aircraft was in a very poor condition and we lost bearing on the two forward ships, Brian managed to bring the aircraft under control and we turned to attack the Prinz Eugen. Now by that time we were at 50 feet and we closed to about 1,200 yards, which is always reckoned to be the best dropping distance for a torpedo, and we dropped our torpedo, and immediately after we dropped it Brian called back to me through the Gosport tubes, 'I'll try and put her down astern of the fleet'. So we broke away, and I was still watching aft because the aircraft were still attacking us, and what I didn't see, but Brian told me afterwards, was that we almost flew into the stern of the Prinz Eugen. We were about fifty feet and just flew over the stern, and then we broke away astern and flew right over the rearmost destroyer because we had very little control of the aircraft. As we passed over the destroyer, of course she gave us everything she had, and we finally crashed about a mile beyond the rearmost destroyer.*

The navigator on the *Scharnhorst*, Helmuth Giessler, was intensely moved by the courage of Esmonde's squadron:

*Such bravery was devoted and incredible. One was privileged to witness it. Although they were shot down by our anti-aircraft fire before they could get into position to release their loads, they knowingly and ungrudgingly gave their all to their country and went to their doom without hesitation.*

All six Swordfish were destroyed and thirteen of the eighteen crew were killed. No hits were scored by their torpedoes. The German ships were by now almost past the danger point when the RAF at last stirred itself. From all over southern and eastern Britain hundreds of bombers were going into action, though few were to find their targets and none secured any hits. Meanwhile, Beaufort torpedo bombers began to arrive. Arthur Aldridge of 217 Squadron describes the scene at Manston, where a mass of escort fighters were trying to find the bombers they were supposed to escort.

*When we arrived at Manston we saw all these aircraft circling the airfield, a lot of aircraft on the ground. They were all circling. I'd never seen so many aircraft before at an aerodrome, so this was obviously something very big. There were so many aircraft, and it was this that made me convinced that it must be the* Scharnhorst *and* Gneisenau *and so that's why I landed, to get the correct position. The other two aircraft who were with me, they went off for the wrong position, of course, but we landed, and it was confirmed that it was the* Scharnhorst *and* Gneisenau *and we were given the correct position.*

By now, the Navy, or what there was of it, was in action as well. But, of their wounds, many were inflicted by their own side. One wonderful example of the 'fog of war' involved the destroyer *Campbell*. Commander Tony Fanning was not laughing when the following curious incidents occurred. First:

*Our first excitement really was when a Hampden bomber of the Royal Air Force suddenly appeared out of the murk and flew straight over our force, I suppose probably at about 500 feet. We actually watched with some amazement as we saw his bomb-bay doors opening and then he went on ahead of the ships and came back again and dropped his stick of bombs between the two lines. We could hardly believe it, but I think to our credit the gunnery officer stopped anyone firing at it and said that aircraft is friendly, although it's got a funny way of showing it.*

Next:

*I must mention this. When we received fairly frequent attentions from German aircraft, mainly Messerschmitts who were the cover for the German fleet, they obviously mistook us for the ships they were meant to be escorting just the same as the Hampden bomber had done, but when we fired at them, which we did, they were very indignant and quickly fired off their German recognition signal, saying, 'Don't, don't, don't!'*

It was a wise destroyer that knew its escorts: 'I think it was the first time that we had been escorted by Messerschmitts after being attacked by our own side.'

The Germans must have felt by now that they were home and dry. After avoiding everything the RAF and Coastal Command could throw at them, it was perhaps fitting that just before reaching safety the *Scharnhorst* should hit a mine and suffer serious damage. To the Germans the whole operation had been a vindication of Hitler's shrewd assessment of how the British would react: with a kind of slow-motion panic like an old man looking for his glasses. When Dudley Pound finally told Churchill that the Germans had escaped, the Prime Minister uttered one word – 'Why?' – and slammed down the phone. Arthur Aldridge was furious at the escape of the German ships:

*We'd lost forty aircraft, and they'd still got through in spite of us losing forty aircraft. That seemed to me to be a dreadful thing, not just that they got through, but that we lost forty aircraft without stopping them getting through, and that someone must have blundered somewhere because how did they get so far without being spotted off Brest?*

At any other time the Prime Minister would have resigned. To preside over a war effort that could manage no more than this was to make Chamberlain's Narvik blunders seem very slight. The *Daily Mail* commented:

*It is symptomatic of the general feeling that there is something wrong with Britain's war direction, and this feeling is crystalized in an almost universal demand for removal from high places of the tired and incompetent.*

Fat chance. Dudley Pound survived in office and finally died in office, on 20 October 1943. By then he had perpetrated several more catastrophic blunders, including the terrible scattering of Convoy PQ17 in July 1942, which cost Britain twenty-six merchant ships carrying 210 aircraft, 430 tanks and 100,000 tons of stores destined for Russia. Leigh Mallory survived and the following year became both commander-in-chief of the Allied Air Forces for the invasion of Europe and Eisenhower's chief air commander. As such he perpetrated the disastrous Operation Cobra, during which 111 American soldiers were killed by their own bombers.

# THE SCHLIEFFEN PLAN

⚔

The trumpet played the last post and the margarine was ceremoniously lowered into the grave. The officer barked out an order, and the burial detail fired three rounds into the wintry sky, scattering the birds from the nearby trees. When the news of this curious ceremonial reached England, smirks tugged at the edges of the stiff upper lips in Whitehall, while in Berlin another red-faced and bewhiskered professor took up the pen that had become his cudgel and began to berate the 'perfidious English'. The land of Bach, Beethoven and Goethe had lost yet another round in the battle for the hearts and minds of the neutrals. Throughout the war the British benefited from the winning start in the propaganda battle that they had been handed them by Germany's march through Belgium in August 1914. The Belgian atrocities – real, like the burning of Louvain, and imaginary, like the famous 'corpse factory', in which it was said the Germans melted down the corpses of soldiers for margarine or soap – were a military consequence of Germany's being tied to an inflexible plan that could tolerate no delay. Anything that stood in the way of the Schlieffen Plan must be ruthlessly swept aside, regardless of the consequences.

For almost three generations, historians have accepted a version of the opening of the First World War in August 1914 which has taken the following form: Germany placed all her hopes on the famous Schlieffen Plan, a massive 'hook' by five German armies that were to pass through Belgium, Artois, Picardy and then to the west of Paris before crushing the French against two remaining German armies in Lorraine. However, by violating Belgian neutrality the Germans brought Britain into the war alongside France and Russia, and ironically it was to be the tiny British Expeditionary Force that was to administer the *coup de grâce* to German hopes on the Marne in September 1914.

The Schlieffen Plan had supposedly been a brilliant concept, aimed at winning the war in the west in six weeks, before moving German forces east to deal with the Russians, who, it was thought, would be slow to mobilize. Thus, the Germans would avoid the old Prussian strategic nightmare of a war on two fronts. But in reality the plan contained flaws that should have been ironed out before being used in 1914. Simple geometry should have shown the German planners that von Kluck's 1st Army, on the extreme right of the German 'hook', would have to travel much further – and much faster – than the Crown Prince's 5th Army on the inside of the wheel. Any delays encountered by von Kluck from unexpected Belgian – or British – resistance would be disastrous. In the event, it was resistance by the BEF at Mons and Le Câteau that disrupted the German timetable. Meanwhile, a thousand miles away in East Prussia, an invasion by two Russian armies prompted Moltke to send two army corps from his right wing in Belgium to reinforce his beleaguered 8th Army. This – according to the accepted view – was a catastrophic error. Moltke had apparently made the cardinal mistake against which the dying Schlieffen had warned: he had not kept his right wing strong. Ironically, the troops he sent east did not reach Prussia in time to fight against the Russians at Tannenburg and were in trains crossing Germany when the Battle of the Marne was lost.

Holger Herwig, however, believes the Schlieffen Plan was doomed from the outset:

*The plan sought through a General Staff brain centre to dictate not only the opening moves of the campaign but also all subsequent operations of millions of men in a foreign land. Not only would this deny front commanders initiative, but the slightest disruption of communications threatened to unravel the overall timing of the advance.*

△ Count Alfred von Schlieffen, chief of the German general staff, and author of the famous plan. He liked to read military history to his small daughter and set his students intractable planning problems which he insisted they completed on Christmas Day.

In addition, so entrenched had the German fear of the war on two fronts become that the German military planners were willing to gamble on a plan that would certainly violate Belgian neutrality and would probably bring Britain into the war against them. In addition, so inflexible was the operation of such a plan in the west that nothing could be allowed to interfere with its smooth operation. The bureaucratic minds of the German planners found they could justify atrocities against civilians in order to keep the plan in operation. The consequence, in the long run, was that British propagandists were able to win the struggle for neutral opinion, helping to bring America into the war against Germany. Thus, Germany's gamble became a very costly error indeed, the price being nothing less than defeat in the war. As Niall Ferguson, of Jesus

College, Oxford University argues:

*The question you have to ask yourself is at what point does a gamble become a blunder, and I think the point is when there is an alternative which is less risky and we know there was an alternative for the Germans in 1914 which was less risky because almost every intelligent German businessman said what it was. Max Warburg, the banker, and Hugo Stinnes, the great coal industrialist, both said it, and they said it directly and publicly, in the case of Warburg to the Kaiser, in*

the case of Stinnes to the Pan-German leader. 'We will control Europe peacefully if you just allow us to carry on our economic expansion; if you avoid a war, German business will take over Europe peacefully,' and they were right.

The truth is that the Schlieffen Plan was the albatross of the German Army in 1914, and Helmuth von Moltke, nephew of the great Moltke, was condemned to work in its shadow and finally to put its fantasy into operation, for which he received the blame that should truly belong to the German General Staff. For the Schlieffen Plan – if there ever really was such a plan, and the latest research by Terence Zuber insists there was not – was more fantasy than fact, as Niall Ferguson explains:

*When Schlieffen devised his famous, notorious plan in 1905–6 he imagined an army which in the west had twenty more divisions than the German Army actually had in 1914, so there was a fictional quality to this planning. These are imaginary divisions being deployed,*

△ German field artillery on the right wing of the Schlieffen Plan, entering France in early September 1914.

*and the whole notion of being able to sidestep the French by going in through Belgium was in many ways a fantasy designed to make a point, the point being 'We have a problem here; we need twenty more divisions'.*

The problem was that Germany did not have those twenty divisions either in 1905 or in 1914, and yet many officers at the German Staff acted as though they did. An order issued from the grave was more powerful than the thoughts of living men. The plan, though Schlieffen himself knew it was impossible, became Germany's only reality. To make it work, the Germans were apparently prepared to stop at nothing. Professor Denis Schowalter shows us that the German General Staff was so smug that they never gave adequate attention to what the other side was planning:

The failure of the German General Staff is a lack of empathy; they are, one might say, like surgeons. They think everyone else is a surgeon, that every officer, every reserve lieutenant and sergeant, every recently mobilized civilian in the German Army will be not merely willing but able to do what these professionals can do, and do so under conditions of extreme physical and psychological stress. They do not pay enough attention to the fog and friction of the human elements of the Army. Germany's General Staff officers fail to understand the mindsets, the attitudes, of their opponents because they do not care about them. Increasingly, as the Schlieffen Plan becomes as much a set of mantras and principles as a military plan, the enemy is expected to be forced to conform to the German intentions. Therefore it is not particularly necessary to know much about his psychology, his military structure, how generals in Russia or France will react: they'll react the way the German plan makes them react, and so paradoxically you have human beings abandoning the great original skill of a German Staff officer, which was imagination or, if you will, empathy.

The Schlieffen Plan was a nightmare of logistics. For example, von Kluck's 1st Army needed daily 2,000,000 pounds of fodder for its 84,000 horses. Food for men and horses had to vie for roadspace with ammunition being brought up from miles behind the front line, which was constantly moving away from the railheads at a rate of over twenty miles a day. Such logistical figures make for dizzy reading. Each German soldier was loaded like a donkey, as Barbara Tuchman writes in *August 1914*:

*Each soldier carried 65 pounds: rifle and ammunition, knapsack, canteen, extra boots, entrenching tools, knife and a multiplicity of implements and kits strapped to his coat. In one bag was his 'iron ration' containing two tins of meat, two of vegetables, two packages of hard tack, one of ground coffee, and a flask of whisky which was only to be opened on permission of an officer and was inspected daily to determine if its owner had cheated. Another bag held thread, needles, bandages and adhesive tape, another held matches, chocolate and tobacco…As they marched, the Germans sang. They sang* Deutschland über Alles, Die Wacht am Rhein *and* Heil dir im Siegeskranz.

▽ 20 August 1914. German troops of General von Kluck's 1st Army march through Brussells. In spite of his urgency it took von Kluck three days and three nights to move his huge army through the streets of the city.

Denis Schowalter asks:

*How are these men going to be fed, going to be kept moving, how is their everyday health going to be maintained, because four-fifths of them are not professional soldiers and they're not even serving draftees. They are officers and men called back from civilian life who have very often forgotten much of their military training. They are not particularly physically fit; they're not emotionally geared for marching twenty and twenty-five miles a day under the stress of potentially having to fight a battle at the end of it.*

▷ The irresistible advance of the 'Hun'. Inflexible planning set German commanders impossible timetables and contributed to the atrocities committed by German troops in Belgium during August 1914.
▽ German troops post notices threatening reprisals if the local Belgian population resist the German advance.

Relentless schedules prepared by military hierarchies, based on calculations applicable only to fit, regular soldiers and assuming ideal conditions, make the Schlieffen Plan as much a regimen of torture for the Germans as for their opponents. Denis Schowalter explains how most of the German reserves and new conscripts must have floundered:

*Strictly speaking, a platoon commander in the German Army is supposed to check his men's feet at the end of a day's march for blisters. That's regulation in every army, the British, Russian, French. But a young reserve officer at the end of a fatiguing march might very well neglect to inspect his men's feet. When he does, the blisters become worse, feet become infected, men start dropping out of the ranks, and stragglers in turn will feed themselves by stealing or looting from the country. You could say, too, that as rations don't come forward, the officers and sergeants, again mostly reservists, mostly guys that were, you know, in civilian life a few days, maybe a couple of weeks earlier, will requisition food. But to see that the men cook it properly is quite another problem. They requisition stimulants, brandy, wine to keep their men going. Well, again, to see that only the amount of liquor that gets drunk is the amount necessary requires levels of discipline and professionalism that are just very often lacking, and the Schlieffen Plan takes no account of these things. The Schlieffen Plan assumes that every soldier, every officer, every horse in the German Army will do his duty as the plan provides. Well, you know, the horse never heard.*

The friction of war began to rub Germany's heels just as the new boots rubbed those of her soldiers. As Holger Herwig writes:

*Field kitchens fell behind. Horses slowed owing to utter exhaustion. Motor transport broke down. The horse-drawn artillery lagged even further behind the advancing infantry. By 4 September, both the First and Third Armies reported the exhaustion of their troops.*

Ultimately, so great was the threat of breakdown and failure to the plan that it drove the Germans to a form of military atrocity that has coloured the world's view of the German military machine since 1914 until replaced by the holocaust in 1942. The 'Hun' was born. Niall Ferguson explains the atrocity stories:

*You have a lot of inexperienced troops, who've only known about the war for a matter of days since they get*

△British Royal Marines arriving in Belgium in September 1914. Within days of being welcomed by cheering Belgian crowds the British were retreating.

their mobilization orders, having to march at a furious pace in very hot weather into Belgium, where very few of them have ever been before. Not surprisingly, after the main Belgian military resistance had crumbled, there were still some people who weren't aware that it had crumbled, who carried on fighting, and there were also misunderstandings, confusion and a sense of paranoia on the part of the German troops which led them to clearly enormous overreaction when they encountered problems. We know that in those days in August and into September 1914, when the Germans were moving most rapidly through Belgium, thousands of Belgian civilians were shot in response often to imaginary attacks on

German troops. This notion that there was a kind of sinister guerrilla army which you had to root out before you lost men to sniper fire was deeply embedded in the historical memory of the German Army, and this must explain why so many casualties are inflicted on the civilian population. However this happens, whether it's trigger-happy inexperience or in some cases a really overdeveloped Prussian sense of ruthlessness – i.e. in this situation this is an emergency; therefore we throw away the rule-book and we really hit them hard – there's no doubt that some lower-ranking officers did take that attitude. However it happened these thousands of civilian deaths had massive political consequences for the war as a whole. Nothing did more to mobilize British and later American opinion against the Germans.

This was what Clausewitz meant by friction in war.

*It was all very well to stand in front of a map and say the 1st Army goes this way through Belgium. On the ground that meant tired, dirty, sunburned German squaddies tramping through quite built-up areas. I mean, Belgium was one of the most industrialized countries in the world, and although our conventional images are of fields full of poppies, a lot of the action in 1914 is going on in highly urban areas. Now, you're a junior officer and all you know is that you've got to be at point B by 0600 hours, otherwise the entire fate of the German Empire is on the line, and you suddenly encounter some resistance, or somebody lets a gun go off, or one of your own soldiers lets his own gun go off and kills himself, which is precisely the kind of thing that happened. You panic, you think we're encountering resistance, we have to be at point B by 0600 hours, therefore we need to completely dispel any resistance by making some examples, shoot those two men over there and that's the kind of thing that happened. The decisions to shoot civilians were being taken at quite a low level.*

The commander of the German 1st Army, sixty-eight-year-old Alexander von Kluck, a 'strange, dark, fierce-looking man', took his role as the 'hammerhead' of the German right wing very seriously, constantly disputing the 'pace' of the advance with von Bülow, commanding the 2nd Army, on von Kluck's immediate left. Naturally, von Bülow's men were set a slower pace than von Kluck's, and so there was the ever-present danger of a gap developing between the armies on the extreme right wing, which is, of course, what eventually developed, allowing the British Expeditionary Force and Gallieni's Paris garrison to penetrate the German line. Von Kluck's men were responsible for most of the German atrocities – or, as he described them, 'severe and inexorable reprisals'. Many Belgian towns have graveyards dating from 1914 bearing the inscription 'Fusillé par les Allemands'. Travelling with von Kluck's army were a number of American journalists who brought to the world's attention the progress of the 'Hun'.

The problem was that the German military machine was out of step with the attitudes of the Western democracies. If it came to a choice between injustice and disorder, the Germans would choose injustice every time. While the general public in Britain, France and the United States were horrified by the reports of the American journalists with von Kluck's army, the German authorities tried to spread counter-propaganda, which was merely laughable. Against British stories of Belgian nuns being used as the clappers in church bells, Canadian soldiers crucified with bayonets through hands and feet, and babies skewered on German bayonets, the Germans responded with stories of 'thirty German officers in hospital with their eyes put out by Belgian women and children'. When the Germans burned the medieval city of Louvain, with its priceless medieval library, they lost the

propaganda war at a stroke. Their excuses were simply farcical. The German Foreign Ministry issued a communiqué claiming that 'the entire responsibility for these events rests with the Belgian government' and that 'women and girls took part in the fight and blinded our wounded, gouging their eyes out'. The French writer Romain Rolland spoke for many when he wrote to German writer Gerhardt Hauptmann with the question: 'Are you descendants of Goethe or Attila the Hun?' The Kaiser did not help much when he wrote to President Woodrow Wilson of the United States, saying 'My heart bleeds' for the suffering of Belgium 'caused as a result of the criminal and barbarous action of the Belgians'. Ninety-three German professors issued a manifesto emphasizing Germany's civilizing role in Europe. Britain responded with the 'corpse factory' story. The land of *Kultur* was hoist by its own petard.

Martin van Creveld has shown that the German plan of 1914 – whether 'Schlieffen', 'Schlieffen/Moltke' or 'Zuber' – was doomed because 'the sheer size and weight of the German Army in 1914 proved wholly out of proportion to the means of tactical transportation at its disposal.' A war involving millions of men and horses required mechanization and mobility on a scale not available for another generation, as Niall Ferguson shows:

*I mean, if you think about ultimately trying to move 2,000,000 men and 600,000 horses for when they ran out of train line, you're needing at least 11,000 trains. That's only the fifth stage of German mobilization; that's the military transport plan which is part five of this vast operation, all of which has to happen in a matter of days. And all the time the pressure is growing because basic starting assumptions are from the 1890s: like the Russians are crumbling away. But with every year the Russian railway system improves, and with every year the speed of Russian mobilization increases, so that by the time you get to the end of Schlieffen's career in 1905 the central ideas that the Russians are going to be slow off the mark, or that the French are going to be quite easy to beat are looking shakier and shakier. And therefore the plan – or plans, to be exact – are looking less and less convincing.*

Schlieffen – or Moltke – was planning a war within a vacuum, which did not allow them to take account of technology, transport or communications. It has been estimated that each of Germany's thirty corps consumed 130 tons of food and fodder, requiring twenty miles of road and a whole day to resupply them – and this while they were standing still. The mind boggles at the logistical horrors of trying to follow a fast-marching army advancing through successive battle zones with everyone's evening meal. The 320,000-strong 1st Army of Alexander von Kluck on the outside of the wheel was the biggest problem of all. Continually in action against French, British and Belgian forces, it was also required to maintain a killing pace of twenty to twenty-five miles a day for three weeks. Niall Ferguson explains the plan's obvious drawbacks:

*The first thing that was wrong with the Schlieffen Plan was that it assumed everything would go right at all levels. It assumed that from Supreme Headquarters down to the rifle companies, officers and men would understand what they had to do, implement what they had to do against an enemy that would oblige them by making all the right mistakes. So first off, the Schlieffen Plan has to go right at all levels. Secondly, the Schlieffen Plan overlooks the practical problems of effectively supporting – logistically, administratively – a massive sweep through the Low Countries by men who are going to be marching on their feet, and horses that within a few days can eat their own weight of forage. The logistical elements were something that had been expected to go along with the system. Thirdly, the Schlieffen Plan assumes not merely an obliging enemy but an enemy that will accept defeat, an enemy that will be unable or unwilling to rally from the kinds of defeats the Germans expect to impose in the war's early days.*

To the German military bureaucrats it was a vast war game, and it was unfair of the enemy to cause them to miss their deadlines. *Franc tireurs* and guerrillas were not proper soldiers; they were criminals, and the Germans had not included them in their calculations. Moreover, what were the British doing in Belgium? They were sailors, not soldiers. Bismarck had summed up the German attitude towards the British Army even better than the Kaiser's 'contemptible little army'. When asked how he would respond if the British Army landed on Germany's Baltic coast, the Iron Chancellor replied: 'I would send the local policeman to arrest them.' The German planners did not believe Britain would go to war just to protect Belgian neutrality. As Niall Ferguson shows, this involved a basic misunderstanding of traditional British foreign policy, with its defence of the Channel coast:

*You had to attach far more significance to British intervention than Moltke did, and so when he and then Bethmann-Hollweg, the German Chancellor, dismisses the treaty of 1839 by which Germany and the other powers, including Britain, are pledged to uphold Belgian neutrality as just a piece of paper, it's one of the great underestimates of modern history because it underestimates the significance of giving Britain this wonderful pretext for getting involved in the war. If the war is going to be over by Christmas, it doesn't really matter much, but Moltke really knows in his heart of hearts that it is not going to be over by Christmas. He's always known this, and in that sense I think they were in denial about the implications of British intervention, they really didn't want to face this possibility that what was six or seven divisions in 1914 could turn into a vast Continental*

*army by 1916, and in that sense one can see the limits of German war planning, the myopia, really, with which the whole plan was constructed.*

Niall Ferguson concedes that the German General Staff certainly contained the brightest and the best military minds. But the problem was that in everyday terms they had less common sense than the average German householder because they tied themselves into knots of their own creation. They had made an impossible plan and, when faults were found with it, they simply continued to work, day in, day out, making the impossible plan better. By 1914 they had an almost impeccable plan, but one that could work only in the never-never land of their own minds:

*A quick war with France is unwinnable, but to assert that a quick war is unwinnable is to say that the grand strategy and the policy of the German Empire is wrong-footed. It's also to say that the best and brightest of the German General Staff don't know their jobs, that they can't solve a problem set to them, so you sit down and you develop a solution to the problem and you do it in terms of the bureaucratic staff system and in terms of a bureaucratic planning method, which means you try to do the same things you're doing only better. The aphorism is a hammer is a very good tool but not every problem is a nail. However, the better the hammer you have, the more likely you are to try to make every problem into a nail, and that is I think what the Germans are doing after 1890. They put their emphasis on solving the problem that is originally set to them, as opposed to redefining the problem or submitting the problem as insoluble.*

There were no contingencies for the Schlieffen Plan, so that after the failure on the Marne in 1914 the General Staff found its cupboard literally bare of ideas. In Denis Schowalter's words, 'it had orientated itself into becoming a doomsday machine in which the plan worked or nothing mattered afterwards.' For Niall Ferguson, once the plan had failed there was nothing left except either a gambler's resigned shrug or, as happened, 'a long day's journey into night':

*The shortcomings of the German system were that in 1914 it put the fate of an army, a country and a people on one single throw of the dice. The Schlieffen Plan was a gambler's gambit requiring everything to go preternaturally well, to succeed. If it did not succeed, well, in the words attributed to one senior General Staff officer, it was a good time, it was a good trip. The image that I have is of a gambler at Monte Carlo putting the last of his fortune on the roulette wheel, and when his number doesn't come up he smiles, turns and walks away. Well, that's the kind of* beau geste *about which romance novels may be written and movies made, but it's one hell of a way to pursue and develop a national strategy.*

# OPERATION
# EAGLE CLAW

✄

When eight twin-engined Sea-Stallion helicopters led by marine Lieutenant-Colonel Edward R. Seiffert took off from the US carrier *Nimitz* to begin Operation Eagle Claw, unknown to their crews they carried an extra, unwanted passenger. His name was Murphy, and he was a regular stowaway on military missions. He took up little space, but his weight was enormous – and his law was absolute. The task of the marine pilots in each chopper was to fly to a rendezvous in the Iranian desert, but before they did so Murphy would have a lot to say on his own account. Director of Operations, General James B. Vaught, knew Murphy well:

*Murphy's Law is a common thing in the military. It says in effect: if it can go wrong, it will go wrong. And my experience has been that when you're practising and putting plans together, Murphy sends a liaison officer, but when the time comes to execute the mission, he comes and brings a whole A team and he bugs you from the beginning to the end, and he's always there.*

On Sunday 4 November 1979, the American embassy in Teheran was attacked by followers of the Ayatollah Khomeini and sixty-six Americans were taken hostage in a bid to force the USA to hand over the deposed Shah of Iran. The militants were threatening to put the American hostages on trial for spying, and even the idea of public executions was mooted. It was the start of a psychological battle with the United States. Thirteen black and female hostages were subsequently released as a gesture, but the remainder of the white males were clearly to be used as political pawns. American flags were burned in the streets, along with effigies of American President Jimmy Carter. And – as during the Vietnam War – all of this was brought into the homes of ordinary American citizens through the medium of television.

△ The captured American embassy in Teheran on 11 May 1979. Iranian students are already daubing the roof with anti-American slogans.

In response, President Carter and his advisers sought a peaceful solution, playing by the rules of international diplomacy, contacting known moderates in Iran, calling on the United Nations for support or for economic sanctions, but all to no avail. Moderation was clearly not working, but would a more forceful reaction prove any more successful? President Carter faced enormous problems in considering a military response. He had an obligation to try to bring out the hostages alive, and a military response, however successful, was unlikely to effect a rescue. Moreover, failure would bring with it not just the death of the hostages but virtual political suicide for Carter as President.

If war was not an option, what was available to Carter once diplomacy had failed? As one of the President's aides made clear: 'President Carter has never lost sight of the fundamental truth that, painful as it was to have American diplomats held prisoner in Teheran, there were other possible outcomes

that were even worse.' Could US Special Services offer Carter an option like an undercover rescue mission, carried out with such precision that the Iranians suffered no casualties themselves and hardly knew how their hostages had been ghosted away? Attractive, maybe, but was this 'mission impossible'? Hindsight shows us that the United States did not have the capacity to stage such an operation and was deficient in special operations in comparison with Britain and Israel.

However, Hollywood had shown the way, and where cinema pointed could the US military be far behind? National Security Adviser Zbigniew Brzezinski believed that such a raid was possible, though Carter was adamant that if carried out it should be 'quick, incisive, surgical', with 'no loss of American lives'. Wade Ishimoto, Intelligence Officer of the recently formed Delta Force, was not confident about the success of such a mission:

*I didn't think we really had a high chance of succeeding, and the reason I say that is that this was an awfully complex plan. It was a plan bringing in a number of different organizations that had not necessarily worked effectively together for any lengthy period of time.*

Richard Gabriel, author of the book *Military Incompetence*, agreed with Ishimoto. Inter-service rivalry played a serious part in weakening the planning for Eagle Claw. Although Air Force pilots, with experience of flying in Vietnam, were available to pilot the helicopters, marine pilots were chosen instead and they had neither the requisite skills nor experience. As Gabriel explains:

*The reason why the selection of marine pilots was a problem was because from a fundamental perspective what you had to do is fly eight helicopters 700 miles. Now, the best way to do that is have them track on C–130 aircraft, refuel them in the air, never stop and go right to your destination, and that was what the Air Force proposed. It was vetoed. The choice of the marine pilots created enormous complexities for the following reasons: one, they had no experience of flying that helicopter long-range over ground; two, they could not even use the existent navigational systems, three, their own doctrines required no navigators aboard, so they end up flying long distances with essentially dead reckoning, which was with a map and a compass, looking out of the window. Even with all that and perhaps more dangerous was the assumption that because they could not refuel in mid-air they could not track on C–130s, and had to stop in Desert One. And that's where it all went wrong.*

Carter was sold on the 'surgical operation' and met the mission commanders, General James Vaught and Colonel Charles Beckwith, who would lead the ground operation to rescue the hostages from within Teheran. Carter found their detailed description of the operation reassuring and told them that they had his complete confidence. However, Vaught and Beckwith were beginning to realize that they faced problems with intelligence. Apart from the fact that the United States could not gain permission from any of Iran's neighbours to launch the mission from their territory, nobody in the usual intelligence agency seemed to know anything about Iran. General Vaught relates a farcical intelligence briefing at which he lost his temper:

*Well, we asked for a comprehensive intelligence briefing at the Pentagon, and what we got told by the senior intelligence officials of the United States, namely the Director of CIA was 'The best we can*

*tell you is the same thing you see on the TV. We don't know any more than you do, we don't have any reliable sources there that are reporting to us, and we don't have at this point any way to get in there. All we can do is look at 'em, but we can't deduce much from that.' So we really ended up with very little. A man from the CIA read a kind of encyclopaedic thing that said in effect: 'You know you're going to be operating in a desert.' We said, 'Yes, we understand that,' or I did, whereupon he said, 'Well, when you're in the desert it's dry, it's dusty, and when it rains it's muddy.' I said, 'Yes, I appreciate that, and I can get that out of the encyclopaedia. What else can you tell me?' And he couldn't tell me anything else: where the roads were, where the potential airfields were…*

General Vaught admits that he lost his temper at the paucity of the intelligence work:

*It was kind of an exasperated reaction on my part that the intelligence we were getting was the same thing we could read in the encyclopaedia, and I ripped out a page and pinned it to the wall so people could see and compare the exact words of what we were given with the exact words in the encyclopaedia. I'm not saying that it wasn't the truth, but that was the kind of sort of dead-end analysis that we were getting.*

In spite of the severe limitations of the intelligence work, the mission went ahead. On D-day, aboard the US carrier *Nimitz*, eight helicopters led by Lieutenant-Colonel Edward R. Seiffert took off to fly to a rendezvous at Desert Base One with Delta Force, which was already on its way from Masirah Island, off the coast of Oman, in four-engined C–130 transport planes. Other transport planes – EC–130Es – were each carrying 3,000-gallon fuel reservoirs to refuel the helicopters. In the lead plane were transport commander Colonel James H. Kyle and ground-force commander Colonel 'Charging Charlie' Beckwith. With them flew Wade Ishimoto and Logan Fitch. The transports encountered little difficulty and arrived safely at Desert Base One. However, Murphy arrived with them and soon began to practise his full repertoire.

Desert Base One – on the Dasht-e-Kavir salt flats – had been selected because it was far enough away from habitation to avoid the risk that the American preparations could be disturbed. Although the Yazd–Tabas highway ran by the base, it was rarely used. But as fate would have it, the road proceeded to see as much traffic in a few minutes as it generally saw in a day. No sooner had the American transports landed than a Mercedes bus carrying some forty-four Iranian peasants – mostly women and children – came bumping along the road, as Logan Fitch relates:

*Obviously, once we'd selected Desert One as the place where we would land and refuel and transload, we kept the place under surveillance by satellite imagery and so on, and there was hardly ever any traffic – totally desolate, nothing around – but as soon as I stepped off the airplane, and I got off immediately after the initial security element, through all the dust and all the noise and everything I looked over to my right and, lo and behold, there's this new modern Mercedes bus with all the lights on, and it stopped. There are a lot of people on board and I thought, what in the world is going on?*

Next, a fuel tanker, driven at near-suicidal speed, came thundering along the lonely road. The American checkpoints were knocked sideways by the tanker, and it was only brought to a standstill by an anti-tank weapon that ignited the fuel, so that the sky was illuminated by a fireball visible for many miles. The driver leaped free of the inferno, but instead of seeking medical aid he sprinted back down the road to where a small truck had appeared, apparently driven by his partner in crime. Before the Americans could react, the truck had left the road and set off across the desert. In fact, as Beckwith suspected, the men were petrol smugglers who thought they'd been stopped by Iranian police. At that moment Logan Fitch could see the funny side:

*I remember the second aircraft landed and some troops came off, and one of my colleagues came off, and when they landed there was a fuel truck on fire. There were forty-four hostages sitting there, on this modern bus, totally unlike anything they might have expected, and he came off and said, 'How you doing?' I said, 'Welcome to World War Three.'*

Another witness to the fiasco with the fuel tanker was Wade Ishimoto. He and his colleague Rubiell weren't laughing:

*I'm waiting on the back of the motorcycle. Its engine is running, so it's pretty noisy, and all of a sudden we see these lights whirling through the dust. The next thing I hear is kaboom! I learned later that Littlejohn had fired a 40-millimetre grenade at the bus. It missed the bus, but none the less caused it to come to a stop, and he and Logan Fitch moved towards that bus, unknown to me at that point. I said to Rubiell, 'We can't wait.' The bus was coming from the direction where we needed to establish our roadblock, so promptly we started heading across the desert. This is all within just a few minutes after landing in the great salt desert of Iran, 7,000 miles away from the United States. Rubiell looks back at me and he says, 'Sir?' I said, 'Yes, I see 'em. Move off the road to the left.' So he pulled the motorcycle off the road, and we saw vehicle lights coming at us. At that point I got out in the middle of the road and I told Rubiell: 'Grab one of your light anti-tank weapons. Come up on me and take cover.' So he went forward of me and went down on the ground, then took*

*out his light anti-tank weapon as I stood in the middle of the road. The lights came down on me. I knew they could see me clearly because they were illuminating me. I had my hand up. The vehicle started towards me, and I opened fire with my M-16 rifle, and the vehicle was still coming. Finally I hollered over to Rubiell, I said: 'Rube, cock your lock.' 'Yes, sir.' 'Ready?' 'Yes, sir.' 'Fire!' And then the next words out of my mouth were: 'Holy mackerel!' We hit a 5,000-gallon fuel truck in the middle of the Iranian desert, and now fuel was venting upwards in flames at least 90 to 100 feet into the air. It was quite an experience, and I was having flashbacks to Vietnam. Things were happening fast, and when things happen that way time has a way of slowing down as you perceive different things. So I moved in on the truck to see if anybody was alive, and I heard this bizarre sound coming from it. I couldn't figure out what it was until I got closer: the guy had his radio playing Iranian music at full blast. The flames were jumping out every place. He was hidden in the cab of the truck, and as I moved in I saw another vehicle behind it. I'm saying to myself, 'What next, Murphy must be alive and well on this night!' I hollered in Farsi for the guy to get out of the truck, but saw no movement. Then I saw movement from the truck to the rear, so immediately I went back towards Rubiell, because nobody had heard a word of English spoken so far. I got back to Rubiell, and said: 'There's another vehicle behind. Jump on the motorcycle. Let's go after 'em.' And he said: 'Sir, somebody just jumped out of the front truck.' I said: 'OK, he's probably running back to that rear truck. Let's go. Let's try and catch him.' So we jumped on the motorcycle, and nine kicks later it finally started.*

Everyone, meanwhile, awaited the arrival of the eight helicopters from the *Nimitz*, little expecting the problems their arrival would bring. The helicopters were absolutely vital to the operation, and it was now obvious that too much reliance was being placed on machines liable to mechanical failure and instrument malfunction. The choppers and their marine pilots were being pushed beyond their limits, with disastrous consequences. One problem that all the choppers faced was the fact that the Americans were paying too much respect to the Iranian radar and had ordered all of them to fly under its imagined umbrella by skimming the desert floor at not much more than fifty feet, a nightmare for the pilots, who knew that a moment's loss of concentration could result in a fatal crash. The next emergency occurred when chopper number six was forced to land because of a damaged rotor blade. There was no alternative but to abandon the helicopter, the crew being picked up by chopper number eight.

As if the problem of mechanical failure and the threat from low flying were not enough, the choppers now encountered something for which they had not been prepared. Clouds of sand and dust known as haboobs – thousands of feet high, and miles in width – lay in their path. With the sand clouds thickest nearest to the ground, where the choppers were forced to fly to avoid radar, one pilot commented that it was like 'flying in a bowl of milk'. Ed Seiffert described his impression of flying through a haboob:

*I was looking out, and it looked like a fog bank to me. It had the characteristics of a rolling fog bank coming in off the Atlantic coast, a lot higher, but it had those characteristics. It looked like a billowy ground cloud; it wasn't turbulent, it was kind of a pumicey environment, highly reflective because there are lots of particles in the air. It degraded the capability of night vision goggles because you couldn't see very far, and you couldn't see without night vision goggles either, so it really didn't make much difference whether they were on or off. This is something that was not forecast, OK, and we had a great deal of confidence through our training in the Air Force weather service. They hadn't ever missed a weather brief at all. They were a hundred per cent spot on. We had satellite imagery the day we left.*

Not only was visibility obscured but the temperature inside the helicopters rose dramatically, adding to the discomfort of the journey and making breathing difficult. And beyond the first haboob was a second, even larger one. It was now that the pilot of chopper number five made a fateful decision, one that was to affect the whole mission. Uneasy about his instrumentation, chopper five turned away and limped back to the *Nimitz*, reducing the helicopter force to just six, the bare minimum for the mission to be given the go-ahead.

The arrival of the choppers at Desert Base One was an anticlimax for Logan Fitch, whose heart must have leaped as he heard the throaty sound of the rotor blades emerging from the dark sky overhead. His first meeting was with the pilot of chopper number three, Major James Schaeffer. Schaeffer was in no mood to exchange pleasantries with Fitch:

*Finally two helicopters arrived. I happened to be the senior officer*

△ Colonel Charles Beckwith, leader of the abortive rescue attempt in Operation Eagle Claw.

*immediately in the vicinity, so I ran up to the pilot and said: 'Gosh, I'm glad you're here. Where are the rest of your people?' And he said: 'Well, I think they're coming.' Then he said, 'Logan, you don't know what we've been through.' And I said: 'Well, you're here now, we're glad, get fuelled and as soon as the other ones get here we'll take off.' Two more helicopters arrived, and again I was in the immediate vicinity. I talked to one of the pilots, who told me that he'd had a mechanical problem, that his primary hydraulic system had failed.*

*And I said: 'Does that cause the mission to abort?' And he said: 'No, this is not an uncommon occurrence with this aircraft. We've got backup systems and we'll be able to proceed.' Two more helicopters arrived, the last of the six that finally arrived, one of which was piloted by the commander of the marine helicopter unit. I immediately went to him, briefed him and told him he had four aircraft on the ground that were fuelled and ready to go just as soon as he could get fuelled. We'd load, and we'd be ready to proceed because we're way behind schedule. He immediately said: 'Well, I've got to go talk to my people.'*

The marine pilots led by Ed Seiffert seemed to be less than keen to go on, and when news reached them that another chopper had technical problems they seemed almost relieved. Six choppers was the minimum possible for the mission; five fit machines would not have the carrying capacity. Beckwith now faced the decision he must have dreaded: should he abort the mission? Tempers frayed as the Delta Force men saw their chances disappearing. They were entirely dependent on the marine pilots to get them to Teheran, but had the marines got the guts or were they looking to chicken out?

Beckwith and Colonel Jim Kyle of the Air Force used the satellite transmitter to contact the operation commander, General Vaught, in Egypt. Beckwith explained the difficulties with the helicopters. Vaught asked him to consider going ahead with just the five choppers rather than aborting the mission, but Beckwith was resolute. It had been agreed before the mission started that six choppers was the minimum number needed to carry out the mission in safety, and that was now Beckwith's prime consideration. To the tough army colonel it would be better to get out cleanly with nothing lost and 'come back in a few days' for another attempt. And so the decision was taken to abort the mission.

To the north of the highway some of the C–130s had been parked with four of the helicopters behind them, while to the

△ President Jimmy Carter pays the political price for military failure.

south were positioned the other transports and the remaining choppers. Jim Kyle ordered the helicopters to return to the *Nimitz*, but before they could do so number four needed to refuel. Major Schaeffer in number three moved his chopper aside to let number four pass, but as he did so the helicopter was lifted by a sudden blast of wind and dropped on top of the nearest transport. Its rotor blades cut through the C–130's cockpit, and there was a sudden fireball as both planes burst into flames. The transport had only just been boarded by members of Delta Blue, who imagined that they were under attack. Logan Fitch described what happened next:

*I was in the back of the airplane near the left door, and I heard and felt a thump, a series of thumps, actually, and my first thought was that we were under attack and that someone was firing on the airplane. So my first thought was to get off the airplane and get my men off, and the crew chief and I opened the back...and I looked up and I saw sparks and fire up towards the front of the cargo compartment, up around the flight deck. So I went to get my people off there, opened the left door, and the whole left side of the plane was on fire outside. You couldn't get out there. Obviously, we couldn't go out the front, so the only way to get out was through the right troop door, they call it, and that one door was opened and the men started getting out and running away from the plane. Someone started yelling, 'Get out of here, get out of here', and my sergeant-major — I credit him with saving a lot of the lives — he just said, 'Everybody calm down and get off in an orderly fashion'. They followed that direction, everybody got off but before that I had in mind that I would be the last one off, and at this moment I still think we're under attack, and so I grab my weapons and so on, and I would be the last one off and make sure everybody got off. But you could see the flames and the fire advancing from the front to the back of the cargo compartment, and I knew in my mind then that we wouldn't all make it off. So I thought I'd waited as long as I could, and then I got out of there. Even after I got out, other people still came off. In fact, one of my sergeants went back in and pulled one of the crew members out and saved his life, for which he was awarded a soldier's medal. We ran away from the plane, and I mean you can't imagine a fourth of July like that. There was fuel on board, there were explosives, ammunition, and I remember thinking, Hell must look like this. It was an awful situation. We simply tried to get away from it. The other planes were taxiing away from that plane so they wouldn't catch on fire, and we started loading people on aircraft as they became available.*

It was a hellish scene that Logan Fitch was never to forget:

*The aircraft was burning, and the helicopter which crashed into our aircraft was sort of sitting on top. It looked like a locust or a dragonfly or something preying on the airplane that we'd been on. Ammunition was exploding, rockets were going off, the fuel vapours obviously were burning. I mean, it was a huge, huge, huge fire: explosions, bullets whistling everywhere, a dramatic moment...*

In the inferno that now engulfed the two planes eight American servicemen died and five more were seriously injured. Many soldiers abandoned their equipment in their panic, and all the helicopters were left in the desert, leaving their secret maps and equipment for the Iranians to collect the following day. As the Americans took off and left their desert base, now littered with debris, the puzzled occupants of the Iranian bus watched in silence.

This emotionally searing moment scarred all the participants. However, commentators in the United States have wondered at the precipitate retreat of Delta Force from Desert Base One. Richard Gabriel believes they simply cracked:

*I think, if you ask me, the people on the ground were psychologically defeated: that's to say that events got beyond their control. Here you are at Desert One looking around and you're launched with the full desire of taking out this mission and going on, and everything starts to go wrong. You don't have what you think is enough lift, you don't have what you think is enough daylight, you don't know what the heck...the fuel tank is burning down the road because you've been discovered...Oh, I imagine that the pressure on the commanders and Colonel Beckwith must have been enormous, and he could have concluded that this is just crazy, this is all out of control.*

What had gone wrong? According to Ed Seiffert, the problem was easily summed up: 'Aircraft broke, plain and simple.' Not everyone, particularly those on the mission, was prepared to accept this interpretation. Anger and bitterness coloured their responses, and accusations rained on the helicopter pilots, particularly from the Delta Force soldiers. The Holloway Special Operations Review Group later noted twenty-three different factors that had contributed to the failure of the mission, ranging from inadequate weather reconnaissance to mechanical deficiencies in the helicopters. Yet, in a sense, the overriding problem was the mission itself. Within the constraints imposed by President Carter – the surgical nature of the operation and the unwillingness to accept or impose casualties – the question had to be raised as to whether the operation was feasible or indeed worthwhile. The consequences of failure were so serious that one is tempted to consider Carter's decision to give it the go-ahead as irresponsible. As one of the hostages said, on hearing of the failure of Eagle Claw, 'Thank God for the sandstorm'. The losses in American lives – both military and civilian hostages – not to mention Iranian casualties, if the plan had backfired in Teheran rather than at Desert Base One, should have been part of the military equation and as such sufficient to consign the plan to the trash can. And the consequences to relations with Iran, the Soviet Union and the Muslim world of a shoot-out in downtown Teheran are almost too serious to contemplate. Richard Gabriel feels that not enough was done before the mission was given the go-ahead. Eight months were to pass before the hostages were released alive. During that time Jimmy Carter lost the presidency to Ronald Reagan. One suspects that Murphy voted Republican.

Carnage at Desert Base One. Wreckage litters the ground.

# CHAPTER THREE

# UNDER-ESTIMATING THE ENEMY

A strong sense of purpose and self-confidence, and even a touch of arrogance, binds together an army. In training and tradition, this sense is encouraged. But it can go too far, and a false sense of racial or social superiority has been the cause of many blunders. Military arrogance can lead to underestimating the enemy, which can be fatal. Too many soldiers have felt the shock of betrayal, when they find that the enemy whom they have been encouraged to ridicule and belittle as far inferior to themselves proves to be different in practice than had been expected. Far from being inferior physically, mentally, racially or even technologically, an enemy can prove to have unexpected skills: for example, the Zulus were able to outrun the British cavalry horses over difficult and broken ground, and the Japanese, short of motorized transport, achieved remarkable mobility through the use of bicycles. The Asiatic soldiers of Japan and Vietnam, though slight in comparison with their Anglo-Saxon or French opponents, proved remarkably tough fighters, able to endure hardship and to survive on minimal supplies. Defeat by such militarily 'inferior' opponents had remarkable effects on the mainly Western troops. From underestimating an enemy for whom one felt only contempt one could swing to absurd and equally dangerous overestimation.

▷ This *Punch* cartoon is appropriate not just for the British after
their defeat at Isandhlwana, but for many colonial armies in the
nineteenth and twentieth centuries.

A LESSON.

# ISANDHLWANA, 1879

⚔

The story of the Zulu War, and in particular the great Zulu victory at Isandhlwana (or should I say the great British disaster at Isandhlwana? Usually the winners get to write the history; in this case, however, it was the losers…) is well illustrated in the words of two British officers, both serving in Africa between 1879 and 1902. Captain Edward Hutton, serving in Zululand with the 60th Rifles in 1879, summed up his feelings about fighting the Zulus thus: 'It is to me like a shooting expedition with just a spice of danger thrown in to make it really interesting.' Less than a generation later, Lieutenant F. P. Crozier of the West African Field Force, in 1902, helped explain Kipling's 'White Man's burden' to the local inhabitants: 'I proceeded to become very annoyed and told the interpreter to go into the village again and to inform the king that if he did not come out forthwith and do homage to the British flag, I would set fire to the village and make war on him and his villagers.' In the words of two doubtless courageous British officers, the matter is encapsulated. Sport and the flag, the enemy faintly more dangerous than wild animals but to be hunted, nevertheless, shot, stuffed and displayed in the regimental mess, above the silverware and the polo trophies. A century of colonial warfare reduced to a formulaic game to entertain troops in far-flung parts of the Empire who were short of women, booze and cheap entertainment. Hilaire Belloc summed it all up in the lines: 'Whatever happens we have got/the Maxim Gun, and they have not.'

Superior fire power gave European armies an overwhelming advantage in colonial warfare, but some commanders failed to understand that the non-European, non-white opponents did not 'play the game' according to the rules that said that the white man always won. In the Zulu War Lord Chelmsford, otherwise an efficient, professional soldier, allowed the virtues of his own army to blind him to the virtues of his enemy. The outcome was one of the most famous – where it should be the most infamous – British disasters of the nineteenth century. In their way the British – media and public alike – seized on the setback and remoulded it so that it became more memorable in defeat than most victories were in victory. The 'savage, barbaric Zulu' was transformed into the magnificent semi-Viking warrior, his hair almost an honorary blond and his eyes a Nordic blue. His assegai changed to a great battle-axe, and out of the pages of Rider Haggard's novels stepped the 'son of Shaka', himself now the 'black Napoleon', in the shape of Umslopogaas, friend of Alan Quatermain and companion to many late-Victorian and Edwardian boy's dreams. The Zulus might have believed they won the battle of Isandhlwana militarily, but culturally they lost it and Zululand fell into the hands of Britain's novelists, journalists and film-makers as much as its soldiers.

In 1878 the confederation policy of British Colonial Secretary Lord Carnarvon in South Africa faced a hurdle, the removal of which would hopefully persuade the Boers of the Transvaal, recently annexed by Britain, to accept their new status as British citizens. The hurdle was the powerful, independent Zulu nation, created by Shaka in the early years of the century and an enemy to the Boers. The British authorities knew that while the Zulus probably posed no immediate threat to the neighbouring British colony of Natal, there could be no peace between the Zulus and the Boers, who had been at odds for fifty years since the Boers first trekked into Zulu territory. If the Boers were to be brought under British protection, then that protection needed to be clearly demonstrated by the removal of what the Boers feared most – the Zulu army of King Cetshwayo. But the British faced a Catch-22 situation: if they removed the Zulu threat, then why would the Boers need further protection?

British leaders in South Africa, from High Commissioner Sir Bartle Frere to commander-in-chief Lord Chelmsford, simply tied themselves in webs of deceit. On the one hand, Frere and Sir Theophilus Shepstone presented the Zulu army as such a threat that only its immediate disbandment or destruction in battle would enable white settlers in Natal to sleep quietly in their beds, while, on the other, Chelmsford questioned the efficacy of the Zulus as opponents and appeared to rate them no more highly than the minor Bantu tribes he had recently defeated in the 9th Kaffir War. Never was the aphorism that the first casualty in wartime is the truth ever more clearly illustrated.

The Boers tried to give the British a more balanced picture. The Zulus were formidable warriors individually: they could outrun a horse over broken ground and travel long distances with minimal supplies. Zulu regiments adopted strategy and tactics that had been tried and tested over half a century and

△ Popular novelist Rider Haggard's Zulu character, Umslopogaas, hero of *Nada the Lily* and companion to Alan Quatermain in many of his adventures.

were led by able leaders, while a full army using the 'buffalo chest and horns' formation was a threat to any opponent who did not accord them respect as opponents. Conversely, they were a primitive enemy, lacking missile power and a mounted element. Faced by a modern army with concentrated rifle fire they would fall victim to their own courage, willingly suffering enormous casualties in frontal assaults. While enjoying an enormous numerical advantage – as was always likely against European opponents – the Zulus could triumph through the sheer weight of their assaults and the cumulative effect of their stabbing spears. However, the assegai was not a weapon to equal the European rifle and bayonet, which gave the redcoat considerable 'reach' advantage in a one-to-one combat. The most important lesson, the Boers insisted, was never to let the Zulus come close enough for one-to-one situations. The Europeans should entrench or *laager* themselves to prevent the Zulu 'horns' outflanking them and concentrate heavy rifle fire on the Zulu 'buffalo chest'. Once the buffalo formation was broken and dispersed, the Zulus could easily be ridden down by mounted riflemen or by cavalry using the sword, lance or revolver. In the opinion of the Boers, a European reverse at the hands of the Zulus should never take place if a few simple rules were obeyed. What would be fatal, however, was if these rules were ignored and the Zulus undervalued as opponents. The Zulus should never win a battle against Europeans, however heroic their performance. It would be against all logic, like a triumph for Achilles and Odysseus over Napoleon and Wellington. The Boers spoke sense – they had, after all, survived for fifty years alongside the Zulus and had nothing still to prove – but were the British listening?

If a concentration of fire power was the key to victory against the Zulus, Lord Chelmsford began his invasion of Zululand by making an absolutely fundamental mistake in colonial warfare against a primitive but numerically superior enemy: he divided his army into separate columns, challenging the Zulus to concentrate their numerical superiority against each column in turn. Underestimating the mobility and flexibility of the Zulus, he allowed them to operate on internal lines to strike at his fractured command so that it was not just the central column, which he commanded, which came close to annihilation. Both at Kambula and Hlobane, Colonel Evelyn Wood's column was attacked by large numbers of Zulus but survived through adopting the correct tactics of concentrated fire power from a defensive position. In fact, at Kambula the Zulus displayed an underestimation of the British and suffered a terrible defeat, losing over a thousand men killed to a mere handful of British casualties, thereby reversing the effects of their victory at Isandhlwana. In the final battle – massacre is a better word – at Ulundi, Chelmsford accorded the Zulus the respect of forming infantry squares and massing his cavalry in the centre, ready to exploit the inevitable. Zulu courage cost them nearly three thousand lives for the cost of ten redcoats.

However, Lord Chelmsford had a steep learning curve to negotiate before he reached Ulundi, Cetshwayo's capital. Zulu military expert Ian Knight points out that Chelmsford did do his homework before invading Zululand – yet somehow failed to draw the right conclusions:

*Chelmsford had taken steps initially to do an in-depth study into the fighting tactics of the Zulus and he got hold of a document compiled by a border agent by the name of Finney and in that* document...there was remarkable detail about how the Zulus fought the enemy. He took advice from none other than Paul Kruger, who had been in earlier skirmishes during the Great Trek as a young man. He had heard about the Zulu fighting power, he knew the might of the Zulu nation – that was all at his fingertips – and he even wrote that into regulations on what precautions should be taken on the march, but he himself when he got here never adhered to it, he threw that away, he threw all that away.*

In Chelmsford's case, he was a victim of his own experiences, as South African historian Paul Naish writes:

*He's again under the opinion from his experiences in the eastern Cape that he's going to have to lure them into the field and engage them in the open and take them on under his own terms. He tried that in the eastern Cape, and what had happened was the enemy would vanish into the hills.*

Chelmsford simply tried to shortcut the army regulations about entrenching camps because he was in such a hurry to bring the Zulus to battle. What he appeared to fear, above all, was that he would become embroiled in another drawn-out Kaffir War, but this time against a numerically powerful enemy that could maintain their guerrilla tactics almost indefinitely. Like Navarre a century later at Dien Bien Phu, Chelmsford wanted to draw the enemy into an open battle that they could never win. However, such tactics were fraught with danger if a commander neglected his intelligence work and failed to maintain excellent scouting. As we have seen, Chelmsford had read all that there was to read on the Zulu. Unfortunately, he did not believe it as Ian Knight explains:

*Certainly, Lord Chelmsford was offered a great deal of advice by various colonial settlers in Natal on fighting the Zulus. He must have weighed that up against his own professional competence; inevitably, he must have thought, Well, OK, these people have fought the Zulus but when did they fight them? They fought them perhaps in the 1830s when the Boer Voortrekkers fought against King Dingaan's army. I, Lord Chelmsford, however, have recently been on active service on the Cape frontier, I've been through Abyssinia, I've been through the Crimean War, I actually know a great deal more about what the British Army is capable of than these local settlers who are advising me.*

Suffering from 'cognitive dissonance', he refused to accept that the experiences of settlers – Dutch and British – could really form the basis for the tactics of a professional army. Colourful descriptions of Zulu customs and habits were undoubtedly accurate but surely of more relevance to the Royal Geographical Society. Paul Naish writes of Chelmsford:

*One doesn't want to speak ill of Chelmsford because he was a product of his time, and if you look at the British generals of the day there were some certainly brave men and there were some certainly very foolish men at the same time. Chelmsford of course had been born with a silver spoon in his mouth and he'd been an equerry to Queen Victoria.*

When his scouts reported that they had detected the Zulus to the south-east, Chelmsford, apparently without qualms, divided the central column and personally led half of it away from his encampment at Isandhlwana, hoping to bring them to battle. Ian Knight shows how Chelmsford suffered from poor scouting:

*Chelmsford has a number of problems when it comes down to scouting, certainly there is an element of complacency there, but he's also working in terrain which was hardly even known to the European world. A lot of the maps that Chelmsford and his officers were working from still had huge tracts that were marked 'unknown' on them, so they didn't really understand what they were trying to operate in anyway, and being a typical British Army in a colonial environment he was under strength, he had far too few mounted men to scout properly, and he was forced to rely really on local volunteers, on African auxiliaries. Having said that, such was the imperial mindset that the regular officers were often wary of information that was brought to them by colonial volunteers and African auxiliaries.*

Lord Chelmsford left the camp at Isandhlwana in what he felt to be the capable hands of Lieutenant-Colonel Pulleine with six companies of the 24th Regiment, as well as native troops of the Natal Native Contingent. With Chelmsford out of the camp, Pulleine continued to send out patrols. One, led by Charlie Raw, made an alarming discovery:

*Raw and his men trotted to the rim of that plateau, they peered over it, there were no Zulus to be seen. All that they could see going off into the blue haze were these little deserted beehive villages and then way off in the north-east they saw a large herd of black cattle being shepherded along by little Zulu herd boys, and they thought, Well, they're up here, they might as well loot these cattle, so they started to canter out across this huge expanse of open rolling country. They were not really concentrating, you must imagine: it was a hellishly hot day and they'd cantered for a couple of miles and then they looked up and the cattle and the kids had gone. In open country they had simply*

△ Zulu King Cetshwayo. Always friendly towards the British, Cetshwayo found himself involved in a war not of his own choosing in 1879. Dressed in a frock-coat and top hat Cetshwayo visited England after the Zulu Wars and met Queen Victoria.

*vanished; we think they'd been scuttled off into one of those fingers of erosion, and all these men trotted through the place where they thought they'd seen the cattle and the kids, they trotted up that little stony slope. Dear God, suddenly they had to rein in their horses to prevent them from falling into a huge valley, and they gazed aghast at what was in this valley: below and beyond them, stretching off along the course of that stream, off in an easterly direction as far as the eye could*

△ Frederick August Thesiger, 2nd Baron Chelmsford. Professional arrogance rather than simple racialism caused his downfall. He took advice on how to fight the Zulus from the Boers, but still felt he knew best, as an experienced British officer.

see, packed in there squatting, in absolute silence, upon their great war shields, regiment by disciplined regiment, were the Zulus of the main Zulu army, so the main Zulu army was not to the south and to the east, where Chelmsford was looking for it; the Zulu army was here...between 20,000 and 26,000 warriors accompanied by several thousand teenage boys carrying their older brothers' spare porridge and sleeping mats and several thousand women. What a moment that must have been!

Colonel Pulleine was in his tent when a rider brought in the startling news that there were thousands of Zulus advancing towards the left front of the Isandhlwana camp. Pulleine sat down at his portmanteau in his tent and scribbled a note to Lord Chelmsford. Next he walked across to where the men were having their breakfast and he ordered them to leave their breakfast unfinished and to don their webbing, which contained ammunition pouches holding between fifty and seventy rounds of ammunition per man, and these men were now told to take their rifles and to form up in a skirmishing line to face the threat.

David Rattray believes that after his natural anxiety had subsided Pulleine's confidence reasserted itself. After all, he had 1,774 men in the camp, and of these 1,000 were veteran soldiers equipped with modern breech-loading, lever-action Martini-Henry rifles, which could deliver twelve rounds per man per minute accurately at ranges up to 800 yards. Given such fire power, Pulleine must have thought: roll on, Zulus, roll on and we'll thump the blighters in the open. Pulleine clearly underestimated the Zulu threat even at this pregnant moment, for he sent another note to Chelmsford, without any sense of urgency or appeal for help. Significantly, in an act of insubordination, the captain who delivered the message to the dispatch rider pencilled on the bottom, 'I think you should know, Sir, that Henry Pulleine has strung out his firing line three-quarters of a mile in front of the camp,' a huge and obvious implicit criticism in this postscript.

Outnumbered twenty to one by the Zulus and with no entrenchments, the redcoats had no realistic chance. In such a battle only a defensive position, as at Rorke's Drift, or a laager of wagons interspersed with thick thorn bushes would have held back the Zulu charge. Even concentrated fire power would not triumph if it was not maintained for long enough. At first the Zulus found the British fire power almost impenetrable, and it was problems with ammunition supply that first began to erode the British position. In various parts of the Isandhlwana battlefield the Zulus managed to outflank the redcoat units and roll up their lines. The Zulus record that at one moment the outcome of the battle hung in the balance. Their casualties had been so shocking that even these supremely brave warriors began to hang back, and an old warrior, one of the regimental commanders, forced his way to the front and addressed his men, bullets flying all around him. Zulu battlefield expert David Rattray tells what happened next as described to him by Zulus present at the battle:

*The Zulus were appalled, they were horrified because these warriors started to fall back under this hail of lead, they were horrified because the whole thrust of the whole attack of the horns of the buffalo was going to fail because of that one thing, and then an event occurred which in its own way changed the passage of this great nation's history. An old Zulu left his position right at the back behind the depression – you can see there's a little stony slope – he was one of the chiefs of this regiment, old, wizened, grey beard…and we watched this old man pick his way down through the slope, we watched him stride through this depression recklessly exposing himself to British bullets, and above the row of battle we heard him scream at these young warriors who were falling back. He shouted at them: 'You in the front line, don't even think of running away. Cetshwayo never told anyone here to run away.' And with that a British bullet struck him smack between the eyes and killed him in his tracks, and so struck were the Zulus with what this old man had just done for all of them that afterwards not one Zulu fell back even an inch.*

Once the Zulus broke into the British camp, among its tents and wagons, the British lost all cohesion, and panic set in. David Rattray describes the final stages of the battle:

*The Zulus went berserk in the camp. They slashed at the tents, they set fire to everything, they smashed the medicine bottles, they stabbed the tinned meats, they were tossing these wagons on to their sides and hacking at the oxen and the mules, they were tossing the bodies of British soldiers on to their backs and disembowelling them, often incorrectly described as a needless mutilation: no,* ukukaka, *to disembowel, was a politeness that was extended to the deceased to allow his spirit to escape with dignity, and if he was a brave man the man who'd killed him would cut out his gall bladder and suck out the* inyongo, *the repository of bravery. He would clench his fists and shout: 'God, I have eaten.'*

Meanwhile, Lord Chelmsford was twelve miles away with his column following a Zulu will-o'-the-wisp. Films and novels have ridiculed Chelmsford for his activities that morning. At a time when his camp was being overrun and his troops massacred, he is often portrayed as conducting almost a social event in the hills of Zululand. Zulu Chief Mangosuthu Buthelezi, great-grandson of King Cetshwayo, feels this displayed an underestimation of the Zulus:

*Well, I think that they had a picnic attitude towards the whole thing. It would just be some kind of picnic, and I think that is very dramatized by the fact that Lord Chelmsford himself had breakfast that morning where he was. I mean, with all the silver and things, you know. I mean, during that war there is an element of disdain in their attitude.*

Ian Knight points out that Lord Chelmsford was very much a man of his time:

*I think it would be very wrong to believe too much in the stereotype of the sort of racist, arrogant imperial army, but all stereotypes I suppose have an element of truth in them, and that's why they gain credence in people's imaginations, and I think it's certainly true that the British army really from top to bottom, from Lord Chelmsford down to the ordinary soldier, had an innate belief in their own superiority. They felt that their white skins and their discipline and their technological superiority actually made them pretty much superior to anybody. After all, they'd fought just about everybody in the world and beaten them at some time or another.*

The arrogance of the redcoat officer, perhaps fresh from the regimental comforts of a cantonment in Britain, and now finding himself plying his profession among the heathens and savages – white as well as black – in the colonies, is very much of its time and should not attract our historical scorn. In an intensely class-conscious society, as Victorian Britain undoubtedly was, contempt for one's social inferiors was as predictable as it was deplorable. Thus, when Lieutenant-Colonel Henry Crealock, for example, commented on receiving a report that the Zulus were attacking the camp, 'How very amusing! Actually attacking our camp! Most amusing!', he was reacting in a manner laughable to us, but acceptable to his peer group around him. No British officer could react with other than scorn at the idea that a savage race, stereotyped by his commander as needing to be forced into the open and virtually forced to fight, would come knocking on the door and asking him to step outside.

Ultimately, the British disaster at Isandhlwana – notwithstanding the achievements of the ancient Zulu commander, Tshingwayo, and his magnificent regiments – was Chelmsford's disaster. He had painted a picture of what he expected to happen and had joined up the dots. When completed, he found the picture very different from what he had expected. Naturally, the most common criticism he faced was that he did not fortify the camp at Isandhlwana as local opinion – Boer and British – had warned him to do. Was this underestimating the enemy or was the error forced on him by necessity?

Battlefield historians like Paul Naish and David Rattray give an accurate assessment of what options the British commander faced. Paul Naish describes Chelmsford's first arrival at Isandhlwana:

*Chelmsford arrived later and he was asked about what plans had been made to laager the camp. He decided that this was not necessary. The ground, he said, was too hard to make entrenchments, and the wagons and the carts were needed to go back to Rorke's Drift down yonder to bring in fresh supplies, and so it is we see the first discord, as I said earlier, about the unsatisfactory nature of the laagering of that camp. The Boers had successfully fought the Zulus forty years earlier at Blood River, and none other than Paul Kruger had warned Chelmsford: 'When you fight the Zulus you must throw your scouts far out in the distance so they can see where they're coming from, and*

△Lieutenants Melvill and Coghill try to save the regimental colours after the battle of Isandhlwana.

*when you stop at night you must laager your wagons because forty years earlier, when we fought them, that was the only way we could beat these men warriors. The Zulus are like nothing that you've ever come across before.' And, of course, Chelmsford was quite disdainful. 'Thank you, Mr Kruger. That is very good of you to warn us.' Kruger, of course, was not fighting with the modern technology we have today. Of course, what Chelmsford was referring to was the Martini-Henry, the breech-loading Martini-Henry, the most modern weapon in the world 120 years ago.*

David Rattray points out that *laagering* the camp was easier in principle than in practice. Armchair critics have never seen the sort of wagons the British Army used at that time.

*Chelmsford failed to entrench the camp. He did not dig a peripheral trench around the borders of that camp. Now this was a stipulation in the general orders, and by not doing so he effectively disobeyed the standing instruction, and when this was pointed out to him he quite correctly pointed out that if he tried to dig in, in this hard, coal-bearing shale, it would take at least a week to do so, and his intention was to be here for two days, so for good logical reasons this camp was not entrenched. Chelmsford was to be flayed in history for not entrenching this camp. He fails to draw his wagons down here into a defensive arrangement, a laager. Chelmsford had been told by Paul Kruger himself that he must laager, he must defend every bivouac, but laagering for the Boers was a different matter. The Boers took into battle with them little fighting wagons; five of us could push one around. On the other hand, the British wagons were transport wagons; they carried up to eight tons of commissary. You needed a whole company, a hundred men, to push a laden transport wagon; you needed fifty to push an empty one, and they were full. Fifty of these wagons were always shuttling supplies from Rorke's Drift. The area that would be subtended by such an enormous number of wagons would be so large as to be unmanageable. Chelmsford doesn't laager for good logical reasons.*

Yet Chelmsford has been rightly criticized for not defending the camp at all. Imperial armies in primitive areas have been fortifying their camps since Roman times. It was an article of faith among professional soldiers that to be ambushed was the crime beyond forgiveness, simply because it was so easily avoidable. Reconnaissance and entrenchment were the watchwords, and Chelmsford failed in both departments. The Zulus surprised him on an open hillside, and after that no amount of Martini-Henry rifles could save his redcoats. If he knew he could not *laager* the wagons or entrench the camp, then clearly the site was the wrong one to choose for an encampment.

Few British defeats seem as clear cut as Isandhlwana. David Rattray sums up the military errors:

*One can actually explain from a British point of view why the machine failed: the line was too far out, the line subtended only 90 degrees of the 360, the men on that line were between three and five yards apart, they were armed with between fifty and seventy rounds of ammunition per man, they ran out of ammunition. On the line, possibly the lever-action Martini-Henry rifles got hot and jammed and malfunctioned. The supply of ammunition was faulty because of pigheaded quartermasters; there is a possibility that there weren't screwdrivers to free the strapping on the boxes. There are all sorts of military reasons why this failed. They split the force, they split it again,*

*they split it again on top of that: three huge columns, two little columns split into five, the big strong central column then splits again...Oh, yes, complacency has crept in here, there's no doubt.*

Rather than ending with Lord Chelmsford's errors, it is surely better to conclude with these splendid words of David Rattray, drawing on the accounts of Zulus he had interviewed over many years: *Boy's Own* stuff, maybe, but ringing true to its time. For once the raw courage of Britain's soldiers was not enough to redeem the failures of their leaders:

*In this bloody bedlam Henry Pulleine stepped into that tent one more time, this time to fetch out the Queen's colour of the 1st Battalion, 24th Regiment of Foot, to which all regimental honour was attached, and he stepped out into this chaos and he saw Lieutenant Teignmouth Melvill, the adjutant, and he said to him: 'Melvill, the Queen's colour, you're to take it to a place of safety. God speed, and God be with you, boy.' And Melvill took this huge field case colour, placed it across the pommel of his saddle, and these two men saluted each other solemnly and Melvill wheeled his great roan horse and punched a way through the Zulus, and off he goes on his epic ride which was to end for him in tragedy at the Fugitive Drift.*

*Younghusband's men had their backs to this rock, and that's what they saw. There are some fantastic Zulu accounts of this. One man explained how he was in the camp; he said there were quite a few of us Zulus in the camp, he said suddenly the sun went dark like night. I mentioned that, the solar eclipse: the computer tells us that it started at ten minutes past one. The tumult and the firing, he said, were wonderful. Every warrior shouted 'Usutu!' as he killed. One man said: 'We looked from the camp and we saw on the side of this hill there was a man standing on this rock with big black moustaches and a great knife on his belt, and the men stood around this rock with their bayonets fixed.' One said he ran up the slope and he came over this lip and saw to his relief that these soldiers here had by now run out of ammunition and 'we forced them quickly, easily, killing a number of them along the way, we forced them right up against the crag of the hill, and they stood with their backs to that mountain and their bayonets fixed, and they glared at us and we glared at them.' One Zulu account intimates that they gave Captain Younghusband time to shake hands with all his men before they killed him. Only the Zulus would do something like that, and then one man said: 'This man of yours with the big black moustaches and the great knife on his belt, he pulled the knife from his belt and he whirled it around his head, all yelling and screaming were they, and they came running down the mountain at us, suicidal bayonet charge it must have been, and we fell upon them and we killed them all.' He said: 'We really respected those men; they were men of enormous courage.'*

A British epic. The Battle of Isandhlwana as it probably never was.

# THE BALANGIGA MASSACRE, 1901

⚔

I ronically, the high point of the colonial age, the period at the turn of the century when Kipling's 'White Man's burden' acted as a kind of 'international anthem' for the colonial powers of Europe and America, saw some of the greatest military disasters in colonial history. For every triumph of the imperial legions, as at Omdurman, there was a disaster, as at Isandhlwana, Adowa, Anual or even Balangiga. It really did not help white troops in the colonies to pay too much attention to Kipling's verse, at least to the use the press made of it. The outcome was that it fed their own racial prejudices and fuelled atrocities against the so-called inferior races. In addition, it led soldiers to underestimate their enemies, usually a prelude to military disaster.

One of the least known colonial disasters occurred during the war between the United States and the Filipino revolutionary forces in 1901. Overshadowed by the Second Boer War, this incident and its consequences have earned little more than a footnote in American history books. It is not difficult to see why. The racial attitudes of American soldiers, generals and enlisted men alike provide a chilling introduction to a century that has seen genocide on a level undreamed of in earlier times. In a sense these American servicemen were reflecting the prejudices of the age in America. The massacre of 3,000 Filipinos in Manila in 1899 had provoked the following editorial from the *Chicago Tribune*:

> *The slaughter at Manila was necessary but not glorious. The entire American population justifies the conduct of its army at Manila because only by a crushing repulse of the Filipinos could our position be made secure. We are the trustees of civilization and peace throughout the islands.*

The development of guerrilla tactics by the Filipinos was similar to that of the Boers in South Africa and produced the same response from the frustrated white professional soldiers. While in 1900 General Kitchener in South Africa had complained, 'The Boers are not like the Sudanese, who stood up to a fair fight. They are always running away on their little ponies,' US General Wheaton responded to a comment that the Filipinos were brave with, 'Brave! Brave! Damn 'em, they won't stand up to be shot.' If the British responded to guerrilla warfare with the harsh logic of the concentration-camp system, in the Philippines the Americans resorted to the widely employed 'water cure' torture, which involved pumping water into the victim until he was hugely distended and then jumping on his stomach.

The German atrocities committed in Belgium in 1914 were chillingly anticipated by General Arthur MacArthur, father of a more famous soldier-son, Douglas, who insisted that guerrilla fighting was 'contrary to the customs and usages of war' and that guerrilla fighters 'divest themselves of the character of soldiers, and if captured are not entitled to the privileges of prisoners of war'. This German logic – it could be General von Kluck talking prior to the Belgian atrocities of August 1914 – was but a small step away from an official policy of military atrocities. What the American Founding Fathers would have made of such a description of the heroes of Concord and Lexington would have been enlightening. Certainly, the mentality of the American soldier of the time was not in line with the niceties of the Age of Enlightenment or even the Geneva Convention. Arthur Minkler, a soldier from Kansas, boasted in a letter home: 'We take no prisoners.' An American journalist wrote: 'There is no question that our men do "shoot niggers" somewhat in the sporting spirit...They do not regard the shooting of Filipinos just as they would the shooting of white troops. This is partly because they are "only niggers".' While the US Army vehemently denied killing prisoners and injured Filipinos, it had to find an explanation for the wayward battle statistics. Figures from the American Civil War had indicated that five men were generally injured for every man killed. In the Philippines, however, the figures were at odds with all hitherto known wars. Fifteen Filipinos were killed for every man injured! Clear racialism was manifest in the curious explanations used by both General Otis and his successor, General Arthur MacArthur. Otis attributed the high kill-count to the excellent marksmanship of the rural Southern soldiers. MacArthur added a nasty twist by explaining that Filipinos simply died more easily than the Anglo-Saxons because they were of an inferior race.

Underestimating their enemies was the downfall of the 9th US Infantry in Balangiga on the island of Samar, in the Philippines, on 27 September 1901. Seventy-four men, led by Captain Thomas Connell, had been moved into Balangiga to protect the town from General Lukban's Filipino rebels. The American soldiers, mostly young and poorly educated, showed little appreciation of the skills or military prowess of their opponents. American military intelligence should have warned Connell that evidence linking the mayor of Balangiga with rebel General Lukban had been in American hands for months. Instead, Connell naively walked into a trap by allowing a hundred of Lukban's best fighters to masquerade as street cleaners in Balangiga.

Connell seemed more concerned with the morals of his soldiers than with their safety, forbidding his men to fraternize with local women and punishing any of them who used the word 'nigger' when referring to the Filipinos. Connell probably meant well, but his men condemned him as a 'nigger-lover', and General Lukban decided to make use of what he saw as Connell's weakness to surprise the American garrison. The final error that Connell lived to make was when he received the tragic news on 26 September that President McKinley had been assassinated. Even such a shock should not have caused Connell to drop his guard in enemy territory, but the puritanical young captain took the bad news almost personally. He insisted that every one of his men should spend Saturday night sewing black crepe mourning bands on their sleeves. Connell himself retired early to prepare the service and eulogy he intended to deliver the following day for President McKinley. The danger posed by General Lukban's fighters seemed to have slipped everybody's minds.

The American sentries in Balangiga were scant that Saturday evening. Even so, the few that were on duty observed a strange phenomenon. The church was virtually besieged by hundreds of women, heavily dressed and wearing headscarfs in spite of the heat, who were carrying small wooden coffins. When questioned, the women told the guards that the coffins contained dead children who had succumbed to a cholera epidemic. Unsurprisingly, the Americans were disinclined to open the coffins. If they had, they would have found them filled not with dead children but with machetes and knives. Moreover, had the guards dared to investigate further – they had been warned by Connell not to touch any Filipino woman – they would have found that many of the women were in fact men, burly fighters sent by General Lukban.

On Sunday morning the American soldiers assembled for breakfast, while Captain Connell fretted about the eulogy he had been writing for the dead president. Unknown to the Americans, the coffins had been opened and the weapons distributed to the town's supposed street cleaners and to the mourning women of the night before. Suddenly the town's church bells began to chime and Lukban's fighters responded to the signal. The American soldiers were unarmed, on

Connell's orders, so when the Filipinos poured into the canteen they found their enemy helpless – but not for long. While many of their number were hacked down, the Americans fought back with whatever came to hand, including baseball bats, cans of food and pots of boiling coffee. The Filipinos burst into Captain Connell's room, but he fought back armed only with a prayer book, before leaping through his window into the street. Here he was decapitated and his head set on fire by the frenzied Filipinos. In a space of minutes all the officers and half the men had been killed, but Sergeant

▷ American troops in the Philippines extract information by the use of the 'water cure'.

◁ American troops using dogs against the Filipino rebels, much as they did against escaped slaves in America before the Civil War.

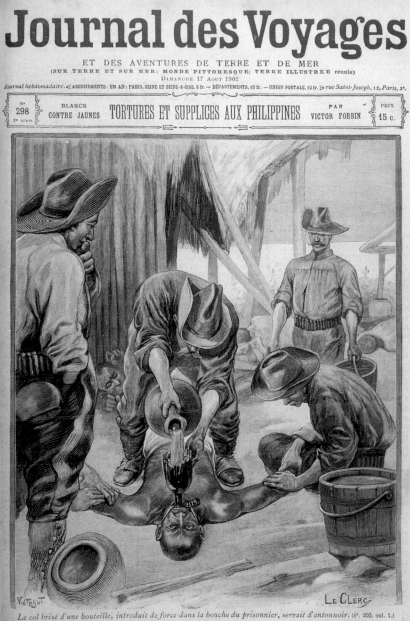

**Journal des Voyages**

ET DES AVENTURES DE TERRE ET DE MER
(SUR TERRE ET SUR MER; MONDE PITTORESQUE; TERRE ILLUSTRÉE réunis)
DIMANCHE 17 AOUT 1902
Journal hebdomadaire. ❧ ABONNEMENTS: UN AN: PARIS, SEINE ET SEINE-&-OISE, 8 fr. — DÉPARTEMENTS, 10 fr. — UNION POSTALE, 12 fr. ❧ rue Saint-Joseph, 12, Paris, 2ᵉ.

N° 298 2ᵉ SÉRIE | BLANCS CONTRE JAUNES | TORTURES ET SUPPLICES AUX PHILIPPINES | PAR VICTOR FORBIN | PRIX 15 c.

VINTRAUT                                                                LE CLERC

*Le col brisé d'une bouteille, introduit de force dans la bouche du prisonnier, servait d'entonnoir.* (P. 203, col. 1.)
N° 298. (Deuxième série.)                                    N° 1310 de la collection.

Breton organized a fighting retreat towards the shore, where the survivors escaped to the nearby American fort at Basey. Fifty-nine Americans had died in the attack and a further twenty-three had been seriously wounded. Just six escaped unscathed. Once the survivors reached Basey the American commander, more typically racist than poor Captain Connell, set out for Balangiga to avenge the massacre. What his men found there further fuelled their anger, if that was necessary. American bodies had been mutilated, with stomachs slit open and stuffed with flour, jam, coffee and molasses from the mess hall. Even the company mascot did not escape: Connell's dog had had its eyes gouged out and replaced by rocks. The Americans now massacred the inhabitants of Balangiga, burned the town and returned to Basey full of righteous fulfilment. The enemy they had thought beneath their contempt or notice had proved how dangerous American complacency could be. Suddenly, the inferior 'nigger' had become the dangerous, marauding blood-crazed killer in American imagination. What followed was the worst series of American atrocities before Vietnam. General 'Howling Jake' Smith ordered his men to turn the island of Samar into a 'howling wilderness'. He instructed his officers: 'I want no prisoners. I wish you to kill and burn; the more you kill and burn the better it will please me.' Everyone capable of carrying arms — anyone, in fact, over ten years of age — was to be shot.

Shockingly, although General Smith was court-martialled, when he returned to the United States he was welcomed as a national hero. The docks at San Francisco were lined with people cheering the returning general, and his medical officer defended him to the press in the following terms:

*It makes me sick to see what has been said about him. If people knew what a thieving, treacherous, worthless bunch of scoundrels those Filipinos are, they would think differently than they do now. You can't treat them the way you do civilized folks.*

# THE FALL OF FORTRESS SINGAPORE, 1942

⚔

In 1781 at Yorktown, near Williamsburg in Virginia, the 8,000 British troops of Lord Cornwallis surrendered to George Washington and ended at a stroke the American War of Independence and the first British Empire. It was the greatest British disaster until, 161 years later, it was to be surpassed by a second, far greater surrender that ended Britain's second Empire: the loss of Fortress Singapore to the Japanese. Unlike the redcoats of Lord Cornwallis, permitted the honours of war and marching out with Union flag and regimental standards flying, the British army commander at Singapore, Lieutenant-General A. E. Percival, was accorded no such privileges; he was filmed walking up the road carrying a white flag alongside the Union Jack.

The fall of Singapore in February 1942 was not only the most humiliating defeat ever suffered by forces of the British Empire but was also a symbolic moment of great importance. It marked – as no other event could – the end of Britain as a world power and the final stage in Britain's centuries-long adventure in the Far East. It was not only the fact of defeat that was important; it was the nature of that defeat. Britain's imperial presence was humbled by an Asiatic power. Her forces were not overwhelmed, as in some Victorian disasters, by seething masses of tribesmen. They were rounded up, many reduced to little more than drunken looters, by Japanese soldiers riding bicycles. The 'fortress' that had been the image of Singapore portrayed in the hollow words of politicians was found to have left the back door unguarded and unlocked. The great naval guns remained as poignant gestures, pointing out to sea and defying the Japanese to come that way. If it was a growl from the British lion, it frightened only the seagulls. The airfields, dotted throughout the jungle clearings of Malaya, were largely untenanted, the few Buffalo fighters outnumbered by the buffalo that drank from the water holes on the edge of the runways, untroubled by warlike preparations.

◁ Yorktown in 1781. British General Burgoyne surrenders to the Americans, marking the end of the American War of Independence.

Complacency ran through the colony in the interwar years. Singapore resident Elizabeth Choi reflects on this:

*Well, you know, all along we were told that Singapore would never fall, it's the pride of the British Empire. You know, we had a very well-defended island called Santosa. There you have all the big guns, you know, facing the sea, and if enemies were to come from the sea, well, they have no chance, no chance of taking Singapore, and we had a very good naval base, brand-new one, very posh…We were very confident that Singapore would never fall, until 8 December the Japanese dropped the first bombs in Raffles Place and people came and told us that, you know, bombs were dropped in Raffles Place, and we said 'Don't talk nonsense.' They said, 'Yes, we saw some corpses being put into lorries.'*

British perception of the Japanese military threat was tied up with racialism and a profound contempt for the Asiatic. The expats who dominated Singapore society regarded the Japanese as quaint and colourful but essentially second-rate producers of shoddy goods, as military historian Dr Brian Farrell of the National University of Singapore records:

*Oh, I think the British were very racist in those days and so were the Australians, and you speak to the people of the day, they were very racist in their view towards the local population, Chinese, Malays,*

*Indians and particularly the Japanese. The Japanese were regarded as little men, short-sighted, scared of heights…*

The military officers who served in this comfortable billet set a bad example for their troops. The following quotes are by no means unusual and reflect unprofessional complacency right at the top. The commander-in-chief of the Singapore garrison, Air Chief Marshal Brooke-Popham, described his first experience of some Japanese prisoners he had seen in China in December 1940:

*I had a good close-up, across the barbed wire, of various subhuman specimens dressed in dirty grey uniforms, which I was informed were Japanese soldiers. If they represent the average of the Japanese Army, the problems of their food and accommodation would be simple, but I cannot believe they would form an intelligent fighting force.*

Brian Farrell describes the other side of the coin: the British overestimating themselves:

*It's certainly true that the British underestimated the Japanese right from the very beginning, and I think it's also fair to point out that they overestimated themselves. This was particularly so regarding the Japanese Air Force. Brooke-Popham's famous remark that the Brewster Buffalo was good enough for Malaya not only showed that he'd failed utterly to absorb any of the warnings about how good the Japanese Army and Navy and Air Force fighters could be, but also that he had supreme and baseless confidence in the ability of his enthusiastic but almost completely inexperienced pilots.*

General Percival himself reported on the overconfidence prevalent in navy and airforce circles:

*At a Joint Staff Defence Conference held, I think, about August 1941, the view was officially expressed by the C-in-C's Air Representative that we could rely on the Air Force destroying, I think, about 70 per cent of the ships of an invading force before it landed. The trouble all along was that most of the Naval and RAF senior officers were far too optimistic as to what they would be able to do.*

Subordinate commanders, taking their lead from above, were not slow in denigrating the abilities of the Japanese. Louis Allen records the comments of just two such officers:

*'I was amused by one battalion commander,' Brooke-Popham wrote to General Ismay, 'who while we were standing together looking at the men said, "Don't you think they are worthy of some better enemy*

*than the Japanese?"' I also got a similar remark from the colonel of the Argyll and Sutherland Highlanders yesterday. He has trained his battalion to a very high pitch for attacking in the type of country one gets near the coast and said to me, "I do hope, sir, we are not getting too strong in Malaya, because if so the Japanese may never attempt a landing."'*

The attitude of the ordinary British soldier is seen here in the words of Arthur Lane, a machine gunner with the Manchester Regiment:

*In Singapore at the time, it was a holiday camp: everybody was happy, everybody was fooling around, and dance halls were going at full steam. We'd no idea that there was going to be a war.*

As a regular soldier, Lane had confidence in his own ability but not in that of the reinforcements sent out to swell the Singapore garrison:

*We were safe inasmuch as that we knew our own capabilities and we were a match for any Japanese or any Japanese unit, and by that I'm saying we who were on Singapore at that time – I mean the Manchesters, the Argylls, the Loyals and the Gordons – well, nobody could get past us, we were the best… Then they sent in the reserves, and the reserves were obvious…even after six months they were obvious. They'd got white knees, they'd got white faces, they'd got white hands, and we knew then that we'd got a hell of a job on our hands.*

The common soldiers demonstrated the sublime ignorance so typical of Britain's fighting men throughout the centuries. In Lane's words:

*A lot of the soldiers hadn't had the type of education that they get today. Nowadays a soldier is taught, but in those days they weren't, they were getting five shillings a week and that's top pay, so you didn't need to think, and in their eyes we couldn't do wrong. We were the British, so we can't lose, and this was the attitude all the way along.*

It is as well that crystal balls were in as short supply in Singapore in 1941 as tanks and modern aircraft. Such soldiers were themselves victims, inheritors of racial stereotyping by the generations that had won the Empire and set their seal on it. In the opinion of journalist Ian Ward, the upper echelons of the Singapore garrison were little more than a 'cocktail party army':

*Very bad leadership, very bad planning, and nobody seemed to want to criticize the commanding officer. You see, this was a cocktail party army, really. I mean, I'm talking about the officer corps. They lived very well; they lived in camps like this here in Saleta, they lived in Alexandra Barracks. These people had gardeners, they had drivers, they*

*had cocktail parties in the afternoon, gatherings in the mess, their wives were out here with them, they lived very, very well, and a war was something they really didn't need and didn't want to think about too hard, and so they didn't, that's the fact.*

The fall of Singapore was a long descent into darkness. During the First World War Britain had been obliged to keep the cream of her navy locked in harbour at Scapa Flow, playing a deterrent game against the smaller but probably stronger German High Seas Fleet. To patrol the seven seas, she was dependent on older, weaker vessels that occasionally succumbed to German surface raiders, like Craddock's squadron at the Coronel. To help her in the Far East, Britain found herself increasingly relying on the Japanese, who were making immense technological strides under the benign but myopic paternalism of the British Admiralty. The Japanese Navy had been victors at Tsushima under Togo, an admiral truly with the Nelson touch, and pupils of the best in British naval traditions were secretly eager to test their new strength against the master. Japanese battleships, first built in Britain, then later in Japan with British help, were by 1914 wearing the true livery of Japanese genius. Significantly, from 1916 new Japanese battleships combined the flair of British projects with the strength of the best German designs. Britain looked on in nodding approval, her mind now so Euro-centric that she had nothing left to offer the Far East colonies but symbols and gestures. Opportunistic Japan, however, was already revealing incipient anglophobia by 1918.

At the end of the First World War Britain faced the need for two fleets, one in European waters to face the potential of a rejuvenated Germany, the other in Far Eastern waters to protect her colonies against an increasingly aggressive Japan. This was clearly impossible. Financial restraints restricted Britain to merely tinkering with her existing, ageing fleet. During the interwar period Britain built just two new battleships at a time when aggressive dictatorships were breaching the Washington Treaty and equipping themselves with new capital ships of a kind no British warship could match. Short of a massive programme of rearmament unprecedented in a democratic country and merely fanciful in view of Treasury restrictions, Britain faced the collapse of her position as a world power as well as the certain loss of much of her Empire. Her politicians fell back on 'myth-information': the 'myth of the fleet', and then the myth of 'Fortress Singapore'.

The eventual admission that no fleet would be available for service in the Far East while the European situation remained

threatening meant that Singapore would have to defend itself through the efforts of the army and the R.A.F. Thus, the myth of 'Fortress Singapore' was born. But the Royal Navy, unable to defend the naval base in body, was determined to be there in spirit. Instead of Singapore being a fortress with all-round defences, it would simply become an isolated gun turret with five fifteen-inch guns pointing out to sea, as if marooned when the British fleet abandoned its world role and took station off the north of Scotland.

During the 1930s there was never any question of Britain being able to send her fleet eastwards. Moreover, neither could Britain send her best troops to garrison Singapore; nor could she even equip the colony with her best aircraft. Frankly, the British were simply crossing their fingers and hoping that Japan would not exploit Britain's European difficulties in 1939. Historian H. P. Willmott described the limitations of British planning:

*In the whole of military history there can seldom have been a series of strategic decisions that reached such a nadir as did those of the British at this point. For the defence of Malaya the British had placed their faith in warships. When they realized the bankruptcy of this notion they turned to air power in order to economize on troops, and in the end they sent troops to economize on aircraft.*

In fact, everything was allowed to take priority over the defence of Singapore. When war broke out in Europe, the best Australian and Indian troops were sent to North Africa; the best available fighter planes were sent to help Russia, and the most modern British warships were kept in home waters to face the danger of German surface vessels. When war with Japan eventually came in 1941, Britain's bluff had been called. She no longer had the military strength to fight a global war against two first-rate military powers. On the absurd assumption that the Japanese could be deterred by the mere presence of the Royal Navy in whatever strength, Churchill sent out the new battleship *Prince of Wales* and the old battle cruiser *Repulse*, without any air cover. It was war by symbolism – but these ships were symbols of Britain's weakness, not of her strength. To offset the lack of proper air defences in Malaya and Singapore, Britain increased her military garrison. However, the troops were essentially second-rate, consisting of untrained Australian and Indian units, while the best continued to be used against the Germans in North Africa and the Balkans.

The Japanese invasion of Malaya and the subsequent loss of the *Prince of Wales* and the *Repulse* struck a devastating blow to British morale, as Brian Farrell relates:

*The civilians in Singapore were particularly hard hit by the reverses of the first days of the war, when the news arrives that the great bat-tleships that have only recently come out to the Far East, the Prince of Wales and Repulse, have been sunk by Japanese aircraft off the east coast of Malaya…The expatriate civilians in particular, the Europeans, feel almost the shadow of doom crossing across their face, and when barely a week later the oldest British possession in the Far East, the island of Penang off the north-west coast of Malaya, is abandoned virtually without a fight and a large number of European women and children arrive in Singapore as refugees – well, the message is really driven home to the European community here.*

Churchill's bluff had been called, and it was shown to have been a very shallow one indeed. The effect on the ground troops in Malaya was very bad. Defeatism became widespread even though on the ground the British defenders heavily outnumbered the invaders. Preconceptions about Japanese equipment and the fighting quality of their soldiers were now proving to be terribly wrong.

Morale had to be maintained, both among servicemen and the civilian population, by suppressing the truth. In March 1941 the Far East Combined Bureau had issued a Japanese Army Memorandum, of which 10,000 were printed. It gave a rundown of the Japanese military qualifications, indicating that they were high-class soldiers, high-class airmen and had good equipment, particularly excellent aircraft. It was suppressed, however, and never generally issued purely and simply because it would have been bad for morale. Furthermore, the general-ship of General Percival was wholly unacceptable, as Major-General Julian Thompson explains:

*One wonders why Percival had a change of mind because as Chief of Staff to General Dobbie around 1937 he well knew what the Japanese capabilities were at that date, and he'd been updated no doubt since then. Also, he was the guy who first put in writing the idea that if the Japanese did attack Malaya they would attack on the east coast, they wouldn't come and attack paltry Singapore with the big heavy guns that were situated there. It was he that formulated the idea; he put it on a more positive basis: that that was where the Japanese were most likely to attack, on the north-east coast of Malaya.*

In Singapore journalist Ian Ward's opinion:

*The rot begins to set in almost from day one, and if you look at air-fields like Alor Star in the north, they were just deserted. They just left those airfields with food on the table and disappeared south. They were very, very upset by the Japanese arrival and believed that they were going to be overrun and just left the bases. And the Japanese, in the case of Alor Star…the Japanese came in, there was fuel in the tanks, there were bombs in the armoury, and they just loaded up with the fuel, loaded up with the British bombs and dropped them on the retreating British forces.*

Military historian Peter Elphick points out that communications in Malaya were so bad that commanders often lost contact with their troops at crucial moments:

*There was one telephone line from the south to the north, and that was not just a military line, it was a line used by the general populace too. There are plenty of stories going around where operators unplugged General Percival when in the middle of a conversation to one of his generals and said your time's up…The radios wouldn't work in the jungle properly, in the rain they didn't work, and so even local communications were bad as well. There are plenty of instances where units, whole units, were out of touch with their command post for hours and days.*

The Japanese assault on the island of Singapore saw a dreadful collapse of military morale and a shameful loss of fighting spirit by the large garrison that, even as they surrendered, still outnumbered their opponents by nearly three to one. For many reasons, morale collapsed as the fighting spirit of the troops dis-

△ In the country of the blind the one-eyed man is king. Japanese light tanks, feeble by Western standards, dominated the battlefields in Malaya and Singapore because the British had no tanks at all in their Far East command.

appeared. They had been led to believe that the Japanese were feeble soldiers with inferior equipment, and now they found they had been lied to by their officers and by their governments. From Lane's 'ramshackle army', the Japanese had become invincible supermen. Resistance was futile. Professor Richard Holmes of the University of Cranford has something to say about this:

*The British attitude to the Japanese certainly changes. It goes from one of generally underestimating them before the Malaya and Singapore campaign to overestimating them thereafter, and at some stage in the Burma fighting…I mean, for the first campaign or two in Burma there's an excessive regard for the Japanese and they're regarded as supermen who can hide behind a single leaf in the jungle and march*

△ Bespectacled and short as many Japanese soldiers were in Malaya and Singapore they out-fought their much larger British and Australian opponents, who had made the fatal error of underestimating the enemy.

*huge distances and are invulnerable.*

General Percival may not have been responsible for a generation of military neglect by successive British governments, but he was responsible for getting his men to fight. Tanks and planes apart, there were still three British soldiers on the ground for every Japanese invader. Julian Thompson blames Percival for not inspiring his men to do what they had been trained to do:

*I think Percival was too weak as a leader. He'd been a very brave battalion commander in the First World War, but that I think was about his level. He was also actually quite intolerant; he was intolerant of some of the people he commanded because they hadn't been to staff college. He was in a way a sort of mixture of a mili-tary snob and a guy who actually is a bit weak when it comes to moral things.*

At the start of the war in the Pacific – in December 1941 – Britain had a total of 90,000 troops in Malaya and Singapore, of whom 20,000 were British, 15,000 Australian, 37,000 Indian and 17,000 or so local Asian. Now troops found themselves in the front line against a well-equipped and professional enemy whose capabilities had been seriously underestimated. Arthur

Lane reflects on what the British soldiers had expected the Japanese to be like:

*Before we met them, they were a ramshackle army that we were going to defeat. They were a banana republic type of army, you know: rifle slung over the neck and no drills, no discipline.*

The truth was so different it overwhelmed many of the poorly trained men. Japanese infantry tactics came as a complete shock to the British. Their mobility – many of them using bicycles – made light of the difficulties the British had anticipated they would face in advancing through Malaya. At the head of their forces was a 'shock group' of light armour. Even though their tanks were relatively feeble in comparison with the best British, German or American models, they were effective because they were the only tanks in Malaya. Peter Elphick describes their effects on the Indian soldiers:

*The Indian troops saw for the first time in their lives a tank, and they were horrified. They hadn't got the equipment to stop them and they started to fall back, and the rot started there, if you like. There was a sudden realization that all this talk about there's no need for Britain to have tanks in Malaya because they can't be used in the jungle, it didn't count for very much.*

Japanese tactics consisted of using the roads to advance until they made contact with British forces, whereupon they moved into the jungle at the side of the roads to infiltrate, outflank and encircle their enemy. The British were tactically outclassed.

The Australian troops had a high reputation in the British Army, having acted as 'shock troops' in numerous battles on the Western Front in the 1914–18 war. However, their best-trained units were fighting in North Africa, and some of the troops sent to Singapore were poorly trained and dependent on bravado alone. Under pressure from an enemy they had scorned but now found to have underestimated, Australian morale cracked, as Julian Thompson describes:

*The Australians have been going round saying that they can fit three Japanese on to one bayonet because it's long enough and all that sort of thing and this sort of rather macho rubbish talk. And of course it comes as a huge shock when you suddenly find these people are better than you are and are continually surprising you.*

The Jitra Line, which was supposed to hold for three months, broke in fifteen hours because of feeble resistance. Clearly, only brilliant generalship and an influx of experienced reinforcements could save the whole of the peninsula. Of brilliant generalship there was absolutely no sign, but London decided to send more troops as if – at this eleventh hour – it was really

possible to turn back the tide. It was decided to send the 18th British Division, which had been earmarked for North Africa, to Malaya instead. It was remarkable how troops that had been unavailable when they could have been of some use were suddenly discovered in time to swell the number of prisoners-of-war. Julian Thompson reflects on the fate of the men of this division, many of whom were to spend the war building the Burma Railway for the Japanese:

*Percival had quite a lot of troops, and of course he was given a division, the 18th Division, poor chaps, who were bound for North Africa with all their vehicles painted yellow, and at Durban they were turned off and said off you go to the Far East. So they'd been mentally attuned to fighting in the desert and suddenly they found themselves fighting in South-East Asia without any preparation at all. The whole…all of them went into the bag. I mean, can you imagine anything more lowering to morale than that?*

Churchill's response was to call on the garrison to 'fight to the last man'. These were brave words spoken in London, thousands of miles away, but in Singapore the garrison was not listening. They were trapped, and they did not intend either 'fighting to the last man' or waiting to become prisoners of the Japanese. What followed was mass hysteria on the part of the troops. Thousands deserted, going back to Singapore, to get drunk and loot the place before the Japanese could, as British Colonel Ashmore described:

*I myself saw five Australian soldiers, naked except for a pair of dirty shorts, no boots or socks, lying and sprawling in the gutter of one of the main thoroughfares leading west from Singapore on 10 February. They had their rifles and were drinking from bottles. Such a spectacle reduced any confidence and respect the native population may still have retained for the white soldiers.*

The story of the *Empire Star*, which sailed from Singapore on 11 February, supposedly carrying women and children and civilian escapees, was particularly shameful. Believing the boat to be the last to leave the harbour, Australian deserters forced their way on board, barging women and children off the gangplank and also, it was rumoured but never proved, shooting a British officer who tried to stop them. The boat eventually sailed with over 150 deserters aboard, occupying space that should have been given to helpless civilians. Some of the Australians who had failed to get aboard showed their dissatisfaction by machine-gunning the boat as she sailed.

The Australian commander, General Gordon Bennett – who shares with a few unfortunate military officers the stigma of having escaped leaving most of his men behind – claimed that the military collapse resulted from the inability of the

△▷ Different views of the same event. British prints cut out the white flag on the extreme left. Japanese prints show the white flag obscuring the Union Jack.

Eastern races to withstand the strains of modern warfare. The British commander-in-chief, General Wavell, had another explanation:

*As in all other warfare, in thick or open country, in Asia or Europe, in advance or retreat, in attack or defence, the leadership of the officer and the fighting spirit of the soldier – the determination to beat the other man whatever happens – is the deciding factor. There are three principal factors in all fighting: good equipment, tactical skills and guts. But the greatest of these is guts.*

Wavell continued by adding: 'For the time being we have lost a good deal of our hardness and fighting spirit.' General Percival, British commander at Singapore and owner of a white flag, might have hated to hear this judgement, but the facts were clear. His command had crumbled in panicky rout, and Britain had suffered the worst defeat in her history because her soldiers had lacked the guts to hold back a Japanese army a third of their own strength. The Chinese and Malays who watched their imperial masters being marched away into captivity by Japanese soldiers could never feel the same way as they once had about the Empire 'upon which the sun never sets'. The new red on the world map would stand not for the British but for the Communists.

# THE BATTLE OF DIEN BIEN PHU, 1954

The French, it seemed, learned nothing from their humiliations at the hands of the Germans and Japanese in the Second World War. The scorn of France's arrogant officers, basking in the traditions of a great martial race, was turned in 1945 on the freedom fighters of her Colonial Empire. In Indo-China – now Vietnam – the French returned to find that the previously servile peasants were now responding to new masters in the shape of the Communist politician Ho Chi Minh and his military ally, Vo Nguyen Giap. The French attitude towards their new opponents was summed up by General Salan's description of Giap as 'a non-commissioned officer learning to handle regiments', and by constant references to Ho Chi Minh's early career as a pastry cook in London and Paris. Not unlike the British in Singapore, the French military had enjoyed a luxurious and decadent lifestyle in Indo-China during the interwar years and had drawn the wrong conclusions from their colonial presence. Simplicity on the part of the Vietnamese was mistaken for incapacity, and the rural peasantry was seen as not far removed from the beasts of burden on which they depended for their livelihood. The military and bureaucratic domination of the colonial power was accorded a permanence that was instead merely a thin veneer on an ancient civilization. The triumph of Communism in China under Mao Zedong, with its promise of land reform, allied to the new feelings of national identity and resistance in Indo-China engendered by the ending of the Japanese occupation, meant that the native peasantry now felt they had a cause for which to fight their colonial masters. The returning French found that the servility of their previous subjects was transformed into an irresistible fervour. Their underestimation of the danger posed by Giap's new Vietminh fighters was ultimately to lead to the downfall of French rule in Vietnam. In the words of Richard Holmes:

> *In very general terms, Western opponents tend to underestimate their opponents. There is very often a tendency to believe in technology, that technology is the answer, that technology is the panacea,*

△ General Vo Nguyen Giap, Minister of War in the Vietminh Government and commander-in-chief of the Vietminh Army. One of the great commanders of the twentieth century, Giap later triumphed over the Americans, just as he had the French.

*I think there's little doubt that getting your image of the enemy wrong is a real problem. If you lead your soldiers to believe that they're going to be fighting an enemy who is incompetent, who has low technology, whom they can easily beat because they've got the technology, and he actually turns out to be competent and with good technology of his own, their confidence will be badly shaken.*

For eight years, from 1945 until 1953, a bitter war raged through Vietnam. Even with the support of the United States, the French were unable to defeat the Vietminh, and by the time Henri Eugène Navarre took command of French forces in Vietnam most people in France were thoroughly sickened by the cost in lives and money that the war had imposed. As the Americans described it, this was 'the wrong war at the wrong time'. Armed with the past, the French were trying to subdue the future. By 1953 the French government made it clear to Navarre that they were looking for a way out of the war.

However, Navarre had convinced himself that control of the air would enable him to place a large French force in a forward base and keep it supplied with food and munitions, even during a siege by the Vietminh. He hoped that such a challenge would persuade Giap to abandon his guerrilla tactics and concentrate a large force around the base, which would give the French the chance to use their tanks to inflict a decisive defeat on him. Navarre selected a village named Dien Bien Phu, some 200 miles to the west of Hanoi, right on the border with Laos. The village was in a long, narrow valley overlooked by mountains and surrounded by thick undergrowth. On 20 November 1953 French paratroopers landed around Dien Bien Phu and succeeded in taking possession of the valley. Soon an airstrip had been built, and thousands of French troops were brought in, along with tanks, heavy artillery and equipment, to erect a series of powerful blockhouses.

When Giap heard what was happening he could hardly believe his luck. The French were offering themselves as bait, obviously planning a trap. But where would the French assemble the ambushing force? It was impossible. And then the truth

*that it enables you to hold the enemy at arm's length, to punish him without him being able to punish you. An overreliance on technology, on fire power, on air power, on modern logistics often lies at the heart of a Western army's defeat by an outside army, by what Kipling would have called lesser breeds without the law.*

As so often, the god of technology, revered by soldiers in Europe and the United States, demanded a high price from his worshippers:

struck Giap. The French were so dismissive of his Vietminh that the bait *was* the trap. There was no ambushing force. Navarre believed the garrison at Dien Bien Phu would in itself be strong enough to crush the Vietminh. The French commanders were underestimating the enemy's strength, as French General Bigeard explains:

*Yes. It had been underestimated by the commanding officers. It had been underestimated. But you also have to remember, although we asked what we were doing in this basin to begin with, we didn't expect Giap to build an army like that so quickly, with so many divisions.*

▽ General Navarre, on the left, inspecting French paratroops at Dien Bien Phu on 29 November 1953. Dien Bien Phu became known as 'Navarre's Folly'.

*He would attack with three or four regiments. You would be shooting them, and the others would come up from behind. And it would carry on like that and you would suffer losses. So you were submerged by fanatics, highly trained and commanded by commanders-in-chief from behind.*

The French arrogance deserved an answer, so Giap took up the French challenge and ordered three divisions to begin marching towards Dien Bien Phu. Two other divisions, even closer to the French base, could be there in days. Navarre was matching about 10,000 French troops against nearly 50,000 Vietminh because his personal arrogance convinced him that Giap could not assemble more than 20,000 men and that these would be of poor quality and badly supplied.

Using vast numbers of peasants, some with Peugeot bicy-

cles purchased from pre-war French shops and capable of carrying 500 pounds in weight, as well as every kind of wheeled, human or animal transport, General Giap kept his frontline troops supplied, as he describes here:

*The supplies of food had to be carried from rear base, some 600–700 kilometres [370–435 miles] away from Dien Bien Phu. In order to carry 1 kilogramme [2 pounds] of rice to Dien Bien Phu on the bicycle you would have to eat 24 kilogrammes [53 pounds] on the way. But we could do that. Because of President Ho Chi Minh, who appealed to all of us, 'Everything for the front lines, everything for victory', the whole nation responded to that appeal and they all participated and contributed to the war. We mobilized nearly*

*300,000 young volunteers, male and female…*

In contrast to the French air transport, the Vietminh relied on feet; and against the tractors and tanks of the French the Vietminh offered their invincible shovels. It was a triumph for the human spirit over modern technology. Morale was kept high among the Vietminh, as Colonel Vinh describes here:

*During the training there was singing and dancing, yes, but especially when we were travelling to the frontier we sang a lot. It was great when we met the local volunteer corps. From where we were based in the jungle we received the order to go to Dien Bien Phu, and before we got to Highway 41 we didn't realize that there were so many people travelling to Dien Bien Phu. There were so many joining the campaign. The roads were so busy with people. People came from all directions. Everybody singing, and the people who came from Thanh*

▽ General de Castries, on the right, with senior French officers at Dien Bien Phu.

*Hoa province had beautiful voices…singing 'the hills are very high, but the spirit of the soldiers is higher still.' The atmosphere was great, and I was so happy.*

The French parachute hero General Bigeard describes the problem with French morale: they had lost their will to win.

*What was there to win in any case? Indo-China. It was a country that no longer wanted us. Faced with an enemy taken with Marxism, as Giap was, it was better to get out of there, because they had a doctrine, a common belief…You can't impose yourself on a country that no longer wants you.*

In December Navarre chose the man they wanted to command Dien Bien Phu: Colonel Christian de Castries. De Castries was a dashing tank commander more suited to the warfare of an earlier age. As an exponent of aggressive and mobile warfare, he was a curious choice for a task involving tenacity in defence.

Two Vietminh divisions had occupied the high ground surrounding the valley, and the only way into and out of the base was by air. In the wet, foggy conditions of that area the French Air Force was unable to strike effectively at the newly arrived Communists, who were thus given time to dig in. The French tanks stood rusting in the heavy rain, already immured in the mud. Veterans from Passchendaele might have felt at home here – except for the rice dinners!

By January 1954 Giap's full strength had arrived and had taken up position in the jungle and on the hills surrounding the French base. While they entrenched themselves – to the astonishment of the French they dug 2,175 miles of trenches (as long as the Paris sewers) – Giap spent ten days studying the French position for weaknesses. He was not going to play into the enemy's hands by wasting lives in human wave attacks, as Navarre expected. He had well-established supply lines and, contrary to French expectations, he could keep his troops in action for months. The French defenders, on the other hand, were entirely dependent on airdrops, and in poor flying conditions loads would either be lost to the enemy or returned to base if visibility was too bad. Time was on Giap's side, so he decided to wait. During the foggy, damp weather of February and March, he let the elements work for him to lower French morale. The French were frustrated: they had expected the Vietminh to attack at once and walk straight into their assembled heavy artillery. French underestimation of Vietminh artillery is clear in Navarre's complacent quip: 'They must have a gun or two, but most of the time the shells don't even explode. It's a farce.' But Giap had learned from his mistakes earlier in the war. He had obtained from the Soviet Union better guns and had dug them into the hillsides, out of

sight of possible French air attacks.

Afraid that a peace settlement might rob him of his victory at the eleventh hour, Giap ordered the attack on Dien Bien Phu to begin on 13 March. Colonel de Castries knew when the Vietminh planned to attack but could do little to prepare for it. As it began, he retired to his bunker with the sound of artillery fire in his ears. The onset of the Communist artillery was overwhelming, and the French were shocked to find themselves outgunned right from the start. General Bigeard writes elegiacally about the end of Colonel Piroth, the one-armed French artillery chief:

*Colonel Piroth was a hero, a very fine man. To begin with, he'd said, 'I'm doing my job, defending my country. I will completely annihilate the opponents' cannons. We mustn't withdraw.' He didn't succeed, he didn't even get out one of the cannons, because the Vietnamese had buried them. They brought them out to fire with and then buried them again. So he realized he was responsible. He got a hand grenade and killed himself with it. He did it to retain his honour. It has to be done sometimes.*

As Professor Richard Holmes explains, the reality of the Communist artillery's superiority over the French hit morale in a profound way:

*The impact of artillery fire in any battle is often as much…even more psychological as physical. What artillery does is it demonstrates just how powerful the enemy is. An enemy who can reach into the heart of your position, smash it up, flatten bunkers, change the contours, isn't merely doing you physical damage but he's also having a moral effect on you, he's demonstrating that he's got a moral edge over you, and your own will to fight gets sapped by the physical impact of what he's doing.*

*Artillery fire is…all the more damaging if you've rather undersold the enemy up until then, if you believe that the enemy is really pretty primitive and all right at guerrilla war but not really good at the serious stuff, then his gunners really mark your card for you and that's what happens at Dien Bien Phu. The moral effect of artillery is extraordinary. It proves to the garrison that they're dealing with a very powerful opponent indeed.*

The Vietminh infantry, consisting of hundreds of fanatical peasant-soldiers, stormed into the teeth of a torrent of French rifle and machine-gun fire, blocking the firing slits of French bunkers with their bodies and leaping on to barbed wire entanglements so that their comrades could pass over their corpses. The French strong points were besieged and fell one by one.

News of the plight of Dien Bien Phu had spread throughout Vietnam and inspired many French volunteers to go to the

base to fight alongside their doomed comrades. French para-troopers – some of the toughest fighters in the world – led by the legendary Marcel Bigeard, dropped at night within the French-held areas of the base. They stiffened the resistance but could not turn the tide. Heavy rain continued to hamper the French Air Force, which was forced to fly low and conse-quently suffered heavy casualties: sixty-two planes shot down and a further 167 badly damaged.

The French defenders – like their distant commanders in Hanoi and Saigon – began to recognize that they were doomed. As one man put it, they were in a chamber pot and the enemy was preparing to piss on them. But France no longer had the willpower – or the resources – to do any more for her soldiers. All eyes turned to the United States, the one power that might have been able to rescue the defenders of Dien Bien Phu. Many Americans were prepared to support anyone who was fighting Communism, but the current Geneva talks made it difficult to risk antagonizing the Soviet Union and China, and possibly escalating the struggle into a full-blown Far Eastern war.

On 1 May Giap ordered an all-out attack, and soon the French defenders were hemmed in to an area just a quarter of a mile square. From Hanoi Navarre radioed Dien Bien Phu, ordering de Castries to cease firing. Colonel de Castries put on a clean uniform, with a chestful of decorations, and stood silently as Vietminh soldiers burst into his office. Colonel Vinh records his experience of actually capturing the French commander:

*It was very peculiar that there was not a single French soldier around General de Castries' bunker. It seemed to me they had all gone. So it was a great advantage for us to attack the bunker and force de Castries to surrender…I ordered Nho to throw a grenade, but outside, not into the bunker, to just frighten them, as I thought it was best to capture them alive. The grenade exploded with a big bang. Afterwards, a captain raised a white flag, coming out of the entrance of the bunker. He spoke French and asked to surrender to our commander of the Dien Bien Phu battle. At that time, I was very concerned as I was unable to speak French – I never knew how to make them surrender. I did capture the French soldiers and French officer before, but I didn't know how to make them surrender. I was so worried that I pointed my gun very close to the body of the French officer.*

*He was terrified and spoke a lot of French to me, but I couldn't understand a single word of it, so we were standing still and waiting for each other. At that point, my company leader, Mr Ta Quang Luat,*

△ The last days at Dien Bien Phu. Entirely dependent upon air drops these French troops are surrounded by supply canisters. Poor weather and Communist artillery made French airlifts too hazardous.

arrived with the rest of my company to surround the bunker, so he spoke to the French officer. Then Mr Ta Quang Luat ordered Nam and Heiu to block one entrance, but I and comrade Nho went with him to enter another entrance to the bunker. Before moving in, he told all of us to obey his orders strictly and to act only when he ordered. He told us to put on airs when we moved in, and we must look straight into the eyes of any enemy who was not scared.

I was the first one to enter the bunker. When I looked inside the bunker, I saw about forty French army officers wearing beautiful

army uniform and full army rank. It was the first time I had ever seen them in beautiful uniform like that, so I started and took one step backwards.

Immediately, Mr Luat shouted at me: 'What is this? Comrade Vinh! Forward! Carry on moving forward!' Then I moved forward. After entering the bunker, I walked to one side. Comrade Nho moved to another side, and Mr Luat was in the middle. Three of us walked further to them; they gave way and stepped further back. Mr Luat ordered them in French to hands up. Most of them followed the order and handed up to surrender, except General de Castries.

I remember he was sitting on a chair with his head looking down. In front of him there was a table with many documents on the top. He was watching, keeping an eye on our action. In this situation, Mr

*Luat, my company leader, ordered: 'Comrade Vinh, go forward and force General de Castries to surrender.' I carried out his order and walked straight in front of General de Castries with my eyes looking straight, my lips tightened and my finger on the trigger as if I was ready to shoot him if he gave any reaction.*

*General de Castries was quite worried, I was sure he was. So he stood up and extended his hand to shake my hand. I was quite surprised and had a question in my mind: Why? Why did he want to shake my hand? So I shouted at him: 'Haut le main.'*

*Then he handed up and spoke some French to me. I didn't understand what he spoke to me, but Mr Luat told me that he asked me to spare his life and let him surrender later on. Mr Ta Quang Luat told General de Castries to order his troop in Dien Bien Phu to surrender. De Castries replied to him that he had done it about five minutes ago.*

*Afterwards, we took General de Castries and thirty-nine French military officers out of this bunker entrance that we handed over to the Command Centre of the Division. After handing over the prisoners, I then returned to the command bunker of de Castries. I climbed to the top of the bunker, I drank the water from the ditch and watched the surrender of the French soldiers.*

*There were so many French; the French were everywhere. I saw the French soldiers crowding up their trenches to surrender. Each of them already had a white flag in their hand to wave. I was really very surprised, as we didn't see any French soldier around de Castries's bunker at all when we entered. But now there were too many of them crowding out of their communication trenches to surrender. There must have been at least 10,000 of the French surrendered in this area.*

*I got the impression when the French soldiers crowded out of their trenches at that time it looked like a long line of termites crowding out when it rained.*

As de Castries was marched out under guard, he could see that the Tricolour had been pulled down and replaced by the red flag of the Democratic Republic of Vietnam. Like shrouds, 80,000 French parachutes lay discarded across the narrow, muddy valley.

The French defeat at Dien Bien Phu in 1954 was a result of military arrogance on the part of the French commanders. An American adviser had told the French: 'The Vietminh have no vehicles and no aeroplanes. How can they be mobile?' Such contempt for an Asian enemy was typical of the ethnocentrism of commanders schooled in the colleges of Western Europe and America, rather than in the practical experience of guerrilla warfare developed by Mao Zedong in China in the 1930s.

Professor Richard Holmes sums up the French disaster:

*I think the roots of the French misappreciation are complicated. They're in part the disdain of the professional for the irregular. I think there is in part a racist element in it, although the French Army had a long and honourable tradition of using soldiers from other races, so it's actually got North Africans and Indo-Chinese fighting for it in the Dien Bien Phu garrison, so it's not just racism, but it's a complicated series of factors which tend to persuade the French that a Vietminh enemy is simply not going to be able to take on and beat a position like Dien Bien Phu.*

General Giap described why the French lost at Dien Bien Phu:

*Why did they lose the war? The French and the Americans had become a superpower because of their money. They relied on their weapons, artilleries, B–52s and the marines. They talked about human rights, but in reality these wars were unjustified wars. They trampled down the people's rights to live, the rights of a nation to be independent and have freedom.*

Giap was right. The Vietnam Wars were fought in the mind as much as on the battlefield. For all their military technology, both France and the United States were fighting 'the wrong war at the wrong time'. Anti-Communism forced the United States to take the side of a colonial power trying to suppress an independence movement. Washington, Jefferson and Lafayette might have shifted in their graves while King George III would have revelled in the irony. Yorktown was avenged. Perhaps the final words should be left to Giap. When asked why the Americans fared no better in the following decade, he replied: 'One thing that they cannot understand is the strength of the whole nation, united against the foreign aggressors. We were prepared to sacrifice everything, but not to become slaves.'

⚔

# CHAPTER FOUR

# HUBRIS AND NEMESIS

In ancient Greece, successful military commanders knew the dangers of hubris. The overweening pride of mere mortals in a world dominated by the will of the gods would inevitably bring overthrow by Nemesis, the goddess of retribution. In Roman times, great commanders employed slaves to accompany them, whispering from time to time a reminder that in spite of all their glory they were merely mortal. In more modern times, unfortunately, this sound habit has been discontinued, and military heroes, from Napoleon to MacArthur, have fallen under the power of their own propaganda. Nemesis has stalked many great generals to thwart their ambition.

▷ Major-General Sir Charles Vere Townshend will be remembered as Townshend of Kut, but to his regret, never as Townshend of Baghdad.

# TOWNSHEND OF KUT

Lord Kitchener of Khartoum, Lord Roberts of Kandahar, but Lord Townshend of Kut-al-Amara? Somehow the name did not quite have the ring that Sir Charles Vere Ferrers Townshend had come to expect. 'Townshend of Baghdad'– that was more like it. In a land fit for heroes, it was so important to get these things right. By 1914 his fame rested only on the defence of the tiny fortress of Chitral, on the north-west frontier, against local tribesmen. Nevertheless his action won him national acclaim and a meeting with Queen Victoria, which he never forgot.

By the outbreak of the First World War, Britain possessed economic interests – oil, to be precise – in the Turkish-held area of Mesopotamia, and, with war threatening, the British government decided to take action to protect the oil pipeline from Ahwaz to Abadan. One division of Indian troops should suffice under a British general. The problem, however, was not for once the terrain, the heat or the Indian troops; it was the British general, a charismatic, forceful and ambitious soldier named Sir Charles Vere Ferrers Townshend who was so obsessed with his own career that he was willing to sacrifice his troops and his country's interests in the pursuit of a chimera – a mythical Baghdad, straight out of Burton's *The Arabian Nights*.

Townshend's career was no preparation for such a minor but irritating campaign. He was an able man, meant for better things, and had he been sent to France he may have done very well. But being a big fish in a small pond enabled him to become obsessed with his own career in a way that the Western Front would never have allowed him. The desert and the Turks provided time and space for a man to dream, whereas Flanders and the Boche kept you on your toes.

According to Professor Hew Strachan of Glasgow University:

*Townshend was a cultured man. He married a French wife, he was very fond of things French, and he saw that as part of his character…very keen on the theatre. And in many ways therefore not a typical army officer of the day, another reason for his being seen to be slightly out of the mainstream professionally. In fact, he wasn't a comfortable man from the point of view of others in the Mess.*

Charles Townshend – 'Alphonse' to those who knew his 'Frenchified' habits – had been a playboy as a young man, frequenting nightclubs, theatres and even music halls, 'escorting' young ladies and even playing the banjo and singing bawdy songs. Apparently having sown his oats to his satisfaction, at the age of thirty-four he made a good marriage to Alice, daughter of a rich and noble French family. Even as early as 1895 he was angling for promotion and cultivating those who might be able to help him. In that year he earned national fame by

△ The docks at Basra in 1915. British operations in Mesopotamia began from here but soon faced difficulties on the River Tigris.

defending the small fortress of Chitral on the North-West Frontier of India for forty-six days. On his return to England, he was entertained at Buckingham Palace by Queen Victoria. Sean McKnight, Deputy Head of War Studies at Sandhurst, sees Townshend as 'just about the most dramatically ambitious senior officer I think I've ever come across. He's never content, he's always looking for the second or third job down the line, and one of the most irritating facets of him is, even when he's got something he should be very happy with, he's not content.'

Townshend realized that his campaign in Mesopotamia was far from the decisive battlefront in France. Still, it would be easier to excel in Mesopotamia than in the more competitive Western Front, and any successes achieved in the east – the capture of Baghdad, for example – would appeal to the British public rather than victory at unpronounceable places like Ypres,

Passchendaele or Poelcappelle in Flanders. Once at Basra, Townshend was ordered by General Nixon to advance up the Tigris and occupy Amara, in the process driving the Turks from their defensive positions at Kurna. To begin with, Townshend would conduct a riverine campaign, employing 328 Arab boats called 'bellums' to transport the men of the 17th Infantry Brigade across the marshes to attack the Turks. This was the start of the 'Regatta', as the first week of the campaign was called. Townshend described using the bellums as 'practically the same way as punting on the Thames'. Whether the British soldiers exchanged their helmets for straw boaters and sang the 'Eton Boating Song' is not recorded.

The British artillery – mainly 18-pounders – began their bombardment on 31 May 1915 in support of Townshend's riverine flotilla. There was little response from the Turks, and when the British bellums reached the Turkish trenches they found to their surprise that the 18-pounders had simply over-whelmed the Turkish trenches, built without the benefit of timber and quite unsuited to modern warfare. Townshend had expected the Turks to have mined the river approaches, but, once again, there was virtually no response from the Turkish side. In fact, there were mines, but they were operated from an electric keyboard and the operator – an elderly, white-bearded Turkish officer – could not get them to work. Captured by the British, he happily volunteered to point out the where-abouts of the remaining mines.

After hardly firing a shot, the Turks were in full retreat, pursued by Townshend's motley flotilla. Within a few days, the governor of Amara and all his senior officers surrendered to Townshend. It all seemed too easy. Townshend claimed that the campaign so far had been won by just twenty-five British sol-diers and sailors plus himself. A certain Erwin Rommel was to claim as much – even more – two years later against the Italians at Caporetto. Whether Rommel emulated Townshend in his choice of spoils is unknown. Townshend seized a huge Persian carpet from the custom house in Amara, ordered a dozen Arabs to clean it and had it shipped back to Britain. Hew Strachan sums up Townshend's successes so far:

*Townshend in the first three months in Mesopotamia achieves a stunning series of successes. He was expected to break through Turkish defences and capture the town of Amara, but he was not expected to do this with a motley fleet of steamers pursuing the Turks in his own personal steamer and actually taking Amara with some-thing like seventy men holding 1,000 prisoners. It was a spectacular advance, very bold, very imaginative and, of course, in 1915 nowhere else in the First World War was there any similar spectacular success, so Townshend overnight becomes a British sensation. He's a success story, and that's something that he can build on to make his career go further.*

Townshend was a hero. However, he next fell ill at Amara and was taken back to Bombay to recuperate. Meanwhile, Nixon planned an advance on Baghdad to be led by the currently prostrate Townshend when he returned from India. Townshend had already written to friends at the War Office in London admitting that an advance on Baghdad was ill-advised, as neither in quality nor quantity were his troops adequate. In his letters Townshend revealed two different sides to his character: his high intellect and his high egotism. On the one hand, he wrote wisely: 'All these offensive operations in secondary the-atres are dreadful errors in strategy: the Dardanelles, Egypt, Mesopotamia, East Africa!' Napoleon would have nodded his head in approval. However, in a letter to his wife he wrote: 'I must have the gift of making men (I mean the soldier men) love me and follow me. I have only known the 6th Division for six months, and they'd storm the gates of hell if I told them to.' Sean McKnight relates one amusing story of Townshend's odd sense of humour:

*Occasionally his quirky sense of humour plays quite well with the men. There was an occasion early on in the siege where he does a snap inspection twenty-four hours earlier than was expected and discovers the officer in command of the particular redoubt desperately trying to change into something a little bit more formal with no clothes on. Townshend insists the guy accompanies him on the inspection then and there with no clothes, which obviously the officer hated but would have been loved by the men in the trenches!*

New Turkish troops and new generals were reaching Mesopotamia and all were to be organized by the famous German Field Marshal Colmar von der Goltz. Townshend rated von der Golz highly and seemed almost flattered to be facing him. Nixon, on the other hand, seemed unaware that anything had changed, least of all the quality of the Turkish troops. Townshend was now ordered to advance on Kut. He replied to Nixon that if he routed the Turks as at Kurna, he would advance on Baghdad straight away. Nixon, who showed no more common sense than Townshend, urged him on by prom-ising to join him at Baghdad for a joint triumphal entry. One senses that Townshend would have hated it. The battle fought at Essinn, just below Kut, was a real struggle, and Townshend's victory owed a great deal to luck. Adopting Napoleonic prin-ciples, he launched his 'Principal Mass' at the Turks' weak point only for General Hoghton to lose his way in the desert. This left Townshend's diversionary attack bearing the full brunt of the Turkish Army. Disaster loomed, but the 'luck of the Townshends' then intervened. Hoghton found that he was somehow approaching the main Turkish trenches from behind. He made the most of the surprise, routed the Turkish camp and then fell on the Turkish firing line, which fled in shock. So

heavy had been the British casualties that Townshend was unable to mount a pursuit. After this bloody but relatively minor action, Townshend revealed how far his common sense had sunk by boasting: 'The Battle of Kut-el-Amara can be said to have been one of the most important in the history of the British Army in India.'

Townshend was clearly now trying to bribe Nixon at Basra into recommending his promotion. If Nixon wanted Baghdad, then Townshend would need another division and therefore a promotion. Nixon, consciously or unconsciously, recognized a kindred spirit in Townshend and, meanly, refused to indulge his subordinate general. In fact, Nixon seemed intent on making everything as hard for Townshend as he could, while Townshend himself faced continual discontent among his Muslim troops, who objected to fighting fellow Muslims near the tomb of the Prophet's barber, Suleiman Pak. To avert a mass desertion to the enemy, Townshend sent 1,000 of his Muslim troops back to Basra, asking Nixon, in return, if he could

△ Sick and injured British troops from Kut arrive at the coast at Basra during General Townshend's ill-fated Mesopotamian campaign in 1915.

replace them with the British regulars who were being under-employed in Basra as police, clerks and batmen for officers. Not surprisingly, the illogical Nixon did nothing to help the man on the spot.

Townshend fought the final battle of the campaign amid the ruins of the Persian capital of Ctesiphon, or 'Pissed-upon' as the British soldiers would have it. For a man with the historical knowledge that Townshend possessed, it must have been moving for him to stand on a classical battlefield, as Hew Strachan explains:

*The centre of the battlefield of Ctesiphon is the arch, and it figures in all the photographs of the army when they reached this high point of the advance. And it's immensely powerful for Townshend, the student of military history, because this marks the extremity of the Roman*

△ Indian orderlies unloading a hospital ship on the river Tigris in 1915. Sickness inflicted many times the number of casualties lost in battle with the Turks.

*Empire, this marks the point where Belisarius, the famous Roman commander, had got to, coming in the other direction, of course. But for those with a classical education, as of course just about every British officer had received before the First World War, then this is a very powerful image indeed.*

The battle of Ctesiphon was extremely hard fought. Nevertheless, during the fighting Townshend revealed one of his oddest characteristics. He suddenly turned to Boggis, his servant, and demanded a change of clothing. Boggis had to run a mile across the battlefield, all the time dodging Turkish bullets, to collect the general's clothes. When he returned, Townshend

stripped naked in full view of the fighting soldiers, then put on 'a silk vest, silk underpants, a khaki shirt, his breeches, boots and sunhelmet and, picking up his binoculars, eating a piece of plum cake passed to him by a junior staff officer, resumed his inspection of the battle'.

The Turks under Nureddin suffered 9,000 casualties during the day's fighting and pulled back at nightfall, leaving Townshend in control of the battlefield. But, victorious though he believed himself to be, Townshend's casualties had been too heavy for him to consider pursuing the enemy or marching on Baghdad. His mind was already pursuing a more personal battle with his superior, General Nixon. Nixon had offered him the services of Major-General Sir George Kemball, an officer only marginally less senior than Townshend himself. Was Nixon trying to tell him something? Townshend's personality had begun to disintegrate as he realized that his target – Baghdad

▷ Kut-al-Amarah, the scene of Townshend's disgrace. Here, ten months later, in February 1917, the British have recaptured the town from the Turks.

– was no longer possible. Instead, he fell back on the idea of Chitral in 1895 – the retreat 'to the womb' – the place that had brought him fame. Hew Strachan believes that:

*. . . retreating from the battle of Ctesiphon for Townshend shatters his dreams of a glorious entry into Baghdad, and that clearly has a profound impact on his decision-making. From Townshend's point of view it could lead to the prefer- ment of one of his fellow generals: for example, Major-General Gorringe might get the coveted promotion to lieutenant-general. Even worse, it could lead to the Mesopotamian campaign doing what Townshend's strate- gic brain told him it ought to do, which is becoming a backwater, any hope of seizing Baghdad being abandoned, and of course any hope of anyone making their military reputation and getting their promotions from Mesopotamia also being abandoned: the dire possibility of yet again being in another military backwater while the action is elsewhere and the limelight is elsewhere.*

Townshend began to fall back towards the small Arab town of Kut – this was to be his new Chitral. Although his men could have continued the retreat to Basra, Townshend decided to stop at Kut and allow the Turks to besiege him there. Napoleon had abandoned him at Ctesiphon; now his thoughts were entirely with General Gordon and his entrap- ment at Khartoum. As a young marine, Townshend had taken part in the failed relief expedition to save Gordon. Now England would have to send her best to relieve him instead. As Hew Strachan points out, the newspapers would be full of the story of his imprisonment at Kut and everyone would join in prayers to liberate Townshend – the great soldier – from the hands of the Turks:

*The ability to sustain a siege was one way of guaranteeing a high profile. The Siege of Mafeking had made Baden-Powell's reputation, had made Baden-Powell a household name and had prompted enor- mous jubilation when the siege had been lifted. So he knew full well that conducting a siege was a more satisfactory way to, or more likely to be a successful way to achieve public adulation than simply conducting a very successful fighting retreat down the Tigris back towards Basra.*

However, Kut was no Khartoum, nor was Townshend a new Gordon. The 6th Division's medical officer wrote: 'Our first impression of Kut was not a pleasing one. Approaching it from the east, almost the first thing that caught the eye was a gibbet – always a gruesome-looking object.' The Turks brought up siege guns and settled in to starve the British out. Townshend's attitude was already difficult to understand. He obviously had his own agenda, and that agenda did not accord with that of the rest of his command. One artillery officer, showing more ini- tiative than respect for military tradition, sighted the rotund figure of Field Marshal von der Golz in the Turkish lines and nearly blew him to 'Kingdom Come' with a well-aimed shell. Townshend's reaction was to 'severely reprimand' the officer, possibly on the grounds that he was hoping to surrender eventually to the old German who might have accepted his sword with more old-world charm than the bandit-like Turks who had not read the right books.

Townshend's behaviour during the siege of Kut undid all his heroic work at Chitral. His profound egotism and disgraceful neglect for his men moved him from the rank of military heroes and into the – fortunately thin – battalion of British military blackguards, peopled by men like 'Milord' Sackville and 'Black Jack' Slade. Ironically, when the British began their attempts to relieve Kut the command was given to the very same man who, over twenty years earlier, had relieved Chitral – Lieutenant-General Sir Fenton Aylmer. Poor Aylmer! He had no idea that the man he greeted with the cheery telegraph, 'Have the utmost confidence in defender of Chitral and his gallant troops to keep flag flying till we can relieve them', was going to wreck his distinguished career. His final message took a different tone: 'The War Office say that my conduct of operations has been unfortunate and have ordered my suspension. I need not tell you how deeply I grieve that I have not been able to relieve you. It all looks so easy when you sit in an armchair at the War Office!' Had Aylmer realized that his last comment applied more to Townshend in Kut than to the men in Whitehall? While Aylmer faced three whole Turkish divisions, Townshend took his dog Spot for a walk. When Aylmer hinted that Townshend might try to break out, Alphonse kept the radio operators in Kut busy with hundreds of messages to his friends in London, including 'actors and gaiety girls'. While 26,000 British troops were lost trying to rescue him, Townshend read military history most afternoons.

Townshend urged the relieving forces to make more and more desperate attempts to reach him by claiming that he was running out of food. When, however, Basra command took him at his word and called on him to break out to avoid starvation and link up with Aylmer, Townshend suddenly 'discovered' some food that could keep him going a little longer. From his desk in Kut, Townshend bombarded Basra and London with letters begging for promotion. Then crushing news reached him: Aylmer had been replaced by Gorringe in command of the relief force, and Gorringe – 'But he's junior to me' was Townshend's response – had got the promotion that he had set his heart on. Major-General Sir Charles Vere Ferrers Townshend then burst into tears and wept on the shoulder of a junior subaltern. Embarrassing was hardly the word – psychotic was a better choice.

Finally, after Britain had sacrificed enough men to capture Baghdad two or three times, it was decided that enough was

enough. Kitchener signalled to Townshend that he could surrender, and on 29 April 1916 Kut was handed over to the Turks – but not before arrangements had been made to ship Spot home to England, somewhere few of the captive British soldiers would ever see again. According to Sean McKnight:

*While Townshend was whisked off to Constantinople by first-class rail, his men were marched to the prisoner-of-war camps. Hundreds died en route, many of them through lack of water and the heat, but many of them because of the Arab marauders that robbed and killed any stragglers who fell behind the main body. Once they arrived in the prisoner-of-war camps, conditions were little better and hundreds died every month from starvation or being beaten to death by the odd casual brutal Turkish guard.*

*While this was going on, Townshend was cultivating high society in Constantinople, living in a modest palace and enjoying a very pleasant life indeed, with servants and even his own yacht.*

Townshend was a guest of the Turkish government, arriving in Constantinople with a formal guard of honour and to the acclaim of crowds of onlookers. In the words of Norman Dixon:

*Underneath the agreeable veneer there lay a fatal flaw that showed itself in a ravenous, self-destructive hunger for popular acclaim. Though its origins remain obscure, Townshend gave the impression of a man who at some time had suffered traumatic damage to his self-esteem, which resulted in an everlasting need to be loved.*

Norman Dixon explains how 'cognitive dissonance' must have struck Townshend hard after the battle of Ctesiphon:

*No better example is afforded than that of Townshend's occupation of Kut. Since his advance up the Tigris was totally unjustified by facts of which he was fully aware, his dissonance, when disaster struck, must have been extreme and, to a man of his egotistical nature, demanding of instant resolution. So, again, in the face of much contrary evidence, he withdrew into Kut. The wiser and possible course of retreating to Basra would have been a greater admission of the lack of justification for his previous decision. By the same token, once inside Kut nothing would budge him, because to break out, even to assist those who had been sent to release him, would have emphasized his lack of justification for being there in the first place. In short, an inability to admit one has been in the wrong will be greater the more wrong one has been, and the more wrong one has been the more bizarre will be subsequent attempts to justify the unjustifiable.*

# MONTGOMERY OF ARNHEM

The fact that Field Marshal Bernard Law Montgomery was ambitious is well known. On one famous occasion, the Chief of the Imperial General Staff, Sir Alan Brooke, commented to King George VI at a social function in 1944 that the problem with Monty was that 'every time I meet him I think he's after my job'. The king replied: 'You should worry. When I meet him I always think he's after mine.' Many generals share that sort of ambition, yet to allow it to dominate one's military planning is a dangerous flaw. The obsessional behaviour of Sir Charles Townshend at Kut is an example, as we have seen, and Norman Dixon has observed similarities in Montgomery:

*Montgomery of Alamein, for example, and Townshend of Kut were two of a kind. Both were conceited, vainglorious showmen with an eye to their own personal advancement; both had charismatic personalities, and were popular with their men.*

One is forced to conclude that although Montgomery has a justifiable reputation as a very good general, in the planning and operation of Operation Market Garden he was little better than Townshend was at Kut. Colonel Michael Hickey confirms the fatal flaw in Montgomery's make-up.

*Montgomery, in a speech made towards the end of his career, was asked to list the three great generals of history and unhesitatingly he named Alexander the Great, Napoleon and Montgomery of Alamein. I'd like to think that there was a twinkle in his eye and that his tongue was in his cheek, but Montgomery had not got that sense of humour at all. He wasn't the sort of man who would look in his shaving mirror in the morning and roar with laughter. He was vain, egocentric and really and truly believed his own high opinion of himself.*

Montgomery's poor relations with American generals like Eisenhower, Bradley and Patton stemmed from his own snobbery. He did not regard the Americans as serious military commanders, in the way that he would French or German generals. As Montgomery saw it, when Eisenhower 'robbed' him of command of Allied land forces and took over himself, he was not fit to lead a company of soldiers let alone an entire front. Montgomery feared that an American, probably General Patton, pearl-handled revolvers swinging from his hips, would ride into Berlin on a white horse and steal his glory. With the film cameras rolling to record another American triumph, Patton, Bradley and their poodle, Ike, would swank through the Brandenburg Gate like tourists on a holiday. After all, American cameramen had followed Douglas MacArthur throughout the Pacific as he waded ashore on to yet another white-sand beach, freed for democracy and American tourism. Major Brian Urquhart, Chief of General Intelligence to the First Airborne Division, describes this problem:

*Patton notoriously didn't very much like the British. In fact, when we were going to land on the plain between Orléans and Paris in order to try to boost the Allied advance, Patton, who was by that time moving very fast, said, 'If I see a single Limey in the way, I shall shoot him down,' which wasn't very helpful. I mean, he wasn't very keen on Montgomery, and he didn't like the British.*

American military historian Professor Russell Weighley of Temple University, Philadelphia, explains why the Americans did not like Montgomery:

*The American impression of Bernard Montgomery, even before Americans had close contact with him, was that he was an impossible person. He had trouble getting along, not only with Americans, of course, but also with British officers, except for his subordinates, who had to behave like subordinates.*

Colonel Michael Hickey feels that there was something almost seventeenth century about the relationship between the 'Puritan Roundhead' Montgomery and Patton, the 'Cavalier'.

*Monty was very competitive. I think all his life he was competitive. He wanted, as a battalion commander, his battalion to win all the trophies available in the Egyptian Command in the 1930s, and they probably did. He competed against other generals, particularly in north-west Europe with General Patton, with whom his relationship was a pretty unstable one. They couldn't make each other out as men, because they were so radically different from each other: Patton the dashing, swashbuckling Southern cavalryman in the American Army, Monty the ascetic, non-smoking, non-swearing, non-drinking*

*Cromwellian. And the competition grew to a head as the Allies broke out of the Normandy pocket and made their big bid to go for the German border in the high summer and early autumn of 1944.*

Two very competitive men – Patton and Montgomery – were chasing glory for themselves and their nations. Eisenhower, trying to run a war for an Alliance, was trying to get the best out of both. Montgomery certainly thought he had old scores to settle with Patton, as Michael Hickey explains:

*I think Montgomery felt that once again, as in Sicily, the Americans had got all the glory and he'd done the hard work. If you remember, he'd had an unfortunate experience with General Patton before, when he was slated to do a sort of formal entrance into Palermo and much to his annoyance the whole American 3rd Army was on the side-lines cheering on the British as they arrived. And I think this had a lot to do with what happened later.*

In order to avoid being upstaged again by Patton, the previously cautious Montgomery threw caution to the winds with a Napoleonic vision for finishing the war in one tremendous British operation that would leapfrog German defences and the Rhine in a single giant stride. The advance of 30 Corps' armour to support the 1st Airborne Division at Arnhem was almost 'blitzkrieg' in its audacity and reliance on an iron fist. But Montgomery was no Heinz Guderian. His 'blitzkrieg' was to flounder in impossible terrain. It was not so much 'a bridge too far' as 'hell's highway'. And however much one tries to apportion blame down the command structure, one is finally left with the fact that it was Montgomery's plan and that the plan itself was flawed. Even so, Montgomery's curious behaviour during the operation – instead of supervising it with the eye for detail he usually brought to his operations, he let it take its own course – forces the assumption that he had something else on his mind at the time: his struggle with Eisenhower? Who can be certain? But as many commentators have noticed, 'he took his eye off the ball' at the crucial time and, for want of leadership, Operation Market Garden failed disastrously. Russell Weighley feels that the pressure was getting to Montgomery at this stage and that he was becoming dangerously unbalanced:

*I think one must look at Monty's mind and almost the balance of his mind in September of 1944. The extent to which frustration over this business of command in the field had really pushed him to the edge of mania, madness.*

Michael Hickey presents Montgomery as an obsessive, almost unbalanced character who needed constant reinforcement for his self-esteem:

*Monty was an incredibly complex character. His experiences as a boy left their mark on him. He adored his mother, he disliked his father, who was a bishop, he was unhappy at school, he wasn't really happy at Sandhurst, where he acquired an extraordinary reputation as a hell-raiser. He's been described by many as an emotional cripple. There were a lot of things missing from his personality, and this showed. He was a solitary bachelor for a very long time until he met the widow of an officer who'd been killed in the First World War with whom he made a very happy and successful marriage, until this was terminated very soon, sadly, by her death from blood poisoning as the result of an insect bite. And he then retreated into himself again. He was ascetic by temperament, a teetotaller, non-smoker...*

On 1 September 1944, as he had his portrait painted following the glittering success of the D-day landings, Montgomery's eyes were glaring and his fists were clenched. He had just received two communiqués, the first reporting that he was to be promoted to Field Marshal, the second that he was being relieved as commander of Allied land forces and replaced by Eisenhower. Out of this blow to Montgomery's self-esteem grew Operation Market Garden, an unhealthy

▽ It could be a duel between Patton and Monty, with Omar Bradley acting as referee. All three are smiling, probably insincerely in view of the company. These three generals had no love for each other and General Eisenhower had his work cut out keeping their minds on fighting the Germans and not each other.

◁ Who's a pretty boy then? Montgomery of Alamein as he saw himself.

*Eisenhower was hopeless, and he'd felt that already since North Africa, since the Battle of Kasserine, and that opinion of Eisenhower didn't improve in 1943. He thought the original planning for the invasion of Sicily was dreadful and would have failed unless he'd changed the plans. He felt that the invasion of Italy was absolute rubbish. He felt that Eisenhower couldn't combine the two responsibilities of being overall Supreme Commander and have hands-on control of ground forces in battle, which he said was a job for one single individual. And he wanted to be that individual.*

It was true that Eisenhower, a soldier-politician, had never commanded in battle and, as Montgomery insisted: 'His ignorance of how to run a war is absolute and complete.' But this was hardly fair. Both he and Ike had had meteoric rises, in which luck played as much a part as military greatness. Just two years earlier, who had heard of Bernard Law Montgomery? He had only got command of the 8th Army in North Africa because the man chosen – 'Strafer' Gott – was killed in an air crash. One battle – El Alamein – had made him. It was, say his critics, a battle impossible to lose in view of his immense numerical and logistical advantage. But from it Churchill created a legend. Before Alamein, there were no victories; after Alamein, there were no defeats. Montgomery was transformed from obscurity into Britain's popular military hero. Two years later, he led brilliantly the planning and execution of the D-day landings in Normandy in charge of all the British and American forces. But military expert or not, Montgomery's imperious and dictatorial manner grated on his American allies, and that was a road leading nowhere.

Montgomery wanted all resources to be piled into one final push that would sweep through the German industrial heartland – the Ruhr – and on to Berlin. He envisaged an army of forty divisions of British and American troops which no one could have stopped, with himself at the helm. Eisenhower, the Supreme Commander, and now self-appointed commander of Allied land forces, saw it differently. His generals, Bradley and Patton, would resent accepting Montgomery as their commander. The Americans were now the dominant partner in the alliance, and American public opinion would not stand for American troops being under a British general. Ike favoured a broad advance into Germany on several fronts. Montgomery was infuriated. Splitting up

origin for any military plan. Montgomery felt he had been slighted – and by an American 'amateur' at that, as Nigel Hamilton explains:

*Monty never quite got over that demotion. He was made a field marshal but his head had swollen. He thought he could do this, he thought that he was himself the cat's whiskers and that he'd never lost a battle against the Germans, he'd twice beaten Rommel, and that there was no German commander who could defeat him.*

Montgomery could not believe that a man for whom he had nothing but contempt as a soldier was now going to command the largest army in Anglo-Saxon history. Nigel Hamilton, Montgomery's biographer, describes Monty's relations with Eisenhower:

*Monty didn't have a very high opinion of Eisenhower as a commander in the field of battle. He felt that Ike had enormous qualities as a human being and as a negotiator, as a diplomat and as a chairman of a committee. But as an actual commander in battle, he thought*

△ General Eisenhower with General Montgomery, 'somewhere in England' before D-Day 1944. The relationship between these two men was vital to the Allied war effort and, of all American generals, Ike was the best at getting cooperation from the tricky Monty. But after the Normandy landings Ike found Monty increasingly difficult.

one's forces, as Ike was proposing, would weaken the thrust. Meanwhile, in Montgomery's view Eisenhower was merely a 'château general', good at taking official salutes, attending parades in liberated cities and performing well with a knife and fork. He wasn't a hands-on leader who got things done. The final straw was when Eisenhower could find time for the social affairs that accompanied the liberation of Paris but could not give him the answer he needed: broad front or narrow front? Montgomery or Patton? In the words of Nigel Hamilton:

*Eisenhower says to Monty, 'Well, will you come with me to the liberation of Paris?' And Monty says, 'No, I will not,' – meaning a commander-in-chief ought to be directing the armies instead of fooling around waving to the populace in Paris. This is the moment of decision. The ending of the Second World War in 1944 depends on the commander-in-chief making the right decisions right now. And Eisenhower wouldn't do it. So almost* faute de mieux, *Monty decides he must come up with some kind of plan of his own that has* some possible chance of ending the war in 1944, and that's how Arnhem gets dreamed up.

Operation Market Garden was, in principle, one of the most imaginative plans of the war. However, it was also hopelessly impractical. Monty's planners believed that to advance through the heavily canalized, inundated fields of Holland in the autumn was sheer madness. There were hardly any roads. For the plan to work at all, the bridges across the Rhine would have to be seized by paratroops.

Most studies of the great airborne battle at Arnhem in September 1944 have concentrated on the failures of the air plan, by which members of the British 1st Airborne Division

△ Lieutenant-General Horrocks of 30 Corps discusses Operation Market Garden with Montgomery.

dropped behind enemy lines, and there was no way for them to be relieved within the time parameters that were being used. Certainly a blunder, one would think, but more like madness on the part of the man who planned it. When one considers that the man whose idea it was was renowned as one of the most careful and patient military minds of the Second World War, a man whose experience of the First World War had made him obsessively careful with the lives of his men, the careless waste of an elite division on what was essentially a gambler's single throw of the dice, and Operation Market Garden seems quite unlike any plan by General Bernard Law Montgomery. Why did Montgomery risk his reputation on such a foolhardy mission? Nigel Hamilton tries to explain:

*Arnhem was very unusual in Monty's catalogue of battles because there was no preparation for it really. The airborne troops were all in England, and Monty didn't fly over to England to see any of those airborne troops, and he didn't go round his ground forces to explain to them what was expected of them in following up the airborne forces. So I think it's a case of opportunism, which was very unlike Monty.*

The road that 30 Corps was to use through Eindhoven and Nijmegen to Arnhem could scarcely have been more unsuitable for a fast strike by armoured units. The Dutch Army Command and Staff College had conducted their own survey on the area and had come to the conclusion that the elevated roadway between the rivers Waal and Rhine, i.e. between Nijmegen and Arnhem, ominously known as 'the Island', should be avoided at all costs. It would not support a large-scale attack by armour. This information was known to the Dutch well before 1944 yet, fatally, the British did not consult them and made no attempt to include local information in their planning, as Michael Hickey explains:

were dropped in some cases eight miles from the bridge they were supposed to secure in the midst of two refitting Panzer divisions and without adequate radios with which to communicate with one another. Instructed to gain control of Arnhem bridge and to hold it for three days until relieved by armoured units of the British 30 Corps, the paratroops performed prodigies of valour before being in the main forced to surrender when the relief column failed to break through. Presented in this way, the layman's initial response would be to investigate the likelihood of the relief arriving. Studies that have criticized the choice of dropping zone, the communications problem and the lack of air support miss the fundamental point. A whole British division was being

*The failure to relieve the 1st Airborne Division at Arnhem stems from the failure of 30 Corps to get up the road from Eindhoven to the southern end of the bridge at Arnhem, the northern end of which, of course, was still being held for three days after the landings. People*

*don't seem to realize what 30 Corps, in particular the Guards Armoured Division, had been asked to do. They'd been asked to advance up an axis about forty yards wide on a straight road which ran across a polder on an embankment, with gun positions on either side from which the Germans, with the dreaded 88-millimetre anti-aircraft gun used as an anti-tank gun, could hit the sides of a Sherman tank. Now the sides of a Sherman tank were vulnerable to an enormous degree to fire of this sort. The Sherman tank was known to the Germans as the Tommy-Cooker because it burned when it was hit. And the sight of rows of these tanks just blocking the road, and no way of getting past them or on, was the sight that greeted many people on that awful attempt to relieve Arnhem. So one cannot blame the Guards Armoured Division, which was probably the best we had, some of our best men were in that, but they had an impossible task, and it was fatuous to ask them to do this.*

How much was Montgomery told of the difficulties with the terrain? On the other hand, how much did he ask? Lieutenant-General Horrocks, commander of 30 Corps, certainly knew about the difficulties he would face. The problem, it would appear, was that Montgomery had accepted intelligence reports that the area was lightly defended, and this presumably became just a further part of the gamble – terrain being literally 'flown over' by the airborne troops.

But the battlefield was a fluid concept. What might be the case one day – one week – might change suddenly. How long the two German divisions at Arnhem had been there raises questions about Allied intelligence even at this late stage of the war. What followed, of course, was the famous incident with the aerial reconnaissance photograph and one enters the world of what Norman Dixon has described as 'cognitive dissonance'. How does a commander react when his most profound planning is called into question by contrary evidence? Major Brian Urquhart, Chief of General Intelligence to the 1st Airborne Division, tells us:

*The really telling fact was that there were two SS Panzer divisions rearming literally almost on the dropping zone, I mean they were within a mile or two. We first got that in the Order of Battle reports from 21 Army Group. I just happened to notice it in one of these intelligence summaries that used to come down every day. Then we had very good Dutch Resistance liaison officers with us, and I asked them if they could find out, and they said: 'Yes, indeed, yes, absolutely. We can tell you which divisions they are. Of course they're there.' I somehow couldn't get anybody to focus on this. And I got one of the Spitfire squadrons, which was stationed in Benson, just outside Oxford, to go along on one of the fighter sweeps and take oblique photographs of this particular area. And sure enough, there the German vehicles were, mostly in camouflage, but they were unmistakable.*

*But I think there was somewhere a higher decision, that it was Montgomery's plan, so he must be allowed to try it. I've never understood this. Eisenhower's chief of staff sent somebody to talk to Montgomery and say, 'Look, are you quite sure you know what you're doing?' And Montgomery said, 'Yes, indeed, it's going to end the war, and that's it.'*

*You might think that with the intelligence that was available, particularly about the two SS Panzer divisions, that there would have been a lot of concern at higher headquarters. And I think there probably was. Certainly one or two people I knew were very concerned about it. But there was a general feeling that this was Montgomery's operation, he must be allowed to go ahead, and we mustn't rock the boat.*

*A certain number of people were in denial about how dangerous it was. Incidentally, I should add that the assumption, which seemed to me to be a very frail assumption at the time and since, was that the relieving troops would come swinging up and they'd cross the Maas and the Waal because the good old Americans would have taken the two bridges, and they'd be in Arnhem in maybe three days. It never seemed to me that this was at all likely, but none the less we weren't supposed to say so.*

Then Brian Urquhart was sent on sick leave. What he knew was not going to be allowed to jeopardize the Arnhem operation. At home in Sussex he watched the great armada carrying the three Anglo-American airborne divisions pass on its way to Holland:

*We lived in a place called Amberley in Sussex, which was a beautiful sort of picture-postcard English village. And Sunday 17 September was a beautiful day. The weather quickly deteriorated thereafter, but the Sunday was unusually sunny and pleasant. And there was just this throbbing roar of glider tugs and parachute-bearing planes and fighter escorts and goodness knows what. I mean, it was a huge operation. I remember vividly people in the village saying 'Ooh, well, that's going to show Hitler!' You know, that's the end of it. And I thought to myself, Goodness me, well, maybe it is, wouldn't it be wonderful? I remember that the headline on the Monday was: Airborne operation goes off without a hitch. It was in the Daily Herald. And I thought, Well, that's nice. And then on Tuesday it was very low-key, Wednesday bad. And I couldn't wait to get out of there, because it was horrible, you know, it's horrible to be totally out of it. I'd always thought before that people like Browning and Montgomery always got it right in the end and that they knew things that one didn't know, they had all this experience behind them, and they never did things for personal or subjective reasons and that it was all discipline and so on. And after that I realized it wasn't true, that this was a nice sort of façade, that actually generals are just like everybody else, they get swept away by emotions of various kinds, their egos get in the way. And it left me with a great feeling of distrust. Whenever I*

'The bridge too far'. The bridge at Arnhem for which the British parachute division was sacrificed in Operation Market Garden.

*saw a leader of any kind, military or civilian, I always instantly began to add up the ego factor, the ambition, the vanity and so on.*

Critics have made much of Montgomery's description of Arnhem as a 90 per cent success for what was, in fact, a substantial defeat. Of nearly 10,000 British paratroopers dropped, 1,130 were killed, 6,500 were captured and just 2,163 were rescued. Such figures speak of annihilation as much as defeat. Yet Montgomery knew the truth but could hardly wallow in self-pity with the war still undecided. The king of Holland said that his people would hope to be spared another of Montgomery's victories.

The failure of Operation Market Garden has not sullied Montgomery's reputation as a general, partly because he stood so far back from it that many commentators placed the blame on the actors rather than the director. This is unfair. Even if the airborne planning was deficient, the intelligence reports, as Brian Urquhart has shown, could have saved the British from blundering into a no-win situation. The very keenness of the paratroopers at all levels was their own undoing. They should have insisted on better dropping zones and more air support. Men like Browning can hardly carry the blame as they appeared to fear to question Montgomery's decision. Eisenhower, one feels, and his planners should have seen that the road down which 30 Corps must travel was impassable. It is not too cheap a point to wonder whether Eisenhower would have given the go-ahead to the mission if one of the American airborne divisions had been allocated Arnhem bridge. Ultimately, however, Montgomery was to blame because he planned an operation, apparently in pique, and pushed it through against mountains of contrary intelligence.

His plan for 30 Corps to 'charge' down the road known as 'hell's highway' would have earned a subaltern a reprimand in a Montgomery-run staff course. For anyone with experience of the Western Front and Flanders in the First World War, like Montgomery, to believe the low polder of Holland was suitable tank country defies belief.

Why did Montgomery gamble away an elite British division by marooning it behind German lines in an area where it could not be supported or relieved? Historians have a variety of opinions.

For Russell Weighley:

*A great general ought to be able to subordinate personal issues to the higher issues of the campaign and the cause, and all that sort of thing. And Montgomery in fact was never able to do that. Till the end of the war, Montgomery's own glory always stood in the forefront of what he was trying to do. And his quest for personal aggrandisement really did get in the way of his effectiveness as a general.*

For Michael Hickey the problem was in Montgomery's mind:

*I don't know if anybody's ever done a psychological study on Montgomery, but he'd be meat and drink for one, I think. It wasn't fashionable to do psychological studies on generals at the time that he was growing up and became one. But there can be no sensible rationale for his rashness, if you like, in sanctioning the Arnhem operation in direct contravention of his track record thus far: one of precise planning, superb logistics, massive air and artillery support, overwhelming numerical superiority, surprise, and the application of force at the critical point. All these are missing from the Arnhem operation, which cost us an airborne division.*

# MACARTHUR
# OF THE YALU
⚔

**M**any generals have pursued successful careers in the military services as an attempt to overcome damaging blows to their self-esteem, often in childhood but, more unusually in the case of Douglas MacArthur, in early marriage. Sexual inadequacy may be at the root of the tremendous and ultimately tragic career of the first and last American 'emperor' of Japan. MacArthur's first wife told her brother that her new husband may be a general, but he was 'a buck private in the boudoir'. At social events and cocktail parties she used to humiliate Douglas by waving a cocked little finger at him, telling people, when intoxicated, that 'Douglas doesn't know what his penis is for except to pee with'. With a wife like that, Douglas had problems enough. But his background, as son of a successful general and with a mother who was determined to push him relentlessly to achieve great things, ensured that Douglas grew up to be a neurotic man, subject to violent mood swings. Professor Allan Millet of Ohio State University describes some of the problems Douglas faced in his early life:

*The MacArthur family was certainly one orientated to achievement. Douglas MacArthur's father, Arthur, was well known because he'd won a Medal of Honour during the Civil War, he'd been a regimental commander at a very early age, and so he wasn't just another soldier, he was somebody of some prominence. Douglas MacArthur's mother was from the Norfolk area, very affluent family, name was Pinky Hardy. And she was even more demanding than Douglas MacArthur's father. She really took it upon herself to be his mentor in every way. Some people speculated that she had almost a schizophrenic effect on him, because she demanded that he be a real man and a real soldier like his father, but at the same time she treated him in ways that suggested that there was a kind of neurotic, sensitive, effeminate side that she cultivated as well. His mother and father kept on to him*

◁ Five-star General Douglas MacArthur A self-portrait – in needlework!
▷ 'The Great Fight of MacArthur'. This *Punch* cartoon shows a Nordic warrior – in the stars and stripes – facing the threat from the East.

*about his grades…he was the kind of poor kid child psychologists would have a wonderful time with. At West Point he was called Sarah Bernhardt, and I think again because some of his contemporaries thought that there was something a little feminine about him. This was a guy who was very moody and tended to cover his own sense of insecurity by being excessively egotistical and self-centred and dramatic.*

Few generals have earned so high a military reputation on such flimsy grounds as Douglas MacArthur. His failures in the Philippines in 1942 were disastrous, and he deserved much of the blame for the humiliating American collapse there. When he abandoned his doomed command at Bataan in 1942, it brought back memories of the unfortunate precedent of British general Charles Townshend at Kut in 1916, abandoning his men to the horrors of a death march across the desert. As MacArthur left Bataan, he earned taunts of cowardice from the Japanese and even from some of his own men, who called him 'Dug-out Doug'. The American public knew none of this. To them MacArthur was a homespun hero, and radio audiences hung on his every word. He was on the front cover of *Time* magazine and MacArthur-mania swept the US.

His background in the Philippines enabled MacArthur to masquerade as an Oriental expert, as Professor Michael Schaller of the University of Arizona explains:

*Most people have enough humility to realize that it's hard to be an expert on the world's largest continent, where people speak hundreds of languages, and there are many different cultures, religions, ethnicities . . . MacArthur would, with little humility, describe himself throughout his life as America's greatest Oriental expert, an expert in Oriental psychology. And by some measures you could argue he was as familiar with the Orient as or more so than many Americans. He had travelled there, he had lived there. But yet his experience in Asia was really circumscribed by the Philippine islands, which were perhaps the least representative part of Asia. During his long tours of duty there, from the early twentieth century through the 1930s, he'd lived in a Manila hotel, he socialized with Westernized Filipino leaders who spoke English, he really knew little about mainland Asia, the peasantry, which was 90 per cent of Asia, China, Japan, and continental south-east Asia.*

In 1946 MacArthur installed himself as (in all but name) emperor of Japan. No American individual had ever held such power, not even 'King' George Washington. As Supreme Commander MacArthur was answerable to no one. Such 'deification' was tolerable only if a person could see the essential unreality of his situation. Like Montgomery, however, MacArthur seemed to lack a sense of humour and took himself very seriously, as Michael Schaller says:

*MacArthur is shrewd, proud, arrogant, successful, handsome, articulate, but he has no humour and no insight into himself, and he mistakes his ambitions and his emotions for principles. And that's his greatest fault, that he really has no insight into himself as a person.*

Yet MacArthur was a man driven by internal demons. Even his closest colleagues declared him paranoid. In 1946 MacArthur began to rebuild Japan in his own image, to sweep away its ancient and corrupt monopolies and powerful families and to make the country a bastion of democracy and capitalism. As a bulwark against Communism, Japan would become 'Little America'. His aide-de-camp, Faubion Bowers, gives us a vivid picture of how MacArthur could influence those around him:

*When I first clapped eyes on MacArthur I fell madly in love. Here was a magnificence I'd never known and I'd never been close to. Here was a man who moved in the highest circles, who held in personal contempt presidents, who had met kings and queens and who knew the world in a way that I had not known up to that time. He was so overwhelmingly impressive, he had a kind of magnetism, a kind of charm that he could charm the birds off the wallpaper in the room. And it was so interesting. I, as a military secretary to the c-in-c, my duties were to take in his mail in the morning, to put the morning newspaper on his desk and to have people come and go. And I once said to him: 'What is it, General, you do that they come in ready to bite and they leave with their tails wagging?' He said: 'I give them a shot of the truth.' I was so stricken with MacArthur that he could say anything and to me it was like a bolt from heaven, it was so marvellously true.*

In many ways MacArthur was a fraud, yet few people ever dared to call his bluff – until Mao Zedong did on the Yalu River in 1950. One wonders how long his military reputation would have lasted in Europe against German commanders.

The extraordinary loyalty that MacArthur inspired was neither good for the general's entourage nor for the man himself, as Faubion Bowers points out:

*One of the interesting things, one of the tragic things in a way, was that all of us who were in the inner sanctum were corrupted by him. All of us, me included, felt that the more we glorified him, the more we ourselves were deified in some way. And it was remarkable how he was surrounded by, well, what Eisenhower called bootlickers, but we were like disciples to a Christ. And I remember one time before I put his mail on his desk, there was a card, an open card written in pencil, and I read it. It was from Anthony Storey, Major Storey, who was his pilot, who'd gone to the Philippines on some sort of business. And he wrote this card and it said: 'To one who walks and talks with God.' And I thought, My God in heaven. That's his own pilot, wrote him that.*

Mao Zedong would have smiled to have heard such nonsense. He knew that arrogant officers provided their opponents with a sure way to defeat them. Professor Chen Jian of Southern Illinois University writes that the Chinese Communists felt that a vain man like MacArthur had half-beaten himself before the fighting began:

*From Mao's perspective, MacArthur's strong point was at the same time his biggest flaw. MacArthur was arrogant, and Mao believed arrogance was very important for a successful military leader. However, on the other hand arrogance can also make a military leader blind. This was exactly how Mao regarded MacArthur as a military commander, with a huge flaw, and he was willing to use that flaw. And also for Mao it was not MacArthur's hostility towards China which made him angry. What made him angry was MacArthur's disdain, ignorance of possible Chinese intention of intervention, of Chinese*

*strengths. And especially when Mao found that MacArthur did not treat the Chinese as a qualified challenge to the Americans, Mao was really angry. And at this point Mao was more than willing to change his own determination to defeat American arrogance into state policy. And at this point he was more than capable of catching MacArthur's fatal flaw, and that is that MacArthur did not treat the Chinese seriously, and Mao said OK, you don't treat us seriously, then we'll force you to treat us seriously.*

At the outset of the Korean War in June 1950, the United Nations appointed MacArthur as leader of a fourteen-nation coalition. The seventy-year-old general's self-belief was as strong as ever, and he called the opportunity 'Mars' last gift to an old warrior'. As usual, MacArthur's preoccupation was with MacArthur, and he conducted much of the forthcoming campaign from the never-never land he had created in Japan.

From the start he underestimated the North Koreans, just as he had the Japanese in 1942, saying: 'If Washington doesn't hobble me, I can handle them with one hand tied behind my back.' Within two days of their invasion, however, the Communists had driven the South Koreans back in disorder, taking the capital of Seoul and forcing President Syngman Rhee to take flight. On hearing this news, MacArthur panicked and began to talk of abandoning Korea and writing it off completely. According to his aides, he was 'a dejected, completely despondent man'. This sort of mood swing was to become a feature of MacArthur's personality in the months to come and should have warned those around him that he was not fitted for the responsibility of such a complex command. Nevertheless, in spite of his known paranoia and the fact that his age and health were against him, his reputation was so great that there was never serious discussion of choosing any other man for the command.

On 13 September 1950 MacArthur turned the tables both on his critics and the Communists in one brilliant gamble – the Inchon landings. Even the Chinese were impressed. The North Koreans were now on the run, and MacArthur was determined to chase them no matter how far it took him. Soon they were across the 38th Parallel into North Korea and heading straight for the Chinese border. At this point, President Truman began to get uneasy. He requested an urgent meeting at the White House, but MacArthur refused, saying he was too busy. The President was forced to fly to the Far East to meet his maverick commander. Truman blanched at the prospect. 'Tomorrow I have to talk to God's right-hand man.' MacArthur was waiting at the foot of the ramp when Truman arrived. Pointedly, he did not salute, as Michael Schaller describes:

*At the Wake Conference in October 1950, President Truman flew halfway around the world, resenting it greatly, to meet MacArthur.*

△ MacArthur and President Truman meet at Wake Island. Truman, as commander-in-chief, awarded MacArthur a medal of merit as a symbol of Truman's superiority in rank. MacArthur however did not salute his commander.

*What they actually said to each other and what they actually felt, there seems to be a wide diversion. Truman wanted assurances that the war was approaching its conclusion, that Korea would be unified without danger of Chinese intervention. MacArthur assured him that that was the case, that the Chinese were bluffing in their various indirect threats, and that he could easily handle a Chinese intervention – if it did occur, which he didn't think it would. In private, each of them expressed contempt for the other. Truman talked about the strutting general who, you know, didn't salute him correctly and wore a dirty uniform and a crumpled hat. MacArthur talked about Truman's ignorance and incompetence and flying to Wake really not for information but to be photographed with him, a successful general in the run-up to the Congressional elections of 1950.*

President Truman returned home convinced that there was no danger of either Chinese or Soviet intervention in Korea. However, MacArthur ordered his troops to drive forward with all speed to the Yalu River, the Chinese border. At the same time he ordered bombers to lay waste to the Korean side of the border, even though it would mean destroying a vital Chinese power station. The Chinese asked themselves whether this might be a prelude to an assault on China itself, from Korea into Manchuria and from Taiwan on to the mainland. If so, the Americans would have to be met in Korea, 'where the risks and consequences were more manageable'. By using North Korea as a buffer zone, China would prevent war from striking her own frontier provinces. Mao Zedong reasoned that the Americans were guilty of misjudging China's attitude to their aggression. If he could demonstrate to the Americans with a short, sharp reverse what the likely costs of a war with China would be, he believed they would see reason and agree

△ A Chinese cartoon showing Communist China's triumph over the Americans.

to a negotiated settlement of the Korean question. But Mao did not know who was really behind the American policy: Truman or MacArthur.

Rarely has the aphorism 'whom the gods wish to destroy they first make mad' been truer than it was of MacArthur in October 1950. Intelligence reports of Chinese troops massing on the border were simply dismissed as 'pure bluff'. With sheer bravado MacArthur declared that he 'had plenty of troops to deal adequately with the Chinese and even with the Russians if they should prove so foolish as to enter the arena at this stage'. American contempt for China's military potential was built on the merest racial stereotype. In any case, MacArthur made clear, if necessary he would use atomic weapons.

China's initial attacks across the Yalu were intended merely as a demonstration of her power, and their sudden cessation on 6 November was designed to give MacArthur a chance to reconsider his options before a full-scale conflict became necessary. Whatever the truth, MacArthur, the Oriental expert, did not interpret them like that. Panic set in, accompanied by dangerous mood swings.

MacArthur would not believe the evidence of his own eyes, namely that the Chinese had defeated his forces only to withdraw on the point of victory. Instead, he continued to express his confidence in being able to handle the Chinese; they in turn noted that Washington continued to follow the decisions taken by MacArthur in Tokyo. Clearly, their warning had not been heeded, and so they would have to face up to American aggression. Allan Millett's view is:

*I think that MacArthur for a short period of time did go into a funk and found it very difficult to make decisions, to accept the fact that he had a disaster on his hands. Really a state of denial. MacArthur is really defeatist, but in a sense his subordinates are fighting the war, and fighting it pretty well with the knowledge that Washington understands their dilemmas.*

On 25 November 1950 the Korean War took on a new and much more desperate character. A massive Communist counterattack – comprising some 300,000 Chinese and 65,000 North Korean troops – swept away MacArthur's preparations for a war-winning offensive. Within two days UN forces had suffered 11,000 casualties and were in danger of a total debacle. MacArthur was first shaken and then plunged into despair. His men were being whipped by an enemy for whom he had nothing but contempt. In the words of Michael Schaller:

*China's massive intervention in Korea at the end of November represented not just a military setback for MacArthur, because almost immediately the Truman administration in effect announced a change of strategy: we're not going to unify Korea, we want an armistice, as close to the 38th Parallel as we can get it, we want to move American troops out of harm's way and minimize commitments to this area. So MacArthur, suddenly faced with a war which defied all of his goals, not only wasn't going to unify Korea, but we were going to seek to avoid a war with China, despite their intervention in Korea. So MacArthur faced a terrible dilemma. At best America would restore the 38th Parallel, at worst might not even do that. There were even contingency plans simply to evacuate Korea and abandon it and draw a defence line somewhere else in Asia. This was a disaster as far as MacArthur was concerned — not only a military disaster, but a political disaster; not just a small defeat, but a big defeat — and it was a real problem for him. And what you began seeing from January until April 1951 were these increasingly shrill communications, sometimes private communications to the joint chiefs, sometimes public via press releases and communiqués and leaks to friendly reporters, that the Truman Administration was not only abandoning plans to unify Korea but was going to abandon the Philippines, abandon Taiwan, abandon all of South Korea, abandon Japan, all as part of an appeasement plan against Red China. I would argue that MacArthur began posterity papers or he was making a case that he wasn't defeated, he was betrayed.*

The entire UN Army was in disarray and began a straggling, humiliating 300-mile retreat, the longest in US military history. Defeat brought on a severe paranoiac reaction. MacArthur blamed everyone, notably the politicians in Washington. To the press he began advocating the use of several atomic bombs against China and suggested saturating large areas of North Korea with radioactive waste. Omar Bradley, the Chairman of the Joint Chiefs of Staff, in his own diaries and notes, said that by early 1951 MacArthur's threats, his tantrums, suggested that he had gone mad. He didn't mean that he was clinically insane but that he had lost any perspective, any professional perspective. The war had become personalized to a degree. Strategy had been reduced in a sense to personal tantrum.

▽ Propaganda print of well-equipped Chinese troops capturing an American tank crew.

△ American troops (with the requisite joker in the middle) retreating along the highway south after suffering defeat at the hands of Chinese troops on the Yalu River.

Truman and his advisers in Washington had the right to sack MacArthur, but they feared that an action so decisive would create severe shocks that could threaten the entire administration and perhaps lead to a total American collapse in Korea. When Prime Minister Attlee of Great Britain arrived in Washington in December, he found to his horror that Truman was seriously considering following up MacArthur's suggestion to extend the war against China to involve 'economic blockade and stimulating internal trouble in China'. Attlee was so alarmed at the possibilities of escalating the war that he made it clear to Truman that if he should extend the war against China Britain would remove her support for America, and this action would be repeated by many European and Commonwealth states.

The alarming decline in MacArthur's mental condition went hand in hand with ever larger fantasies. From mere victory in the war, MacArthur had moved ahead to thinking of not only the defeat of Communist China but the end of Communism itself. He hoped to earn himself a place in history as the man who had turned back and destroyed the peril from the East. America's allies were distressed by the lack of unity among the American leaders. Britain had lost faith in MacArthur and indirectly in Truman as well. The British Chief of the Imperial General Staff, Sir William Slim, was convinced that nothing but removal could prevent MacArthur from fighting a war with China. Slim warned that it was not even safe any more to rely on the judgement of the American JCS, as 'they were scared of MacArthur' and were easily manipulated by him. Truman heard from the British that their principal problem in Korea was MacArthur and that they would not support him in a war against China. Michael Schaller explains:

*A proposal to bring the Chinese to the negotiating table was shown to MacArthur in late March and, to the horror of Harry Truman, on 24 March, the day before Truman was to present this to the Chinese, MacArthur went forward in a press release at a news conference and announced that the Chinese had been exposed in Korea as a third-rate army of barbarians; they had failed in their attempt to conquer*

*Korea, and he would give them one last chance to surrender person-*
*ally to him, which was an important part of what he'd said. The*
*Chinese Field Commander should surrender personally to him; if so,*
*China could avoid destruction. But if they chose not to surrender, he*
*would feel unencumbered and free to release the American Air Force*
*and Navy to bombard Chinese territory. From that moment on,*
*Truman began writing in his diary that the big general in the Far East*
*had to be removed. It would be almost three weeks before the formal*
*removal took place, but clearly, by the time MacArthur released his*
*unauthorized statement about a Chinese surrender, Truman had*
*decided in his own mind to pull the plug.*

Faced with the ultimatum from his allies, Truman realized that
the time had come to act. Truman had a more than adequate
replacement for MacArthur in Matthew Ridgway, and on 11
April 1951 MacArthur was relieved of his command. His
career had been derailed by arrogance and vanity. He returned
to the United States after an absence of fifteen years, and the

American public gave their wayward general the biggest tick-
ertape welcome in history. He was, after all, a hero. Allan
Millett describes his death:

*When MacArthur died – I think he was eighty-four – you didn't*
*expect that he'd be in great shape, but it turned out that in terms of*
*his cardiovascular system it was unusually good, but his digestive*
*system and everything sort of below his lungs was a mess. And that if*
*you look at pictures of him, you think this guy's got cancer or he's got*
*too much chemotherapy or something, because he's shrinking away to*
*nothing. But the truth was that his digestive system had finally just*
*totally collapsed on him, and he wasn't a well man in 1950.*

If Americans were divided over the fall of MacArthur, Europe
and Asia rejoiced. The British ambassador in Tokyo wrote of
his 'tremendous relief' at the news, while a colleague in Paris
echoed his comments, adding: 'the United States administration had almost lost control.' One Pakistani newspaper spoke
for many when it wrote: 'Truman has earned the gratitude of
all peace-loving peoples everywhere by eliminating the greatest single opposition to peaceful efforts and policies in the
Far East.'

▽ MacArthur returns to a ticker-tape welcome in New York. In spite of
his poor relations with Truman, MacArthur never lost the support of
the American people.

# CHAPTER FIVE

# POLITICS

'War is nothing but the continuation of politics by other means' said the famous German military thinker Clausewitz, but many politicians, continuing the logic of the quotation, have seen war as merely another aspect of the political art. In earlier centuries political and military leaders were often the same people, and only in the last hundred years or so has the politician been expected to take a back seat and leave matters to the generals. Even today, the President of the United States is the commander-in-chief of American forces, and during the Second World War Churchill felt he was a match for such pseudo-military dictators as Hitler, Mussolini and Stalin. As a result, political leaders do interfere in military affairs, often to the detriment of their nation's military machine when non-military factors — election success, for example, in the cases of Margaret Thatcher, Jimmy Carter and others too numerous to mention — are allowed to take priority over military ones. The results can be disastrous, as we shall see.

▷ Fantasy war. An Italian propaganda picture showing an imaginary incident: British armoured cars being captured by Italian troops.

# MILITARY NEUROSIS
# IN GRENADA
⚔

After the successful American invasion of Grenada in October 1983, the US Secretary of the Navy issued the following citation on a gallantry award:

*For conspicuous gallantry and intrepid action against a heavily armed rebel force threatening the personal safety of American citizens and the established government of Grenada…Through calculated forethought and incisive action by the officers and men of Task Force 124…the lives of hundreds of American civilians were saved, rebel forces were subdued and the government of Grenada restored.*

It is pleasing to note that in the aftermath of a war, the Secretary of the Navy had not lost his sense of humour. Nor had he and his fellow service chiefs lost their generosity – in contrast to the parsimony of the British authorities, who, two years before, rewarded their forces with a mere 682 medals for three months' fighting in the Falklands against an enemy numbering 13,000. The Americans, on the other hand, awarded their 20,000 troops 15,000 gallantry and distinguished service medals for three days' fighting against an enemy numbered in hundreds. At least the Americans wanted everyone to return home from their trip to the Caribbean with a memento. The American commander-in-chief, Vice-Admiral Joseph Metcalf, narrowly escaped prosecution and imprisonment for trying to take home some mementoes of his trip for his friends in the shape of twenty-four Soviet-made AK–47 assault rifles, concealed in his private plane. Some returning soldiers were content with coconuts; others with what they had looted from Grenadan houses. President Ronald Reagan addressed the nation by congratulating America's returning legions: 'Our days of weakness are over. Our military forces are back on their feet and standing tall.' But this was a politician's verdict. All the service chiefs knew that Operation Urgent Fury had screwed up.

Urgent Fury gave some appearances of being a military operation, yet in reality it was a political act designed to restore American prestige after a series of national humiliations. In military terms the Americans had had their butts kicked so hard and so often since Vietnam that they were looking for a comfort pillow, and Grenada seemed to offer them just that. Failure had been the outcome of every recent American military venture. After the gruesome end to the attempt to rescue the American hostages from Teheran in 1980, a 'hostage neurosis' came to dominate American foreign policy. Never again, her politicians vowed, would the USA allow her nationals to be held hostage by a foreign power. Anything that even suggested a hostage situation would be met by such an overwhelming response from the US military that the outcome would never again be in doubt. The presence of up to 1,000 American medical students in the unstable, Cuban-dominated Caribbean island of Grenada seemed to be an ideal opportunity for an easy win and an opportunity for Middle America to renew its love-affair with the US armed forces.

Ever since the coup in Grenada by left-winger Maurice Bishop in 1979, the Americans had been anxious about the development of the island as a Cuban satellite on their doorstep. Reports of a Soviet military build-up on Grenada, combined with the building of a large international airport at Point Salines, convinced the American authorities that the Grenadans were not merely aiming to expand their tourist industry. Defense Secretary Caspar Weinberger describes President Reagan's attitude:

*He was very well aware of the risks that could come from suddenly facing a island populated by very unfriendly troops with a huge airport, and we kept saying we didn't want another Cuba that close to the United States.*

If the new airport was a military building in disguise, so were the Cuban construction workers building it simply disguised Cuban soldiers. The fact that the average age of these Cuban

△ British governor-general of Grenada, Sir Paul Scoon, whose rescue from prison was one of the main reasons put forward by the Americans to justify their invasion of the Caribbean island.

navvies was thirty-eight and that many were over fifty seemed never to have occurred to American politicians. Congressman Louis Stokes, when he visited Grenada after the war, was not convinced:

*We were taken over to the compound where the Cubans were being held as captured military personnel, and we observed that all of the personnel there, the men and the women in the compound, were dressed in the same manner that we were dressed: that is, they were in casual civilian dress; none of them was in any type of military apparel. So that immediately raised questions in my mind as to what type of military personnel were these persons who were in short-sleeved summer shirts and khaki pants, things of that nature. And I later enquired of our authorities who were in charge if this was the manner in which these people had been dressed who were supposedly the opposition and who were fighting them on the runway, and they said that these were the Cubans who were offering the resistance to the American personnel as they came in. So I enquired whether they were dressed in this manner in which they're currently dressed, and they said yes, that's the manner in which they were dressed.*

President Reagan knew that he needed some further legal justification if he were to invade an independent neighbour which, furthermore, was also part of the British Commonwealth and had a British governor-general, who acted for the head of state, Queen Elizabeth. Without an obvious threat to the welfare of the American students, Reagan knew he did not have a strong enough *casus belli*. He needed an appeal from within Grenada to restore 'law and order'. This is where the governor-general, Sir Paul Scoon, came in. The Americans decided Sir Paul must be in prison at the time of the American invasion and he must have sent a letter from confinement begging for American help. As Caspar Weinberger told our interviewer: 'the British governor-general had spirited a message out of his prison begging us to come in, and we acted on the basis of that.'

The governor-general, however, denies ever having been in prison or having been threatened by anyone except during his rescue. As Sir Paul revealed:

*The only time I had a little fear was when they were firing towards this house during the intervention, when we were in this very room lying on the floor, because they were shattering windows and hitting the walls of this house quite a bit. But I then said to my wife: 'Well, if we have to die like this, so let it be.'*

As for being imprisoned or under house arrest, Sir Paul says: 'A lot has been said that I was under house arrest. There was no hostility against me. I think it's wrong to say that the governor-general was under house arrest.'

If there was a cry for help it must have been from Eugenia Charles, Prime Minister of Dominica, chairperson of the OECS, the Organization of Eastern Caribbean States, who feared Grenada posed a threat to the security of the region and called on America for help. Even so, the Americans knew that they must have a letter from Sir Paul Scoon himself, requesting help. He did not have to write it himself or even know anything about it until the United States justified the invasion afterwards. Then President Reagan knew he would have

to produce the letter signed by Sir Paul and dated before the event. That could no doubt be arranged. He would leave all that to Caspar Weinberger. During his interview for the programme, President Reagan's Secretary of Defense continued to insist that Sir Paul Scoon had been imprisoned, presumably in Richmond Hill Prison, which was why SEALs had been sent to capture it. In fact, SEALs were also sent to Government House, where they found the governor-general and his wife peacefully at home. Curiously, Caspar Weinberger insisted that Sir Paul had been in prison for some time. When the interviewer challenged this, Mr Weinberger replied:

*We were told he was in prison and he also sent a note out from prison saying he was in prison, so we had every reason to believe he was in prison.*

*Our information was, and his testimony in his letter was, that he was being held in confinement in a jail. One of the first objectives after we freed the students was to go up to the jail and, as I remember it, free him.*

The interviewer reiterated that Sir Paul Scoon was not in jail, to which Mr Weinberger responded: 'Well, *he* thought he was!' The interviewer queried the letter that the Americans claimed Sir Paul had written from his jail cell asking for American help. Was it not true that this letter was signed after the invasion and backdated? Mr Weinberger replied: 'Well, that's all news to me.' The interviewer concluded: 'With all due respect, Mr Weinberger, I've met Sir Paul Scoon and he's told me exactly the opposite.'

Whereas Caspar Weinberger has claimed that the Americans actually mounted the helicopter operation against Richmond Hill Prison specifically to rescue him, Sir Paul is emphatic in denying this. And, as to the American allegation that the letter was written by Sir Paul himself in prison, the governor-general is adamant that although he signed the letter he never wrote it and that he never was in prison at all.

The British for once were not playing their usual role of America's poodle. As Grenada was a Commonwealth country, with a British governor-general and the Queen as head of state, they were not in favour of a military solution at all. Reagan had chosen to 'war war' rather than 'jaw jaw' and had not involved Prime Minister Margaret Thatcher, which caused an uncharacteristically unfriendly telephone conversation between her and 'Ronnie'.

Tony Motley, who was Assistant Secretary of State, tells an amusing story about how hard it was to get the invasion of Grenada started. He couldn't get a taxi:

*The final meeting with President Reagan prior to the actual intervention was Monday night. I'd ridden over to the White House with*

△ Twenty thousand American troops took part in Operation Urgent Fury. There were so few of the supposed Cuban enemy that most of the Americans found little to do on the island, except to get sunburned.

*Secretary of State Schultz in his car, and after the meeting I stayed behind to do some things, and so I left the White House about 6.30. Seeing as Schultz had left, I didn't have a ride. So I walked out the front door of the West Wing and walked down Pennsylvania Avenue and it was raining and I'd got these secret documents under my arm here, and I'm about to go out and start an invasion. And I'm standing there, waving down these cabs and they're not stopping. Then one stops and the driver says: 'Where you going?' I said: 'I'm going to the State Department.' 'No, I'm going the other way,' he says. And so on. It took about four attempts, all in the rain, and I'm saying to*

*myself, 'It is the height of the Cold War, you know, the Russians aren't going to believe this, that here am I about to start an invasion except I can't get to my office because I can't get a cab.'*

Motley's 'fury' was matched by the 'urgency' of the operation commander, Admiral Metcalf, who was given just thirty-nine hours to plan the mission and was given his command with the *hors d'oeuvre* at a cocktail party:

*They had to decide who was going to run the operation, sort of an afterthought: who's going to run this thing? Admiral Watkins said: 'Don't you have some kind of a three-star admiral down there in Norfolk? Can't he do this sort of thing?' 'Oh yes, the Commander of the Second Fleet. He'd be ideal. In fact, it's in his area.' And so – bang! – that's how I came to be in charge. That was in the morning,*

△ Troops from the US 82nd Airborne Division arrive in Grenada.

*about 11 o'clock sometime. When I was informed, I was at this party, and away we went. Now, you can say, well, isn't that kind of a slap-doodle way of doing business, yeah, but we were taking advantage of what the armed forces of the United States do best. If we've been trained to do something, we can react very quickly. We had the Navy down there, the Army was all ready to go. And so they just said, 'By golly, we can make this happen', and – bang! – the thing got started.*

Lack of a rapid-reaction force, an intelligence department and any contingency planning rendered Urgent Fury almost uniquely inept. It has become fashionable to turn to Fascist Italy to discover supreme military incompetence. That must cease if operations like the invasion of Grenada are examined. To combat a maximum military force of 1,000 Cuban and Grenadan troops, fighting without air power or heavy equipment, it was thought necessary to send 20,000 Americans, including Special Operations forces. With speed and secrecy the main priorities the American task force approached Grenada like a 'whale in fatigues'. Like the vast majority of Americans, Congressman Louis Stokes only heard about the invasion of Grenada on CNN news:

*I saw no reason whatsoever for the United States to invade a little tiny island in the Caribbean, and it appeared that President Reagan was utilizing his own purposes for that invasion, and it is that type of action on his part that had engendered the kind of controversy that had developed. In fact, most of us as members of Congress learned about the invasion while we were in the cloakroom on the floor working and CNN broadcast the fact that we had just invaded Grenada. So without any prior notice to Congress, as members of Congress you can imagine how silly we felt learning on CNN news about an invasion by our country of another country.*

The invasion of Grenada was under way, but the first 'secret' invasion ended in tragedy. An attempt to land 12 navy SEALs on the night of 23/24 October failed when the overloaded parachutists jumping into the sea sank to the bottom under the weight of their equipment. Four men could not be located by rescue ships and were lost. The 'invasion' was postponed until the following night. The second attempt was just as bad as it had been on the first night, except that no one died. The 'secret' invasion was now cancelled because it was no longer a secret. The 'public' invasion, witnessed by hordes of sightseers and tourists on the shores, would be carried out in daylight.

The rescue of the medical students had to be top priority:

CNN demanded it. But did anyone know where the students were? Much has been made of the fact that the chancellor of the college was safely in New York. But had anyone bothered to ask him where the students lived? Apparently not, for when American troops arrived at True Blue campus, to the east of the new Salines airport runway, they discovered that this was home to just a third of the students; the rest were either in Grande Anse campus a couple of miles to the north-west or scattered in apartments throughout the island. Back in the United States, the parents of the students presumably knew the addresses of their children. However, the National Military Intelligence Center knew best, and nobody bothered to ask Mom. If there really had been a threat of hostage-taking, the Americans would have blown it almost before the rescue attempt got under way. Any desperate hostage-takers alerted to America's fears as well as infuriated by the illegal invasion of their country would have been given sufficient time to round up a few hundred helpless American would-be doctors and

to have settled in for a long siege. That this did not happen undermined the prime American justification for being there in the first place. Dr George Albert, who was one of the medical students in 1983, found a role in American military intelligence:

*I remember students talking to some of the soldiers and helping them try to identify where some of the other students were located, and we realized that what they were looking at were tourist maps, rather crude tourist maps, maps that you could buy at any general store of the island. And it was very difficult for them because a lot of the roads were still dirt roads back then, so they weren't clearly demarcated.*

While the Americans were wading through a chaos of their own creation, unknown to them Fidel Castro of Cuba was reaching a decision that was to ensure American success and to save dozens of American lives. Although the Revolutionary Military Council had contacted the Cuban leader to ask for help, Castro had replied:

*If the United States intervenes, we must vigorously defend ourselves as if we were in Cuba, in our campsites, in our workplaces close*

▽ American troops begin to rescue some of the 1,000 American medical students on the island. This was probably the hardest task most of the invading troops had to do.

△ America welcomes home her medical students from Grenada. Ronald Reagan basks in public acclaim for the nation's first military success since the Second World War.

*by, but only if we are directly attacked. I repeat: only if we are directly attacked. We would thus be defending ourselves, not the government or its deeds. The sending of reinforcements is impossible and unthinkable.*

Right from the start the Americans wrongly pinpointed their objectives: Radio Free Grenada, Richmond Hill Prison and Government House. Faulty intelligence was at work. Even when the radio station was captured, the Americans discovered they could not silence the voice of Grenada, which operated from a studio on the beach and later from a mobile broadcasting vehicle. The prison proved – like the Bastille –

to be symbolic rather than an actual building of political repression. The Americans sent their best anti-terrorist unit to free the political prisoners there. Ultimately, however, the SEALs simply released all the prisoners, so that law and order broke down as murderers, rapists and thieves of all kinds, as well as those who had been late with their TV licence payments or who had played their ghetto blasters too loud, were free to spread a wave of criminality across the island. Everyone ran free except the man the SEALs had gone to release: Sir Paul Scoon, the governor-general. He was at home, where he'd been all the time.

Although Caspar Weinberger has claimed that Sir Paul Scoon was in Richmond Hill Prison and had been for some time – thus justifying the invasion in the first place – the Americans still sent a team of twenty-two SEALs to Government House for Sir Paul and his family. They found him at ease and in no danger. However, the SEALs brought danger with them. As soon as they entered Government House, a veritable siege began, forcing Sir Paul and his wife to lie on the floor of the dining-room for the best part of the next twenty-four hours while the SEALs and the People's Republican Army exchanged fire. With bullets smashing windows and hitting the walls above his head, the governor-general had his 'safety assured'.

The Cuban soldiers on Grenada – all forty-three of them – had convinced themselves that the Americans had come to the island simply to evacuate their students. As a result, Lieutenant-Colonel Orlando Matamoros Lopez was astonished instead at how the Americans behaved: 'We thought the US troops were going to evacuate the students and withdraw, but after they landed they began attacking our positions and taking prisoners.'

The Lind Report, written in the aftermath of Operation Urgent Fury, drew particular attention to what was referred to as 'the cowboy syndrome' among the airborne troops and the Rangers:

*These units may be affected by the 'cowboy syndrome'. The 'cowboys' are people who believe machismo is what defines a competent soldier. The 'snake eater' image of some of our specialized forces and the elite image of the paratroopers tend to make these units magnets for 'cowboys'. In combat, the 'cowboy' tends to fight the enemy even when he can go round him – as some of our forces seem to have done in Grenada – and also to 'come unglued' when faced with the unexpected.*

The extraordinary parachute drop at Point Salines by the Rangers took ninety minutes to complete, with the enemy troops watching the whole time and desisting from massacring the 600 helpless parachutists as they descended. Many Americans alive today owe a debt to Fidel Castro for his firm orders to his troops not to fire unless fired on. The parachuting Rangers were all ludicrously overloaded, one of them getting a hernia from the weight of his kit even before he jumped. Two men died when their parachutes failed to open, but otherwise a single broken leg was the penalty for the most inept airborne operation imaginable.

The American medical students had encountered no danger until the arrival of their 'rescuers'. Now a gun battle took place on their campus, with American bullets penetrating the students' rooms, striking walls, windows and doors from the direction of the beach. Dr George Albert remembers the fighting near his room:

*I remember going to Grande Anse Beach, where one of the dorms was for the students, and noticing the beachfront side of the dorm riddled with bullet holes. The thing that bothered me is that I knew behind the dorm on the island side of that dorm was the Grenadans' military installation. I gathered that the bullet holes were US bullets and that the students were caught in the line of fire between two fighting forces at that time. I don't think that the US intentionally were shooting at students.*

In the absence of jeeps, the Rangers had to transport heavy radios by hand, while twenty-seven 'Stinger' anti-aircraft missile teams had to carry 110 pounds of equipment with them even though the enemy had no aircraft. This did not deter those of the American troops who were spoiling for a fight. While most American soldiers searched high and low for somebody to fight, liberate or imprison, Major-General Trobaugh, commander of the 82nd Airborne Division, who had obviously seen too many war films, demanded of his superiors in Washington: 'Keep sending battalions until I tell you to stop.'

Although the Americans had used the pretext of rescuing potential hostages on Grenada, in the persons of their medical students, it took them an incredible thirty-three hours to reach the Grande Anse campus just two miles or less from their landing point. In fact, no students were hurt, although many claimed they had come close to being hit by American bullets. Even when the Grande Anse campus was 'liberated', there were still 200 more students living in apartments on the Lance aux Epines peninsula. One student house was occupied by the fearsome, potentially hostage-taking PRA soldiers who, after releasing the students unharmed, dutifully locked up the house when they left. Less fortunate were two British honeymooners, who got involved in a gun battle near their hotel. Forced to hide in the bath for much of the day, they were summoned eventually by an American voice bellowing into their room: 'This is the US Army peacekeeping force. Run – and run fast.' The couple leaped from their bathtub and hurried down to the beach, where they were bundled aboard a C–130 transport plane and flown to Barbados.

That Operation Urgent Fury was a political operation can hardly be doubted. Its military justification was minimal, but the President needed it, the military needed it and, by golly, the good ol' US of A needed it. One outspoken young Grenadan soldier complained that while a prisoner of the Americans he found that there was a price to pay for his release. As Keith Phillips remembers:

*The Americans had a condition for them to release you, telling you that you're not supposed to get involved in politics, so I said: 'Who you think you're talking to? You want to come here and tell me I'm supposed to stay out of politics in my own country. This is a joke you're making.' So I was one of the last set of people who was released from*

*Point Salines because I'm a determined young man, and I still remain that way. You can't come here and tell me what to do in my country because I can't come to your country and tell you what to do.*

Apart from the brief fighting, the heat was the greatest enemy the Americans faced. It seemed that American quartermasters had never heard of the Caribbean or its climate. They had kitted out their men for all eventualities, with the result that everyone was overloaded. The polyester uniforms were quite unsuitable for service in the tropics. In one day, for example, twenty-nine soldiers in one battalion collapsed from heat exhaustion; in another there were forty-eight heat casualties, and in a third the entire supply of intravenous solution was used up on heat casualties alone. One soldier reported the effect of his overloading:

*We were like slow-moving turtles. My rucksack weighed 120 pounds. I would get up and rush for ten yards, throw myself down and I couldn't get up. I'd rest for ten to fifteen minutes, struggle to get up, go ten more yards and collapse. After a few rushes I was physically unable to move, and I'm in great shape.*

In the final analysis, 'Operation Urgent Fury' does not bear close scrutiny. Urgent it certainly was, to be the point of rash desperation in too many cases. With politics rather than military necessity in the driving seat, so many mistakes were made that it is kinder to put the blame on the politicians. Of military planning there was hardly a sign. American mapwork was not very good in spite of what Admiral Metcalf thought:

*We didn't have good charts of the area. We operated, particularly when we got ashore to begin with, using an Esso map, you know, doing and setting up grids. I can remember all the instructors and people go to a lot of shenanigans to show how accurate we were going to get these grids, and here we were, making a grid on an Esso map, which goes to show you, when you have to do it, by golly, you can do it.*

When the fighting was over, Grenadan soldier Joe Buyer found that the American troops knew virtually nothing about Grenada:

*This American soldier came up to us and he asked us to point at Trinidad and show him the road that he can travel on to get to Trinidad, which he thought was in walking distance. We tried to explain to him that you have to take a flight to get to Trinidad, and he said: 'No, it's on a map. You can walk. Look at it here.'*

It was left to the American ground troops to interpret the 'fury' aspect of the operation's title. There was some unneces-

sary bloodshed and much looting. Lady Scoon had her jewellery stolen from Government House, possibly by her rescuers, while, as one resident commented: 'As we moved out, I witnessed soldiers literally destroy houses, stealing all kinds of stuff, mostly from people who had retired from England and different parts of the world.' On the other hand, one Grenadan woman found this message in her house from the American troops who had occupied it:

*Sorry we had to bust your door down. We walked your dog. We cleared up the mess in the kitchen. We used your stove to heat up our C-rations. Have a nice day.*

It was that sort of war.

In military terms, Operation Urgent Fury was a close-run thing. It skirted the edge of fiasco. A Cuban officer commented on the problem: 'The US have a lot of training and very good support in terms of hardware, but their morale is based on might alone. Their tactic is to destroy everything with their planes and artillery first and see what's left.' As one Grenadan soldier, Keith Phillips, succinctly put it: 'They're just a bunch of bullies.' Mark Adkin, author of *Urgent Fury: The Battle for Grenada* sums it up:

*In all their undertakings from Korea, Vietnam and Iran, through to Grenada, the United States has fought with enormous technical superiority, particularly in the air. But this has not brought victory. The US military malaise stems in part from the cult of management replacing leadership, from a huge bureaucracy whose aims are often…career advancement, maintenance of an orderly flow of paper within the system, and protection from outside disturbance. The result, obvious in Vietnam, has been a pernicious inability to distinguish between management and leadership, efficiency and effectiveness, and technology and tactics.*

And the medical students? Well, 662 were eventually evacuated and returned to the United States, some to kiss the ground as they landed and earn themselves places in more prestigious American medical colleges. Dr George Albert was not impressed by the experience:

*Of the students kissing the ground, that'd not be something that I would ever do. This event was very political; the students had an opportunity to be on major TV coverage. And many students because of this event were able to transfer to American medical schools.*

Twenty-one future doctors, however, apparently overlooked by their rescuers, remained on the island and never became hostages of either the Grenadan Revolutionary Military Council or of President Ronald Reagan.

# THE FALL OF THE
# ROMAN EMPIRE
⚔

By May 1940 the achievements of an Austrian ex-corporal and failed art student were threatening completely to overshadow those of the new Julius Caesar, renascent south of the Alps. The inheritor of the legacy of ancient Rome could hardly stand by and watch as this parvenu from Braunau-am-Inn toppled nations of far greater culture and history by unleashing the barbarian hordes that had once lived in their dark forests beyond the borders of Rome. A warlord, as Benito Mussolini liked to imagine himself, must eventually put down the pen of peace and unsheathe the sword of war. And, like the jackal he was, he believed that now that the main predator had passed he could identify those of the flock who had been weakened and would succumb easily to his attack. With Britain engaged in the life-or-death struggle with Germany in the skies over southern England, and with her traditional sword, the French Army, knocked from her hand, her scantily defended colonies might fall with ease. Foremost among these, from Mussolini's point of view, was Egypt, with its Suez Canal, adjoining the Italian Empire in Libya. Even Hitler would be impressed if his fellow Fascist suddenly announced at their next meeting that Italy held the Suez Canal and that shipping dues would henceforth be paid in lire.

Shifting from peace to war was no great problem for Mussolini; he did not even need to leave his desk or lift his phone. As well as being *Il Duce*, Prime Minister, Chairman of the Fascist Party (pause for breath), he was also First Marshal of the Empire, Commander-in-Chief, Minister of War, Minister for the Navy and Minister for the Air Force. Sometimes he scarcely knew how he found the time. A Fascists's work was never done: one minute contacting Marshal Graziani in Libya and

◁ Mussolini as he saw himself: sportsman and man of action.

officer who captured him in the desert in 1943: 'Next time it's your turn to have the Italians.' The Italian Mess tents were reported to be bigger than most army encampments, and as a German wrote home scornfully: 'Everyone thinks only of eating, enjoying themselves, making money. Anyone who gets killed is a jerk. He who supplies the troops with cardboard shoes is considered a sort of hero.'

Mussolini's decision to invade Egypt from his Libyan territory was typically the act of a politician rather than a soldier. It looked easy on the maps on his desk in Rome. All his intelligence reports pointed to its being easy. The British had been beaten by the Germans, faced invasion at any moment and, as everyone knows, Britain is a cold country and her men cannot cope with hot weather or the desert. Such intelligence reports were not just postprandial vapours rising from the bottom of a wine glass; they contained information on which the Italian military relied. As Denis Mack Smith says, Mussolini truly believed that:

*. . . the British cannot fight in the heat and, in fact, he even adds on one occasion, 'The British Army's hopeless, so Grandi tells me, and he's been ambassador in London', especially as they have to break off fighting to take tea at five o'clock every day.*

To run a war with such absurd prejudices sums up Mussolini's martial aspirations. Graziani, whether a coward or a patriot, at least tried to face reality. He told *Il Duce* that his Italian Army, numerically superior without doubt, was in every other way inferior to the British forces they would face in Egypt. Without trucks, tanks and water, the Italians would arrive in British territory more like refugees than invaders, hoping to be taken prisoner to save their lives. Mussolini responded to the truth by accusing Graziani of being extremely un-Fascist. Il Duce insisted that the invasion of Egypt should take place forthwith and within a Fascist dictatorship. *Il Duce* always knew best, as Dr Brian Sullivan, military historian and National Security Analyst illustrates:

*The problem, however, is that Libya was a country with very scanty water resources. There's no river in the entire country; what water there is is in artesian wells, but to make matters worse there had been a drought previously, so there was even less water than usual. The Italian Army, the one that was supposed to invade Egypt, was one with very few motor vehicles. The majority of its forces were infantry in the full*

revealing the secrets of how to beat the British, the next selecting the new tank design, as Denis Mack Smith illustrates:

*One of his generals, who was the engineer in charge of the engineering services, came to him and said: 'Look, Il Duce, we've got no medium tanks. You can't have an armoured division without medium tanks.' So he produced four designs of tanks, medium tanks, only ten or eleven tons in weight – really small stuff – and Mussolini pretended to look at them very seriously for about a quarter of an hour. Finally he said: 'Oh, we'll make that one.' And he just pointed to one. The fact that the tank never worked properly didn't matter because the Duce was seen to be taking action.*

Mussolini's hardest job, however, was getting the Italians to fight. The Germans were continually astonished by the 'Italian way of war'. As one German prisoner quipped to the British

△ Marshal Rodolfo Graziani inspecting his troops before the invasion of Egypt.

sense of the word: they were foot-soldiers. Graziani had some tanks and some artillery, but basically he had an army that, if it was going to reach the Nile Delta, was going to have to march there on foot. And, of course, June, July, August, September is a period of blazing heat. In order for him to cross the Western Desert he'd have to supply his men with water, and he had a lot of men: well over 100,000.

Faced with certain disaster, Graziani played for time, and an extraordinary exchange of letters and messages took place which could almost be set to music in an Italian comic opera. Denis Mack Smith tries to provide a libretto:

One moment you find Graziani saying, here am I in North Africa with the finest colonial army that Europe has seen in the last ten years, and the next moment he's saying privately to people, I'm afraid we're without arms. Mussolini talks about having eight million bayonets – next we've got no bayonets at all. We've got a few rifles that don't work, and they date back to the 1880s. We've got no tanks, and he expects me to invade Greece, and Mussolini says you've got ten to one superiority in numbers. For God's sake do something. The peace is coming on soon and I must have a pawn in my hands. He keeps on

inciting Graziani to advance, and Graziani probably quite rightly said: 'Look here, we're not ready. I've consulted all our generals in North Africa and we've all agreed that we must have more preparations, we must have more trucks, we can't ask these people to march a thousand miles in the desert.' In the end Graziani pushes about fifty yards into Egyptian territory.

Meanwhile, an extraordinary decision by Mussolini is not helping the Italian war effort. Denis Mack Smith attempts to make some sense of it:

Another absurd decision Mussolini takes at the beginning of October, two weeks before invading Greece, is to demobilize half his army. This is an incredible story in a way. The army's 600,000 troops are sent home because he says, 'I'll have trouble at home if these soldiers remain for a winter under arms. I don't need them.' He must have known he wanted to attack Greece two weeks later, but 600,000 people go home.

When the Italians reached the Egyptian border, Graziani reported that two companies of his troops had been 'overrun by 300 British armoured cars' – more than the British had in the whole of Africa. The Italian tank drivers confronted by the armoured cars abandoned their vehicles and ran away. Graziani reached Sidi Barrani and dug himself in. Increasingly harassed by Mussolini, receiving threats of dismissal if he continued to refuse to advance further into Egypt, still Graziani dragged his heels. He complained that the weather was too hot and that the terrain was unsuitable. All the while, however, Graziani's diaries record endless fashionable lunches, attendance at Fascist ceremonies and at the Benghazi theatre.

△ Marshal Graziani in more traditional pose. Compared with the Germans and the British, Italian standards in army cuisine were very high and their mess arrangements extensive.

Mussolini's ludicrous invasion of Egypt came to an end when the British decided to put the Italians out of their misery. General Richard O'Connor began a 'reconnaissance in force'. In the space of a few months, the British captured 150,000 Italians and 400 tanks. Many of the Italians were taken prisoner carrying neatly packed suitcases. As Sir Anthony Eden remarked: 'Never had so much been surrendered by so many to so few.'

# FALL GUY AT THE BATTLE OF HATTIN
⚔

Rarely, if ever, has the fate of a kingdom, its people and its religion been gambled so recklessly as it was in 1187 in the kingdom of Jerusalem. The gambler was named Guy of Lusignan, and he was the usurper king of Jerusalem and, as such, defender of the entire Latin Christian presence in the Holy Land which the First Crusade had fought so hard to secure over eighty years before. Guy allowed personal and political motives to outweigh the firm military practices that the Crusaders had developed to combat the Muslim enemies who surrounded them. The loss of the Holy Cross that followed the Crusader defeat at Hattin and the subsequent loss of the Holy City of Jerusalem itself were direct consequences of a military decision taken for non-military reasons. Professor Jonathan Riley-Smith, Dixie Professor of Ecclesiastical History at the University of Cambridge, explains the significance of the cross lost at Hattin:

> *There comes to be an obsession with the cross, now the greatest relic in the eyes of Christians, a splinter which is believed to have come from the cross on which Christ had been crucified which was discovered shortly after the First Crusade. It was kept always in the Church of the Holy Sepulchre, and it was always carried into battle. You've got to imagine this extraordinary scene in the twelfth century: in the front row of squadrons galloping in a charge would be a knight, himself unable to use weapons because he was carrying the relic, with on either side of him two armed protectors; the relic was there going right at the front, charging right into battle. Now at Hattin this relic, the true cross, was lost. Actually, it was taken by the Muslims. Saladin had it paraded upside down on a lance through the streets of Damascus.*

The Muslim leader Saladin, ruler of Egypt and Syria, chose to invade the Christian kingdom of

△ Saladin, 1138–1193, ruler of Egypt and Syria and conqueror of the kingdom of Jerusalem. His shrewd knowledge of Crusader psychology enabled him to exploit schisms within the Christian ranks and brought him victory at the battle of Hattin.

*Crusaders are there as a permanent army of occupation; it is a religious conquest. The* jihad, *which is the Holy War within the Islamic faith, gradually comes to the surface to try to remove the Crusaders. From the Crusaders' point of view, then, what do you do? Do you confront them in battle, or do you take a longer-term view, in which you try to preserve your hold on the coastline and deal with the Muslims through diplomacy, through occasional warfare, through truces and things like that? That's the dilemma that faces them.*

In 1187 King Guy seemed a weak leader, far from the traditions of the ruthless men who had carved out the kingdom from Muslim territory in the first half of the century. Dr Phillips explains the background of Guy of Lusignan:

*Guy became king by being a successful adventurer. He came to the East at the summons of his brother, and friends influenced Princess Sibylla, who was the heiress to the kingdom, to marry him. He was therefore the really ultimate adventurer, if you like, the ultimate gigolo. He carried her off right under the noses of the great barons of the kingdom of Jerusalem, to their absolute fury. Here's a sort of new man. He's been here only a few years; in fact he's been here only a few months, and he marries the heiress to the kingdom, making him the heir presumptive, the next king of Jerusalem.*

Jerusalem in 1187, sensing that political schism among the Crusaders had fatally weakened the Christian state. Saladin was aware that King Guy, who had usurped the throne the previous year, was struggling to maintain his power against 'hawks' like Reynald of Kerak, who aimed for independence for his Moabite lands, and followers of the ousted regent, Raymond of Tripoli, who wanted peaceful relations with the surrounding Muslim states. Dr Jonathan Phillips of Royal Holloway College, University of London, explains the different approaches towards the Muslims adopted by the Christians in Outremer:

*As the twelfth century goes on, the Muslims realize that the*

Dr Phillips describes the most brutal of the Crusaders, Reynald of Kerak (Reginald of Chatillon), whom the Muslims regarded as the devil and whose actions led directly to Saladin's invasion of the kingdom:

*Reginald of Chatillon was one of the most brutal of the Crusaders. He was a man described by a contemporary Muslim chronicler as 'the most evil, the most avid to do injury to us of all among the Christians'. He was an extraordinarily brutal man, but he was brutal to everybody. If a Christian crossed him he would treat him very badly; likewise the Muslims. Perhaps the best example of this with regard to Christians is his treatment of the Patriarch of Antioch, who he hoped would lend him some money. This elderly man refused to lend him some money, so he had him beaten up, bloodied around the head, tied to a chair, had his head smeared with honey and left him on the citadel of Antioch for the bees to swarm around his head*

*— the man gave him the money in the end.*

King Guy needed men like Reynald, but he also needed so-called 'doves' like Raymond of Tripoli and Balian of Ibelin. Whatever their political feelings, all the Christians were needed if the army of the kingdom of Jerusalem was to be strong enough to face Saladin and his fanatics, now inspired by *jihad* to reconquer Jerusalem. Dr Phillips describes the background of the Muslim leader, Saladin:

*Saladin was a very, very effective operator within the political and the religious context of the twelfth century. He had used the* jihad, *the Holy War, and the banner of Sunni orthodoxy to assemble a large coalition of forces within the Muslim world. Although his power base was Egypt, during the 1170s he had gained control of Damascus, Aleppo and Mosul. It was a very, very slow job. He needed to persuade, cajole, bully, to fight his way into taking control of these places. He also needed the mandate, the religious mandate from the caliph of Baghdad. His message is: 'I am the champion of Sunni orthodoxy. You must come with me; otherwise you are a heretic to your faith.' It took him thirteen years to feel that he had the necessary resources so that he could turn his full attention to the Franks.*

△ The Holy Sepulchre at Jerusalem, centre of Christian belief towards which all the Crusaders directed their steps.

News that Saladin had invaded the kingdom and was besieging the city of Tiberias on Lake Galilee united the Crusaders, who temporarily patched up their differences. But reconciliations were shallow and political rivalries might resurface at any time. Thus, when Raymond of Tripoli acknowledged King Guy as his liege lord as a result of the greater danger that Saladin posed, their new relationship was unlikely to last much longer than the military crisis with the Muslims.

Saladin's decision to besiege Tiberias was a particularly cunning one, as it was owned by Raymond of Tripoli's wife, Eschiva, and the question of its defence would drive a stake through the new reconciliation between Raymond and King Guy. Four years before the current crisis Guy had been acting as regent for the ailing King Baldwin IV, a leper, when Saladin had raided the kingdom. Guy had adopted a policy of 'masterly inactivity', refusing to seek out the Muslim army but, instead, standing on the defensive until the Muslims withdrew. It had been a wise strategy, yet Guy's action was heavily criticized by the Count of Tripoli and other political opponents as little less than cowardice. Still smarting from this accusation, Guy was determined that if a similar situation arose he would adopt a more aggressive strategy. However, in 1187 Raymond of Tripoli could see that the situation had changed. Four years before, Saladin had not led the army of a united

Islam and had merely raided the Christian lands. At that time Raymond was involved in a political struggle to secure the power behind the throne of the boy-king Baldwin V, when he succeeded the dying leper-king. In that situation he was willing to malign Guy of Lusignan with accusations of cowardice. But four years later, in 1187, Saladin was now master of the Muslim world, had declared a Holy War against the Christians and had the biggest army that the kingdom had ever faced. Bravado on the part of King Guy was not called for, even to efface an accusation of cowardice. Guy's policy of 1183 was now essential in 1187 or else the whole kingdom could be lost in a single day. But would Guy trust Raymond now that he was advocating the very strategy he had condemned four years before?

King Guy had assembled the whole military strength of the kingdom at Saffuriya, near Acre. He had stripped the castles of their garrisons in order to swell the royal army but must have known that by doing so he was risking everything on a single battle. Defeat would lead to the loss of the entire kingdom as the castles from which the Christians had administered the lands would fall easily to a successful Muslim invasion.

Nearly a century of warfare between the Western Franks and the Muslims had seen the development of specific tactics and strategy on both sides. The massive weight advantage of the heavily armoured Franks in battle must be set against the speed and mobility of the Muslim cavalry. On the defensive, with a city like Acre or Tyre close by, the Christians were virtually unbeatable. Their infantry crossbows were much more powerful than the Muslim bows, and their 'iron' knights always prevailed in close combat. However, the temperament of the Western warriors – notably the Military Orders of the Hospital and the Temple – was always suspect and needed the strongest control. Richard the Lionheart, for example, got the best out of the Templars, King Guy possibly the worst.

The greatest danger the Christians faced was the desert terrain and the Middle Eastern climate. Their way of war had developed in Western Europe, and they had to adapt to conditions that rarely suited them. Harsh experience had taught them that water ruled the Muslim world and that however strong, heavy or forthright the Frankish warrior was in battle the Muslim warrior was the product of thousands of years spent adapting to desert conditions. The Crusaders could not simply impose themselves on an alien environment. Drawn into arid, sandy terrain by the lighter Muslim horsemen, the Frankish knights would succumb to thirst and exhaustion. Their heavyweight charge may be irresistible, but it would only shatter the Muslim cavalry if they were trapped against forest, mountain or river. Otherwise, they would simply outrun the heavier Western

horses and re-form again when the Crusaders had expended their energies in futile pursuit.

The choice that faced King Guy at Saffuriya was an unenviable one. Saladin had set a clear trap for him and was inviting him to fall into it. The Muslim leader had not needed even to conceal his intentions. His close relations with men like Raymond of Tripoli and his spy network within the Christian kingdom supplied him with all the up-to-date information about the political situation in Jerusalem. Saladin knew that if he threatened Countess Eschiva in Tiberias and she called on the king for help, then Guy would feel bound by feudal obligation to come to the aid of his vassal. To reach Eschiva, he would have to lead his army across the barren lands between Saffuriya and Tiberias, with the Muslim army controlling all the high ground on the route. Common sense might say 'Do not go', but Guy had faced the accusation of cowardice once before and if he failed to succour his vassal now he might as well give up the Crown, for none of his other vassals would ever trust him again.

To maintain his political hold on the kingdom, Guy of Lusignan felt that he must take the risk. Several times in Crusader history such marches had been successfully undertaken and, only four years later, King Richard I of England would make an epic coastal march to Arsuf, all the time under the eyes of Saladin's army. Richard's iron discipline kept his command together, with the knights protected by the gambesons of the foot-soldiers and the crossbowmen keeping the Muslim horsemen at long range. Strong leadership of this kind might have made the march to Tiberias possible, but without proper water supplies it would prove disastrous.

Aware of just how much depended on his decision, Guy called the leading knights to his tent on the evening of Thursday 2 July 1187. There he asked the leading figures of the realm to speak. As the march would be through the lands of Raymond of Tripoli and as it was his wife Eschiva who had called for succour, Guy prevailed on him to speak first. Although Raymond was counted as one of the 'doves' and was not trusted by men like Reynald of Kerak and Gerard de Ridefort, he was an experienced warrior who was held in high esteem by the Muslims. His recent alliance with Saladin during his dispute with King Guy made him anathema to the 'hawks' led by Reynald, but he had many supporters, notably the wise and moderate Balian of Ibelin.

What followed was one of the most dramatic scenes of the Middle Ages. Not only the future of the kingdom rested on the arguments of these few knights, but also the survival or otherwise of Christianity in the Holy Land, the land of its birth. Surely it was inconceivable that Christ's Holy Sepulchre could fall once more into the hands of the infidel Turks? We can never recover the words of Raymond of Tripoli as they were spoken or the effect they had on the grim warriors as they jostled for space in the crowded tent. While Ernoul, squire to Balian of Ibelin, has recorded the main arguments for us, it must never be forgotten that Balian was an ally to the Count of Tripoli and an enemy to the 'hawks'. His brother, Baldwin of Ramla, had left the kingdom in disgust after Guy of Lusignan had stolen his intended bride, Princess Sibylla, while Baldwin was imprisoned by Saladin. In Balian's eyes, Baldwin should have been king, not the handsome parvenu Guy of Lusignan. Raymond's speech, as recorded by Ernoul, must be set in context. Raymond had more to gain from staying at Saffuriya than risking everything on the arid march to Tiberias. He knew that he could trust Saladin not to harm his wife Eschiva, and once Saladin withdrew from the kingdom, as he must do if he failed to win a decisive battle, then Tiberias could easily be rebuilt. This was the moment for calm thinking and cool heads. But in the flickering light of the torches held by the servants, the faces of some of Raymond's opponents were contorted with hatred for the man they saw as a traitor.

At first, it seems, Raymond was unwilling to speak, aware of the hostile reception he would receive from the 'hawk' faction. Nevertheless, King Guy urged him to give them his opinion and so, unwillingly, Raymond spoke above the hubbub. His first words stunned almost everyone there – abandon Tiberias, abandon Eschiva. They were bombshells, and even his critics were silenced. The risk was too great. It was nothing less than the loss of the whole kingdom and all the people for one city and one noble lady, even though she was his wife.

According to the chronicler Ernoul, this was the essence of the speech given by Raymond of Tripoli to the assembled Crusader leaders:

*Between here and Tiberias there is no water, only the little spring of Cresson, and there is nothing for an army. And well do I know that as soon as you move from here, in case you do go to the rescue of the city, you will have the Saracens in front of you and they will harass you the entire day, and draw you out until they hold you all day midway between here and Tiberias. They will make you camp despite yourselves, because you will not be able to fight on account of the heat, and because the sergeants will have nothing to drink but will die of thirst, and, if you attack, the Saracens will open out and withdraw into the hills, where you will not be able to penetrate without your sergeants. And if you have to camp there, what will your men and your horse drink? Are they going to remain without water? Such a course would be fatal, and the next day they will take us all, because they will have water and food and will all be fresh. We shall all be killed and captured. And so I think it much better to let the town go than lose the whole land, for surely if you do go there, the land is lost.*

The silence that followed was broken by Gerard de Ridefort, who called out: 'He has a wolf's skin.' Dr John France of Swansea University introduces the Master of the Templars, Guy's *éminence gris*:

*Gerard of Ridefort was an unsuccessful adventurer who came to the East probably in the 1160s as a mercenary, a sword for hire, looking for wealth, looking for position, and he hoped to marry a very rich lady. He was promised a rich heiress by Raymond of Tripoli. Gerard thought, 'Here's my opportunity, here's my golden world.' Then Raymond of Tripoli gave it to somebody else who literally gave him the weight of the heiress in gold, poured out the cash and said: 'Give me the woman.' And he did, so Gerard of Ridefort was an adventurer, and it hadn't worked. He progressed from being a disappointed adventurer to becoming a zealot, a man who was inspired, who was in effect soured in a certain sense by his experiences and sought refuge in religion.*

Other enemies of Raymond's like Reynald found that they were for once in the minority and remained silent. King Guy, weighing up the prevailing support for Raymond's policy, ordered that his argument was persuasive. Apparently, nobody else ventured an opinion. The military argument was irrefutable. The barons left the king's tent and retired for the night. As King Guy received late refreshments, he found that one man had returned, determined to change the king's mind. It was Gerard de Ridefort, Master of the Templars. Dr John France explains the origin of the Templars:

*The Templars were warrior-monks. They were people who took the vows of poverty, chastity and obedience, which were monastic vows, yet they also lived in the world as knights sworn to defend the holy places. That was their job, that was their duty, to help defend pilgrims and the holy sites. They were the crack troops of the Crusader states; they were trained soldiers, mercenaries, who lived in barracks. They had a lot of money. The idea of a warrior-monk is extraordinarily popular, and copied over Western Europe in Spain, in France… The Hospitallers are warrior-monks, a very, very attractive idea. The money that they got allowed them to build large castles and to have lots of horses and equipment, so they really were the standing army, if you like, of the East.*

Personal animosity to the Count of Tripoli had poisoned Gerard's mind and made him willing to risk everything to fight Saladin and to gain revenge for his disastrous defeat at the spring of Cresson only months before. The fact that he, with just 130 knights, had attacked a Muslim force of 7,000 men under Emir Keükburi and suffered annihilation he blamed on the Count of Tripoli. Now he reminded Guy of what had happened four years before when he had sought

△ A painted paper from Fustat depicting twelfth-century warfare. After his victory at Hattin, Saladin was able to capture Jerusalem. It was being defended by one of the few Christian survivors from Hattin, Balian of Ibelin. King Guy's catastrophic decision to march to Tiberias meant the loss of the Holy Land to the Christians for all time.

advice from the Count of Tripoli. Then Raymond and the Ibelin brothers had abandoned him to disgrace, calling him a coward for not confronting the Muslim invaders. Why should the king now believe the Count of Tripoli? Having assembled the strongest army ever seen in the kingdom, Guy would be accounted a poltroon if he stood by and watched Saladin destroying Tiberias without lifting a finger to help the people of Galilee. Guy found it difficult to resist Gerard's arguments. After all, he knew he owed his throne to Gerard and the support of the Templars. And could he be certain that Raymond was speaking the truth?

Gerard saw that his arguments were striking home, so he produced his trump card. He had helped Guy to the throne, but if he withdrew Templar support how long could the new king survive? The Templars demanded revenge on the Saracens. 'Go, have it announced throughout the Army that all should arm and every man go to his company and follow the standard of the Holy Cross.' Gerard was clearly still desperate to avenge his humiliation at Cresson and to pay back the hated Count of Tripoli. No Royal Army had gone into battle without Templar support for fifty years. He knew that Guy would never risk it.

Throughout the camp drowsy men, awakened by a sudden call to arms, tumbled from their beds to the news that the king had changed his mind. Before dawn, the Royal Army would begin its march to Tiberias. The barons and knights grouped together and argued, as their squires prepared their equipment. To advance across a waterless plateau in midsummer heat was madness. Everybody there knew it was a trap – even the king – and that Saladin controlled the high ground all the way to Lake Tiberias. He could choose his moment to

fall on the Christian Army while it was struggling below him.

Guy had made a disastrous military decision for entirely political reasons. As Gerard de Ridefort had pointed out, the loss of Tiberias was a blow to the king's honour. Guy could not afford to suffer another loss of prestige to compare with the accusations of cowardice levelled against him in 1183. He needed to convince everyone – even himself – of his leadership qualities, and this could happen only in the heat of battle. A masterly defensive policy of wait and see – even if successful – would not be enough. Just as Saladin needed to fight a decisive battle before internal pressures broke up his army, so Guy needed to prove himself a king and a warrior, worthy

△ The Gorge of Wadi al Hamam from the Horns of Hattin. In this dry, desert terrain the army of King Guy suffered thirst and exhaustion before it was annihilated by the Muslims.

to stand as successor to the great fighting kings of the earlier part of the century.

Saladin's scouts in the hills overlooking Saffuriya were delighted to see the sleeping Crusader camp ablaze with activity. As the Royal Army began to assemble for the march to Tiberias, the scouts rode to tell Saladin that his ploy had worked: the Christians were choosing suicide to defend their honour.

# CHURCHILL AND THE WRITING OF GREEK TRAGEDY

✤

On 2 September 1898, at Omdurman in the Sudan, there took place the last great cavalry charge of the British Army. The 21st Lancers, under Colonel Martin, interpreted General Kitchener's orders in the loosest possible way. 'Heading off' the enemy became an excuse for a charge to equal Lord Cardigan's at Balaclava. Not surprisingly, 2nd Lieutenant Winston Churchill was there to join in the fun. The *enfant terrible*, who, two years later at Spion Kop in South Africa was to be arrested for interfering with the military plans of General Warren, was not going to miss the chance of a futile, symbolic gesture. This descendant of John Churchill, Duke of Marlborough, was beginning his ride in and out of the pages of Britain's history.

Colonel Martin and his 400 lancers raced across the desert towards a thin line of dervishes, unaware that in a dry watercourse behind these skirmishers there was a concealed force of 2,000 dervish warriors. It was magnificent, but it was not war. Conducted with style, spirit but the sublime ignorance that was to characterize much of Britain's military efforts in the next century, Martin's charge disintegrated into a furious melee in which seventy of his men were lost along with 119 horses. Instead of being dismissed for disobeying orders, Colonel Martin was made a Companion of the Bath, and several of his troopers won VCs. Churchill had tasted battle and he loved it. He had exchanged his beloved toy soldiers for the real thing, and it had made his blood race. A future career in politics would form the basis for military surrogacy. Marlborough had been soldier first and politician second. Winston would be grand strategist, combining both soldier and statesman. After all, he was more than a match for any earth-bound general, yet, as Corelli Barnett, renowned military historian and author tells us: 'The greatest friend of his early life, Lord Birkenhead, once said of him, "Winston has hundreds of ideas a day; unfortunately, he doesn't know which is the good one".'

By Christmas 1940 Britain was on the brink of achieving total victory in North Africa over the Italians. Generals O'Connor and Wavell were about to enter the history books for what should have been one of the most complete victories in British history. Suddenly, Churchill put a stop to the victory march and diverted British efforts to Greece, a hare-brained scheme that inflicted defeat on the British and began a period of two years of terrible setbacks that ended only with General Montgomery's decisive victory over Rommel at El Alamein.

△ General Sir Archibald Wavell was forcibly persuaded by the Prime Minister to support the transfer of Britain's best troops from North Africa to the disastrous 'Greek Adventure'. Churchill was later able to place much of the blame for the ensuing fiasco on Wavell's shoulders.

Corelli Barnett considers Churchill's motives for this disastrous political interference:

*What you have to understand is that, for Churchill, defeating the Italians in North Africa is very much a secondary consideration.*

◁ Winston Churchill's 'Greek Adventure' was one of the worst errors by Britain in the entire war. Control of North Africa was thrown away and had to be re-won after immense losses in men and material.

*Churchill sees a possible British intervention on the side of Greece, to whom the British had given guarantees in 1939, as the first stage towards a much wider political conception that if you can get the Greeks in the war, then you can get the Turks in, and the Yugoslavs, and the Romanians, and the Bulgarians, and you will have this powerful Balkan bloc.*

Tragically, the Greek idea was one of Churchill's worst ideas. Professor John Charmley of the University of East Anglia explains what was wrong with the idea of the Balkan alliance against Germany that Churchill hoped to create:

*The interesting thing about the whole Balkan bloc idea which leads to the Greek fiasco is that it is in its conception entirely political. Churchill has it in his mind, rather like somebody playing a game of diplomacy, that what you can do is get all these powers together and you can help stop Hitler. Now this ignores two things. Even if you add Yugoslavia to Greece, to Bulgaria, to Romania, to Turkey, even if you can get all of them on the same side, it ignores the fact that they wouldn't have fought together on the same side. The idea that Greece and Turkey would have fought on the same side is frankly bonkers. It also ignores the most important fact, which is that added all together and multiplied by two they still didn't balance the Germans. Churchill had spent I think too long in two different mental worlds. He'd spent too long writing the life of his great ancestor, Marlborough, so he was fully au fait with the early-eighteenth-century world of strategy, which would have been fine except for the fact that he was in the mid-twentieth century. Secondly, his own military experience had been of essentially imperial policing. It had been small-scale military operations on the North-West Frontier or the Omdurman battle, the Sudan campaign in the dervish wars; it had not been of moving mass armies with modern technology, and I don't think Churchill had quite caught up with twentieth-century developments in warfare. I think the problem in a sense is that Churchill is rather naive as a strategist, and the criticism is that he didn't listen to those who had slightly more savvy.*

Churchill's blunder in halting O'Connor's conquest of Cyrenaica was all the greater for the fact that matters would have taken a beneficial turn had he not intervened in Greece. In the first place, the Greeks did not want British help. They were doing well enough on their own against the Italians and felt Britain should finish off the Italians in North Africa before turning their attention elsewhere. Such a victory for Britain would have become a symbol of resistance against Fascism in Europe at a time when the British were unable to

strike directly at Germany. In the United States, such a British victory would have strengthened Roosevelt's hands in supporting a Britain that clearly was far from being defeated, as Corelli Barnett explains:

*You have to remember that at the time, when all this debate was going on, our own wealth was running out fast. We had enormous orders in the United States for war material, machine tools, aircraft, all that kind of thing, and we were having at that time to pay cash for it, and our cash was running out. The last of our gold and dollar reserves and investments, all were going, and so the chances were that sometime in the spring of 1941 Britain would be completely bankrupt, and the question then was: how will we carry on with the war or life itself? Therefore the thing for us was to hope that the Americans would pass the Lend-Lease Bill through Congress, and that was in fact I think passed at the end of March, beginning of April…anyway, the point is that so much hung on Congress passing the Lend-Lease Bill, which would permit us to have all these American supplies. We wouldn't have to pay cash for them, and one of the things you had to do therefore was to convince the Americans that Britain was really up and fighting, was not a lost cause.*

The decision to shift Britain's military strength to Greece was an almost indefensible blunder. In view of its consequences, it is amazing that Churchill could have survived such an error in strategy without being toppled from power. As Corelli Barnett points out, it is difficult to find a good word to say about the Greek adventure. Wavell, in particular, was hostile to the Greek plan from the start, telling the Prime Minister in early November 1940: 'Even if we can intervene in Greece, we can't intervene with enough men, so don't stop a successful operation for a possibly botched one.'

On 11 January 1941, however, Wavell received strict instructions to end the North African campaign and to prepare to send his troops to Greece. Wavell tried to change Churchill's mind, pointing out that O'Connor was on the point of achieving an unparalleled success for British arms. The strategic consequences were enormous. But, as Corelli Barnett shows, Churchill wasn't listening:

*By early February the campaign in North Africa was coming to a brilliant success. General O'Connor's great victory at Beda Fomm really opened up the whole of Cyrenaica to the Allies, and O'Connor himself reckoned that with a bit of naval help they didn't really need very large military forces to sweep the Italians all the way out of North Africa. Wavell naturally reflected this in a telegram back to Churchill, arguing very strongly that first of all they were nearly there and the gains were so tremendous, you know, they could get the Italians out of North Africa. They could join up with Vichy in*

△ British troops being welcomed to Greece. In fact, British intervention brought nothing but disaster to the Greeks as Hitler decided to overrun Greece prior to invading Russia.

*North Africa. The response from Churchill was a categoric no: you'll stop at Benghazi and you'll begin to prepare your forces for going to Greece. So from that point onwards, from early February onwards, Wavell was under direct instructions from the Minister of Defence, who also happened to be the Prime Minister.*

John Charmley shows that Churchill the 'politician' was very much in the driving seat at this stage of the war, almost playing the dictator, and was making military decisions contrary to the advice he was receiving from his professional advisers.

*Churchill now began to express some doubts. This was a characteristic Churchillian method: when something was at the crux, always write something down that expresses the other side of the argument. You never know when it's going to come in handy unless you're a historian like Churchill, in which case you know exactly when it's going to come in handy. So it's at this point that Churchill begins to articulate some doubts. But what he then is able to do, having Eden, who had always supported his line out in the Middle East, he's able to say: 'I'm acting on the advice of men on the spot. Here in London we can't keep up minute by minute with the fast-flowing events in the Middle East and in Greece. Eden can; that's what he's there to do. We've given Eden full powers. Eden is saying, 'Let's do this, Wavell is not saying, "Let's not do it," so let's do it.' So when the formal decision is taken in Cabinet on 24 February there's no opposition.*

Master politician Churchill may have been, but this did not hide the fact that the Greek campaign was a disaster, and one that could have – should have – been avoided as John Charmley explains:

*Once the Germans attacked, the fears that Wavell had expressed – that we wouldn't be able to get enough men there quickly enough – were absolutely right. We got about 55,000 men there, we and the Greeks were strung out across too wide a front, the Germans rolled us up and knocked us out of Greece, the British then retreated to Crete, from which they were also kicked out, so in the space of a month the great Balkan bloc was exposed as a myth. Greece was occupied and defeated, and the British suffered their first major defeat under Churchill. Now what was the alternative to that? Suppose they had continued, as the generals on the spot wanted, with the campaign in North Africa. The Italians were so demoralized and so weak that O'Connor would certainly have repeated his victory at Beda Fomm, the Italians would have been thrown out of North Africa, there would have been no Afrika Korps, there would have been no Rommel legend. North Africa would have been safe. The British could then have made political contacts with the French commander in North Africa, and the whole structure of the war would have been quite different. Instead of going for maybe safe gains which were there, Churchill took a grand strategic gamble, not for the first or last time in his career, and not for the first or last time in his career it didn't come off. But what he had done was he had covered himself from every possible angle against being blamed solely.*

Even if the British had been able to stabilize Greek defences against the Germans, Churchill's Balkan bloc was nonsense, as John Charmley points out. Wishing it so does not form the basis of a sound strategy for any nation.

*In my judgement, one weakness of Winston Churchill as a strategist was firstly a determination that what he wanted to happen would happen, and a certain blindness to the real difficulties and a tendency to count divisions without actually evaluating sufficiently what worth those divisions were. In other words, you could count out how many divisions the Yugoslavs had got, and the Turks had got, and the Greeks had got, and you could say: 'Well, this makes a formidable number.' But attacked by German Panzer divisions covered by the Luftwaffe, they weren't worth a row of beans.*

By November 1943, at the Teheran Conference, a more relaxed Churchill – the Americans were in the war and eventual victory was certain, while the Russians were bleeding themselves and the Germans dry in a rerun of the First World War – could reflect on the grim period Britain was going through in 1940–41, standing alone against Hitler. As John Charmley comments:

*At the Teheran Conference Churchill says to Roosevelt and Stalin that history will treat them kindly. When Roosevelt asked why, Churchill says: 'Because I shall write the history.' Not only did Churchill write the history – he's the only British Prime Minister to have won the Nobel Prize for Literature, although not the first who perhaps ought to have won the Booker Prize for fiction.*

# CHAPTER SIX

# TECHNOLOGY

Technology has played a dominant part in warfare since man first used a stone, a sharpened stick or a primitive bow to fight his enemy. From the period of close-range man-to-man combat, with the danger that even the winner was likely to suffer substantial damage, missile power introduced distance into combat and the possibility of avoiding injury to one's own side. From the simplest stone missile to the latest smart weapon, technology has sought to achieve victory in combat without casualties, or at least without friendly casualties.

But technology is a double-edged weapon, creating problems as much for the side using it as for those suffering its use. In fact, it has been at the root of many military blunders as a result of over-confidence in its effectiveness – for example the Patriot missile in the Gulf War and the air campaign in Kosovo. Sometimes, like Frankenstein's monster, it outgrows its maker and imposes itself on national strategy, as with the area bombing by Bomber Command during the Second World War. Perhaps worst of all is where technology has unexpected side effects that, rather than reducing friendly casualties, actually increase them, as was the case with the use of the herbicide Agent Orange by the Americans during the Vietnam War.

▷ Soldiers worshipping false gods. In the twentieth century
technological advances have given military men the promise of easy
victories and low body-counts. Even as early as 1916 the idea of a
Death Ray had immense appeal.

# THE PATRIOT MISSILE

⚜

If they gave ticker-tape processions for successful technology, then the Patriot missile returning from the war in the Gulf in 1991 would have received one. Sprawling across the back seat of its limousine as it passed down Madison Avenue in New York, the Patriot would have represented everything that was good in modern America, notably its cutting-edge, life-saving technology that had put the 'S' in surgical operations and made war 'bloodless', smart and acceptable for television's millions. Above all, it was evidence, if more was needed, that America was still the pre-eminent technological power in the world.

To Joe Cirincione, Senior Associate of Carnegie Endowment for International Peace, the Patriot was part of the American dream. From an over-cost, under-performing weapon it had risen to the heights!

> *The Patriot missile was a hero system, it was a miracle weapon, it was a missile killer, it had a reputation unmatched by any weapon that I've ever encountered. In fact, I went up to the Patriot plant in Massachusetts to take a tour to learn some positive lessons about how to turn a troubled program around. The Patriot had been a program beset with cost overruns and performance problems, but in the Gulf War it vastly exceeded anyone's expectations and we thought, 'Well what can we learn from this? How can we learn to build a weapon right?'*

Joe remembered the pride all Americans felt when the success of the Patriot system was revealed for the first time on television:

*General Norman Schwarzkopf went on television saying: 'On 18 January the first ballistic missile in history has been intercepted in combat.' We heard reports later of thirty-three out of thirty-three Scuds intercepted.*

The American way of war was being vindicated. Surgical strikes kept casualties to a minimum – on both sides – and the advanced technology protected American servicemen and made extensive body counts a thing of the past. And it made good television, with all the video footage of smart weapons homing in on their military targets and not on the homes of America's third-world enemies.

The arrival of the Patriot in the Gulf must have seemed like the answer to a prayer. President Bush's international coalition against Saddam Hussein was in trouble. Including Arab states like Syria, Saudi Arabia and Egypt, as it did, it was vulnerable to the normal pressures of any multinational alliance. However, Saddam Hussein had recognized its Achilles heel in the shape of America's close relations with Israel. The Iraqi leader knew that the alliance would never hold together if countries like Syria believed for one moment they were supporting Israel against a fellow Arab state like Iraq. He reasoned that if he could force Israel to take military action against him, then the Arab members of Bush's coalition would at the very least withdraw their support for the anti-Iraqi campaign and, possibly, even change sides. He therefore began to target Israeli territory with his Scud missiles. The Americans had been aware of this danger, but apart from sending in special service operatives on the ground to find and destroy the Scud sites they had no immediate answer. However, as the threat of Israel joining the war against Iraq become greater, the Americans decided to supply the Israelis with an anti-aircraft missile, the Patriot, which had been adapted to combat missiles.

The dispatch of the Patriot to Israel was accompanied by a PR exercise to convince everyone in Israel that there was no need for them to take military action against Iraq because the anti-aircraft missile would protect them. But who was fooling whom? President Bush appears to have believed what the military men told him. Not quite one giant leap for mankind but certainly a rosy future for the air-defence industry. 'Storming Norman' Schwarzkopf announced the first-ever interception of a ballistic missile by another missile. The problem was that, however it looked on television, it never really happened. Later research showed that there was no Scud in the sky at that moment and that the Patriot battery fired its missile accidentally. The explosion everyone saw was the Patriot detonating itself. But from that moment onwards, the 'damp squib' became a star, and every night television pundits like Sam Donaldson recorded its successes.

In spite of the apparent success of the Patriots, pieces of the Scuds were falling on Israeli towns and, in some cases, the missile warheads were landing and doing immense damage.

△ 'Storming Norman' Schwarzkopf, at a press conference during the Gulf War, announcing the first ever interception of a ballistic missile by another missile.

Israel's Defence Minister, Moshe Arens, did not accept all the Patriot PR razzmatazz. Like many Israelis, he had his doubts about the Patriot, and he was not convinced that the Americans knew what they were talking about – even President George Bush. In the words of Moshe Arens:

*The Americans said to us that they could promise that within twenty-four and at most forty-eight hours they would put an end to the missile threat, that there would be no reason for Israel to retaliate. Prior to the beginning of Desert Storm, they were saying there would be no reason for Israel to take pre-emptive action. It turned out that they were not capable of putting an end to the missile threat in twenty-four hours, not in forty-eight hours, and not during the entire five weeks of the conflict.*

As Scuds continued to fall on Israel, the patience of the Israeli government was stretched to breaking point. If the Patriot

The aftermath of a Scud missile attack in Tel Aviv during the Gulf War.

could not stop the Scuds, Israel would intervene to stop them herself. Moshe Arens was blunt with the Americans:

*By the third week of the war, when in my view there was really no danger any more of the coalition breaking up, it was clear that Saddam Hussein was taking a beating, and the missiles were still continuing to come down in Israel. I told President Bush that the time was approaching when we would have to take military action.*

President Bush seemed genuinely surprised at the Israeli attitude:

*Bush said: 'Why should you be concerned? You've got the Patriot missiles. They're providing an umbrella over the Israeli population centres.' I told him that that wasn't the case. He argued with me. He didn't accept that.*

Bush was astonished and asked his advisers to produce charts showing Moshe Arens how effective the Patriot was. Arens queried the American figures and gave some of his own:

*He didn't accept my figures. As a matter of fact, my figures were optimistic. I told him at the time that the probability of an intercept by a Patriot was no more than 20 per cent. Well, by now we know it was close to 0 per cent, and he thought it was close to 100 per cent, so there was a little gap between us.*

Relations between the United States and Israel reached a low point. President Bush just could not understand what they were complaining about. Moshe Arens, on the other hand, could not understand the apparent American complacency. Arens now visited Bush in Washington with a virtual

▽ Lord of all it surveys or computer malfunction? During the Gulf War the Patriot missile was a product of wishful thinking and corporate propaganda.

ultimatum: unless the Scuds were stopped, Israel would join the war on her own agenda.

*During the third week of the fighting I took a twenty-four-hour trip to Washington with the express purpose of telling President Bush that the time was approaching when we would have to take action. We met in the Oval Office. He had the Secretary of Defense there, and the Secretary of State and his other assistants. I came with my assistants, and it was a rather tense meeting because Bush didn't like the idea at all of Israel taking military action. I think on the one hand he was under the impression that the United States was doing great things for Israel, that it was doing our job, really, so why should we be dissatisfied? And he actually said: 'Do you think that the Israeli Air Force can do more than the US Air Force?' Well, I couldn't possibly reply 'yes' to that question even though maybe the answer was 'yes' at the time. He also felt that the Patriots were providing an umbrella, defending the Israeli population, so what was all the excitement about? Whatever I told him, I told him that it was intolerable and that we simply could not continue to take this beating by ballistic missiles.*

This tense meeting was suddenly interrupted by a telephone call, as Arens tells us:

*Actually, I received a phone call while I was in the Oval Office, telling me that a Scud had fallen on a little suburb where I live. So I left the meeting to find out whether my wife was OK, and fortunately she was, although the Scud hadn't fallen very far from our home. So then I hoped it really brought home to the Americans the kind of problems that we were having, and the kind of pressure we were under, but I'm not sure it did.*

In the event, the ground operation of Desert Storm saved the day and put an end to the Scud menace. But Israel had almost gone to war with Iraq, with unimaginable consequences for the United States and her anti-Iraqi coalition.

America was to learn an even more painful lesson before the Gulf War ended: overconfidence in technology can have disastrous consequences. In the opinion of Professor Ted Postol of MIT, this was what led to the tragedy at Dharhran, in Saudi Arabia, where twenty-eight American servicemen were killed by a Scud missile. So confident had the American personnel in the Gulf become in the ability of the Patriot to protect them from every Scud missile that they failed to take even the most basic precautions, like taking cover if under missile attack.

*I think the tragedy at Dharhran is one of the more disturbing aspects of the false claims surrounding Patriot. What clearly happened at Dharhran was a Scud was arriving, people knew a Scud was arriving. In fact, I spoke to a British officer who had ordered his troops to take cover, but the American troops in a barracks that was actually randomly hit by the incoming Scud did not take cover, presumably because they thought that they were being protected by Patriot.*

David Campbell was a maintenance sergeant with the 14th Quartermaster Regiment at Dharhran when the Scud hit. Before that night he had been supremely confident in the Patriot system:

*We felt really safe. We were far enough away from what they called the front that we didn't think we were in any direct danger outside of the Scuds. And the Patriot batteries were there, so there wasn't much fear.*

Campbell had heard the air-raid siren while resting on his bunk. As he put it: 'Nobody really made any big moves to take cover.' Suddenly, the Scud burst through the ceiling of the barracks.

*When the thing actually blew up, the Scud itself, I witnessed terrific heat and a white flash. And this blast of air – I can remember my whole mouth just blowing up with air, and I don't remember flying but I remember hitting and falling somewhere else in the building. I knew where I was when the missile had come through the ceiling, and where they had recovered me was probably a good eighty feet away. I was at the far end of the building. Again, my first instinct was to get up and leave. My left arm had been pretty much torn off, and nothing seemed to want to work. As much as I wanted to get up and leave, I couldn't. I knew somebody'd be by sooner or later, so I figured it'd be best just to stay there. I could reach around with my right arm and feel the bones sticking out of my left arm, and I knew I was in a pretty bad shape at the time, and I couldn't breathe: I had punctured lungs and broken ribs. So I knew just to stay where I was.*

*There was a total silence after the missile had hit. It had ruptured one eardrum completely and basically ruptured the other one as well. It was very quiet; there was no noise. I could look around and see fire burning, I could see people running around in shadows, but I couldn't actually hear anything. It was an ear-splitting bang.*

*There was lots of chaos. Sheet metal was hanging from the ceiling, the beams were down, but it was 8.30 in the evening, so there wasn't a lot of daylight, and when the Scud had come through the roof it put the lights out in the building. You could just barely see shadows, lights outside, the fires were burning from cardboard, whatever was in the building. And you could just barely make out images of people running, scattering, doing whatever, but nothing in detail. Finally, my eyes would fill up with blood so much that I really couldn't see very far anyway, but I knew just to stay put.*

At the end of the Gulf War the Army testified to Congress that the Patriot missile had achieved a near-perfect 98 per cent kill against Scuds. Joe Cirincione was in charge of the defence

investigations for Congress, and in April 1991 he heard Professor Ted Postol of MIT testifying that his investigations of video evidence suggested the Army's claims were wildly inaccurate. Cirincione also began to hear reports from Israel suggesting that the Patriot's performance had been exaggerated. As a result, Congress decided in December 1991 to launch its own committee investigation into what actually happened with the Patriot in the Gulf. As Joe explained:

*We just wanted to establish the facts. We wanted to know what our weapons systems can actually do. Number two, lives of US soldiers were at stake. If the Patriot didn't perform as well as we thought in future battles, American troops might be committed to believing that they had more protection afforded them than they actually had. And, three, this had a profound impact on the overall debate about ballistic-missile defence. The miraculous performance of the Patriot had been used in 1991 to increase the budget for the Star Wars program by over a billion dollars. Secretary of Defense Dick Cheney came and testified, saying: 'See, we can do it. Ballistic-missile defence works. Give*

△ Saudi troops examine wreckage of a Scud missile that landed in Riyadh on 22 January 1991. The Iraqi missiles often broke up before they landed and the Patriots were unable to stop the warhead doing damage as it hit the ground.

*us more money.' And Congress responded very generously: not only the Patriot program was boosted, but the overall efforts to develop national missile defence increased by a billion dollars because of the Patriot's performance.*

Joe Cirincione discovered to his amazement that the Army had no data to support its claims for the Patriot:

*We asked them the questions that nobody else had asked: where's the data backing up your claims, how do you know it performed this well? They hummed and hawed and said you don't really need to see that. We persisted, we wrote letters requesting the data...*

Frustrated by the lack of proof from the Army, Joe Cirincione now found that the Dharhran tragedy was a direct result of a software fault in the Patriot's computer:

*The problem, as it turned out, was a software problem. The Patriot is designed with a radar that sort of scans and looks at the sky, comes back and looks again, and if it sees a change in that pattern it starts noting that it's got a target, a possible target. It looks at what they call a range gate, and it turns out that the longer the computer was left on, the longer the Patriot was operating, the more that range gate would shift. So after about eight to sixteen hours the range gate would come back on the second sweep and have shifted, so the Patriot radar wouldn't see the target that was there. It would look once and it was on point A; it would look again and it didn't see it, didn't classify it as a target, wouldn't show up on the radar screen, wouldn't set any signals going off for the operator to be warned of anything incoming. That's what led to the Patriot batteries outside Dharhran not seeing the Scud at all.*

▽ Scud 1 Patriot 0. The American barracks at Dharhan in Saudi Arabia hit by a Scud after the Patriot missile malfunctioned. So confident were the American troops they did not even take cover. Twenty-eight died.

Professor Skeel of the University of Ohio explains the software fault in the Patriot's computer:

*The Patriot missile-guidance system relied on a clock which kept time in tenths of a second. The calculations required to determine the location of an incoming missile required the time in seconds, and so it was necessary to multiply the time by one-tenth. Unfortunately, the number one-tenth is not exactly representable in the binary number system that is used by computers; it has to be approximated. However, these approximations can be quite good. In the original software for the Patriot system, the approximation was good to one part per million. Here you see on the screen a value which I call a good tenth, and here's the approximation. It's point zero followed by six nines, so you can see the error is in the sixth digit. However, it was later decided that this approximation wasn't good enough because the clock would keep very long times, and so it was decided to put in a better approximation to a tenth that required twice the storage. And I'll show you a better approximation which I call a better tenth, and now you see a string of about twelve nines. This has an error of only one part per trillion and was more than adequate for anything needed for the Patriot guidance system. Now, in making this change there were about six locations in the computer*

*program where this value was needed. However, when they first made the changes, they failed to put in the more accurate value in all parts of the computer program, so there was one place where the good value rather than the better value was still being used. This unfortunately led to a large error. Because we're using different approximations to a tenth, we get an answer that instead of being one second, as we should expect, is off by three-tenths of a second. Scuds travel at over one mile per second, so in this time a Scud missile will travel a third of a mile, and so the radar tracking, when it did its final confirmation of where the Scud missile was supposed to be, didn't find it where it looked.*

Professor Ted Postol carefully investigated all the video evidence of Patriots in action. At first, he admits, he was, like most Americans, entirely well disposed towards the super-weapon. However, he conducted his enquiries in a scientific manner:

*We very carefully tried to construct any argument that we thought could have merit, that could lead to the conclusion this system had worked, and then systematically investigate whether it had any merit, and we just couldn't find any. Every analysis we did pointed to the conclusion of essentially zero success.*

So enormous was the discrepancy between the Army's success figure (98 to 100 per cent) and that of the Israelis and Postol's own scientific findings (0 per cent) that the professor was left with no alternative but to suspect foul play. As he said: 'There was a wide range of interests all leading to support for this giant fraud that was being foisted on the American people.'

Conspiracy theory now came into operation. Professor Postol found that illegal efforts were being made to remove his security clearance as well as having him accused of security violations. He was accused of political extremism by members of Congress who were not members of the committee and was treated with extreme hostility by army officers who lacked sufficient scientific knowledge to understand Postol's allegations. Postol was shocked by the 'deeply personal assaults' on his character and work during the Patriot debate.

The standard of the Army's response to Professor Postol's evidence is shown in the following example from Joe Cirincione:

*When the Army claimed that the Patriot had intercepted Scuds, the congressional chairman said: 'Well, what do you mean by intercept?' The general testifying said: 'Well, by intercept we meant that they passed each other in the sky.' The chairman said: 'Wait a minute. Let me get this straight. "Intercept" doesn't mean it actually hit it; it just meant that they passed each other like ships at sea.' 'Yes,' said the*

*general. 'That's correct.' That little exchange lasted about ten seconds. It made the nightly news, and it actually hurt this general's career.*

Beaten in scientific argument and forced into the most farcical explanation of 'interception', the Army now fell back on emotional blackmail, not only against their scientific critics but against the American people as a whole. Joe Cirincione explains the Army's last stand, and a thoroughly disreputable one as well. First they refused to let Congress see their reports on the success of Patriot, and then they accused their critics of unpatriotic behaviour – a delightfully ironic pun: 'They wrapped themselves in the flag. They challenged the committee members for questioning the patriotism and integrity of General Schwarzkopf, and the hearing got very testy until we sort of backed off.'

Joe Cirincione reveals the dangers that can result from the misuse of technology:

*You can't always believe what you see. You have to question the information that's being presented to you, particularly about systems that involve billions of dollars. You have to remember that people have agendas here above and beyond simply telling the truth. When it comes to military systems, almost all the services have a fierce pride in the weapons that they're developing, and they feel very strongly that whatever problems these weapons systems have they'll take care of them. They don't need you, Congress, they don't need you, the media, looking over their shoulders. Questions that will be raised will only aid the enemy in developing counters to the weapons. That is definitely the attitude of the program managers and the services. The Army told us with the Patriot: 'We'll fix the problems, we'll take care of them. We'll protect our troops.' That's their attitude.*

According to Professor Ted Postol, America needed the Patriot. It was not just a fraud foisted on an ingenuous President and Congress by a corrupt military-industrial clique; it was also vital to everyday Americans.

*When the Patriot came back from the Gulf War it was seen as the hi-tech hero of the war. The time was an interesting one because the American economy was in a slump, and it was not uncommon to see articles about whether America was no longer the pre-eminent technological power in the world. And when Patriot came back from the Gulf War you began to see articles arguing that the performance of Patriot in the war showed that America was still the pre-eminent technological power in the world, that we've shown the rest of the world what a great technological power we are. Patriot was a big buoy that brought people up high, making them feel like the country was really not in the kind of shape that some people misperceived it was in.*

# KOSOVO

If the war in Kosovo was a demonstration of Nato's capacity to achieve political results through a sustained application of hi-tech weapons, it was a dismal failure. An aerial campaign by itself speaks to the enemy not of strength but of weakness. It indicates a fear of casualties and an unwillingness to involve land troops with all the risks that that involves. The impersonality of aerial technology removes the old adage 'don't fire until you see the whites of their eyes' which, in a sense, encapsulates the primitive element in fighting, the imposition of individual willpower over an enemy. Without this natural body language the enemy cannot be convinced of his defeat if he never sets eyes on the enemy, 10,000 or 15,000 feet above his homeland. Renowned editor and military historian Max Hastings believes:

> It is both morally very doubtful and militarily utterly unsound to attempt to do in Kosovo in 1999 what the air forces attempted so disastrously to do in 1939, which is to achieve an almost bloodless result. Many of the limitations of air power which the Second World War revealed still exist. Dropping missiles of any kind on ground targets, even with all the wonderful technology of the United States, is still a very imprecise art. It is still fantastically difficult not only to assess what you are attacking but what effects you have achieved from aerial photographs, and I believe that it was a grave mistake to attempt to resolve the Kosovo issue solely by air power. If you made the decision, which was a perfectly legitimate political decision, that you wanted to intervene in Kosovo, then I think it would have been far better for the people of Kosovo had the West possessed the courage to do so by a straightforward ground offensive, to move swiftly because what some of us said at the beginning of this was that speed was of the essence. I said on the first day that we

◁ A tomahawk cruise missile fired from an American warship at a target in Serbia, 24 March 1999. The cruise missile, far from being in the forefront of America's clinical strikes, achieved many notable misses, including several strikes into neighbouring Balkan states.

*were engaged in a race between Nato's technology and the ethnic cleansing policies of the Serbs. It was a race that Nato lost because Nato attempted to play the game by the old rules of the air war fantasists whereby you attempted to achieve a victory at no cost to your own lives, and that was a fiasco that in my view brought shame on the United States and on President Clinton personally.*

General Sir Michael Rose was also a critic of Nato's policy in Kosovo. The plan had been to protect a million Kosovan Albanians from ethnic cleansing, but without ground troops how could Nato protect anyone?

*I guess that people wanted a casualty-free war. It was thought that they could solve complex human, social and political problems on the ground in Kosovo from a flight level of 15,000 feet and a speed of 450 knots. And, of course, it was a total failure. Ten thousand people were brutally slaughtered and a million people were driven from their homes because Nato didn't have the moral courage to commit troops to the ground to stop these awful events from happening.*

The swift development of military technology since the Second World War is mostly associated with the enormous growth of the military industry in the United States. America's role as world policeman has seen her troops involved, worldwide, in messy and complex military situations. In an attempt to minimize casualties and depend on hi-tech solutions, the Americans have suffered a series of disasters, from Iraq to Beirut, from Grenada to Dharhan, which might have been avoided with simpler, ground-based solutions. But in Kosovo Michael Rose suggests that Nato's troops might not have been up to the task facing them on the ground, in which case technology served a necessary purpose.

*One of the driving factors, I think, was the political factor that Nato as a collective organization did not have troops that were actually capable of fighting the sort of ground war that would have been required in Kosovo. It would have been a war very much like that fought by the men of the 14th Army in Burma, who drove the Japanese out of Burma down the Mandalay Road. Every bunker would have had to have been fought for with the bayonet and the bullet. Remotely delivered weapons would not have had a part to play in the ground war in Kosovo, and many of the armies of Nato are incapable of fighting that sort of war because of the sort of regime which they become accustomed to through long years of peace and through the sort of peace-keeping missions that they've hitherto embarked on.*

△ One of the greatest military own goals. On 8 May 1999, Nato airstrikes struck the Chinese embassy in Belgrade, killing two Chinese nationals. America's much vaunted military technology revealed its tendency to self-destruct at the most embarrassing moments.

*They are used to health and safety regulations, limited hours of work per day, certain standards of living: all these things legislate against having the sort of fighting capability that would be required. I think many of the Nato countries were politically reluctant to expose their troops to the sort of harsh realities of soldiering.*

Avoiding direct conflict with the enemy soldiers, as the British were forced to from 1940–43, meant that the only way of striking at the enemy was from the air. This was at the root of the British Strategic Bombing Campaign. Unfortunately, of course, it shifts the emphasis of the fighting from serviceman versus serviceman to serviceman versus civilian. As Michael Rose shows, this is what happened in Kosovo:

*I think the first point to make is that Nato, in its use of air power,*

*because it was so constrained by the rules to fly at a particular altitude and use certain sorts of weapons systems, actually killed, I think, three times more innocent civilians, both Kosovan Albanians and Serbs, than they did Serb military. I think that should cause us to review the entire strategy that we embarked on, because if you use inappropriate means in trying to engage a legitimate enemy and you're killing civilians in so doing, then I think you are actually running a grave risk of being in violation of the Geneva and the Hague protocols.*

Ultimately, the effectiveness of the Nato air campaign must be judged by the effect it had in enforcing Nato's demands on the Serbs. In this it catastrophically failed. Far from protecting the Kosovan Serbs, it actually brought about immediate ethnic cleansing, an alarming example of indirect 'friendly fire'. Sir Michael Rose is understandably hostile to Nato's justification of the air campaign:

*I think it is untenable for Nato to say they could not have expected the consequences of launching the bombing campaign, particularly when they told people that they were not going to deploy ground troops because that was politically unacceptable. It almost gave Milosevic a carte blanche to do what he did, and I think some moral responsibility must be borne by the political and military leaders of Nato.*

Sir Michael Rose sums up his views on the use of hi-tech weapons in Kosovo:

*I think it's a natural instinct in human beings when they get a new weapons system to believe that it's going to solve all the problems that they've been grappling with hitherto. But it's only after a period of time and experience that you can really get the optimum use out of these weapons systems, and it's always by integrating them with other elements of the battlefield, not finding a single war-winning weapon, that's always going to solve your problems.*

Perhaps the last word on America's love affair with military technology should be left to Professor John Helmreich, an expert on American bombing of Switzerland during the Second World War, probably the most embarrassing 'friendly fire' errors in history:

*We are so confident and we boast about the wonders of our United States technology that when through a series of blunders we bomb the Chinese Embassy in Kosovo, this is very embarrassing, because the Chinese simply can't believe after all our boasting of our technological wonders that we could make such a dumb mistake. Well, believe me, we can.*

# THE BRITISH ARTILLERY ON THE SOMME, 1 JULY 1916

The First World War was an artillery war with something like 70 per cent of all casualties caused by big guns. Indiscriminate bombardment – often with shrapnel – caused most of the human casualties, but sometimes the gunners were required to be more precise in their activities, notably in counter-battery fire against the enemy's artillery or in barrages delivered against fortifications and entrenchments. Precision firing, however, was still a thing of the future, and even by the end of the war in 1918 the artillerymen were still involved in a relatively imprecise form of war. Their technology, although it had improved out of all recognition since 1914, was still not capable of doing what some generals asked it to do. The best – or worst – example of this was the infamous first day of the Somme offensive on 1 July 1916, when the limitations of the British artillery and of British shell manufacturers were paid for in blood – the blood of nearly 60,000 British soldiers, killed and wounded on that one day. Ironically, 1 July 1916 saw the 'blooding' of Kitchener's new volunteer army containing the 'Pals' battalions, and it was these 'Pals' who were to pay a terrible price for the technological failures of the professionals.

Shell production was not difficult, according to Professor Richard Holmes, but fusing was, in fact, a fine art:

> There are lots of problems if you're trying to produce something like shells quickly. Producing the shell itself isn't necessarily technically that complicated, but the more you rush the process the greater the chance of accidental explosions, and there were several in munitions factories. The real problem is the fuse, and what you're asking the fuse to do is to accelerate very quickly as it leaves the muzzle of the gun and then to burst precisely when you want it to. Inevitably, as you push on to try to produce more shells and more fuses very quickly, there's a risk that you'll not get the manufacturing process correct.

△ During the First World War women's contribution to munitions production was decisively important. Here, a French munitionette dreams of what her shells will do to the Boche.

Mass production in the munitions industry led to a lowering of standards as quality became subordinate to quantity in government demands. Mike Hibberd of the Imperial War Museum in London explains:

*Pre-First World War, the munitions industry was very much limited to perhaps four or five major companies producing this type of material. With the vast expansion of the Army and the vast expansion of the munitions industry post-1914, lots of companies that had never produced munitions began to produce shells, fuses and their components, and they weren't necessarily geared up to the accuracy which is required for one of these fuses to function.*

British offensives at Loos and Neuve Chapelle in 1915 had shown that, without artillery support, infantry and cavalry had no chance in the battle zone where enemy fire power remained unsuppressed. The only solution seemed to rest with the capacity of the British artillery to overcome their German equivalents. For the next offensive, on the Somme, it would be necessary to destroy the German defences with an artillery bombardment of unprecedented weight and ferocity. Once the artillery had succeeded in demolishing the enemy, it would be a relatively simple task for the infantry to occupy the ground won. It all sounded very simple. But on this assumption lay the core of the disaster that was to strike the 4th Army on 1 July 1916.

General Rawlinson was going to demand of his artillery more than it could give. It was technological suicide, and one wonders why the 4th Army's artillerymen did not advise their commander that they could not achieve what he wanted. Rawlinson boasted that 'nothing could exist at the conclusion of the bombardment in the area covered by it'. Somebody should have had the moral courage – masquerading, perhaps, as an intelligence report – to admit that his aims were impossible. Rawlinson demanded that his artillery should not only suppress German artillery fire when the assault began but should already have destroyed the German barbed wire – even though some of it was so thick that light could scarcely pass through its close-meshed coils – and have killed all the German soldiers in their trenches, dugouts and bunkers. There would be no one to scythe down the walking waves of the 4th Army when zero hour came on 1 July. Rawlinson was fooling himself and commander-in-chief Sir Douglas Haig. He never had enough guns, enough high-explosive shells or enough wire-cutting capacity. His 1,547 guns on a 15-mile front were far from adequate. Modern military historians like John Keegan have said it would have taken several small nuclear devices to achieve what Rawlinson expected his artillery to achieve.

How effective was the British bombardment in achieving Rawlinson's three aims? General Sir Martin Farndale, former Master Gunner and chairman of the Royal Artillery Museums explains why it failed:

*Cutting wire with shellfire is not an effective art. All the artillerymen on the Somme knew this. General Birch, the senior commander to General Rawlinson, who commanded the 4th Army, told him: 'We are unlikely to be terribly successful.' There are two reasons for this: first, it is a very inexact science in itself, and, secondly, we didn't have enough high explosive. Seventy-six per cent of the rounds for these guns, the 18-pounders, was shrapnel, and shrapnel is certainly not the right equipment with which to cut wire. To do that, you have to get the fuse burst within inches of the wire, and the only way you can do that is by having forward artillery observers on their bellies, if you like, forward watching this happen.*

Previous barrages had only ever succeeded where the Germans were taken by surprise or had poor bunkers in unsuitable terrain. But this was not the case on the Somme. The Germans had been in their Somme positions for two years and had used the time to build the best and deepest defensive positions on the whole of the Western Front. Renowned military historian and author of *The First Day after the Somme*, Martin Middlebrook explains how the news that the German positions had not been destroyed was received by the British commanders:

*The patrol from the 2nd Middlesex heard the Germans singing in their dugouts, and the feeling was beginning to spread that maybe things weren't going to be quite what they should be. But as these reports got further back, they were treated as being minority reports, and other reports were saying 'yes, everything seems to be all right' and as so often in warfare you believe what you want to believe. There was no question of the attack being postponed or any other method of attack being used. Rawlinson's plan was adhered to.*

Only about 7 per cent of British shells were of high explosive capable of destroying the deepest German defences. Even then, nearly a third of the shells fired – many of poor American man-

△ The barrage over the Somme. Overreliance on artillery meant that the first day's advance was doomed.

ufacture – failed to explode at all, showing how ineffectual was this apparently all-destructive barrage. Richard Holmes tells us why there were so many dud shells:

*A number of shells fired on the Somme didn't explode due to a variety of reasons. Sometimes the manufacture's defective, sometimes the fuse doesn't work – maybe because the fuse is smashed by the impact of the shell with hard ground before it has a chance to operate – sometimes the shells are fired through gun barrels that are themselves worn, which means that the shell doesn't catch the rifling as it ought to and it tips in flight, and if the shell tips in flight there's every chance that it won't land fuse first and therefore won't explode. Something like a third of the shells fired on the Somme didn't actually behave as they should.*

Although Haig remarked fatuously, 'The barbed wire has never been so well cut, nor the artillery preparations so thorough', he did not know what he was talking about and had no idea of what was going on at the front. Rawlinson had, but he wasn't man enough to admit that his artillery bombardment had failed and that when his men went over the top they would suffer heavy casualties. 'I am not quite satisfied that all the wire has been thoroughly well cut, and in places the front trench is not as much knocked about as I should like to see in the photos. The bit in front of the 34th Division has been rather let off.' (The 34th Division later suffered 6,380 casualties, the highest in any British division on 1 July.)

At 7.30am on 1 July, the first waves of 60,000 men went over the top and marched slowly towards the German lines.

Some men were led by officers who kicked footballs, others by those with walking-sticks or umbrellas. It was a jaunt, they'd been told. Within thirty minutes half of them had become casualties. Of the 120,000 from 143 battalions who attacked that day, nearly 60,000 casualties were suffered, including some 20,000 dead. It was the greatest loss ever suffered by the British Army and the heaviest by any army in a single day of the entire war. In fact, British battle casualties that day exceeded those from the entire Crimean War, Boer War and Korean War put together. The cause was simple: the German soldiers had survived the barrage in their deep concrete bunkers and, warned by the cessation of the bombardment minutes before zero hour (according to Martin Middlebrook the worst error on the British side during the entire campaign on the Western Front), they emerged to the sound of bugles from below ground and reached their machine guns before the slowly advancing British troops were even halfway across no man's land. In those areas where the British did succeed in taking German positions, they found them intact and even with the electric lights still on. So much for Rawlinson's crushing barrage.

Martin Middlebrook describes what happened at zero hour:

*Zero hour comes – 7.30 – and two things happen: it goes very quiet, the shelling lifts for a moment off the German front line and falls on the second line and on the other targets further back. The men come out of the trenches: the British soldiers, up the ladders they go, the whistles*

△ British heavy artillery in action. In 1916 precision firing was still a generation away and it was unrealistic for General Rawlinson to base his assault on the Somme on the capacity of his gunners to destroy German entrenchments and barbed wire.

*are blown, through a little gap in their own barbed wire that had been prepared for them, lining up in no man's land. Battalions deploy eight, sometimes ten, sometimes twelve ranks deep and start walking across no man's land, the birds are singing, and then the barrage falls on the German second line. The German machine gunners come up from their dugouts because they realize that the attack has started and the British have lost what is known as the race for the parapet. In fact, they were never going to win. Rawlinson's plan had denied them that, and there are men falling right, left and centre, just falling into the grass. One man saw so many men falling over and he thought, 'What are they doing? Why are they doing that?' He thought they might be looking for shell nosecaps. It didn't sink in that they were being killed and wounded. Then the German artillery falls behind them on the British trenches, and that goes on for twenty minutes. A few men struggle through as far as the German wire, and they try to cut through it with some funny little shears they've got on the end of their rifles, but the German machine gunners are just twelve yards away, coming out, standing on top of their parapet, shooting at them. A few men get into the German trenches – we're talking of one in a hundred overall over the battle front – in little parties of threes and fours and sixes, but nobody comes to support them.*

The British troops encountered not just rifle and machine-gun fire, but they also marched into the face of a counter-barrage from the German artillery, which had similarly survived Rawlinson's bombardment. The uncut barbed wire trapped thousands of men – one battalion of the Newfoundland Regiment suffered 91 per cent casualties on the wire.

The 'Pals' suffered worst. Martin Middlebrook explains the effects of the first day of the Somme on the communities that produced the 'Pals' battalions.

*The Battle of the Somme had a very patchwork effect on communities at home. Kitchener's New Army consisted of thirty divisions. The first eighteen were raised by the Army at regimental depots; they drew the men from all corners of a county or from a regiment's recruiting area. But there were twelve complete divisions, 144 battalions of what we might call 'Pals'-type battalions. 'Pals' battalions were units that had been raised by municipal authorities, by associations: the Tyneside Irish, the Tyneside Scottish, the former public schoolboys' and universities' associations, the sportsmen's associations. There was a whole gamut of them. You've even got complete divisions: you've got a Welsh division, an Ulster division. They were all privately raised and offered to the Army. Those last twelve divisions, what I call the 'Pals'-type divisions, all had their baptism of fire in the Battle of the Somme, so what you got is small communities suddenly receiving news that they'd lost 200, 300 or 400 men killed. In cities, maybe Manchester, Liverpool, Bradford, Leeds, Newcastle, it could be maybe 1,000, 1,200 men killed in the first few days. Small towns like Grimsby or Accrington and a whole host of others had their battalions or a share in a 'Pals' battalion, and they suffered proportionately, whereas other parts of the country didn't suffer too badly. So there was immediate and deep sorrow in these communities, and one of the reasons why the Somme is looked back on by Britain so emotionally is because of the sudden loss of ordinary men, who weren't professional soldiers; they were just home-town lads who had gone off to win the war for the British Empire. No one foresaw that this sort of thing would happen. In the Second World War the Army would not permit the formation of any type of 'Pals' battalion or similar battalions so that this type of experience could not be repeated and inflicted on the civilian population.*

Bill Turner, historian of the Accrington 'Pals', records their experiences on 1 July 1916:

*The men were being told that there would be an artillery bombardment that would last for seven days. This bombardment would be the largest, longest bombardment there'd been in the war, and one general told the 'Pals' as they were grouped together that the result of this bombardment would be such that all the German trenches would be completely destroyed, all the barbed wire would be destroyed, and there wouldn't be a rat alive in the German trenches. This is when they got a little bit suspicious; the optimism was just a little bit too much. They didn't*

*really believe what was told them because they'd been in the front line, they'd seen the barbed wire, they'd seen the effects of artillery fire. The most optimistic of them would expect the German machine-gun posts and the trenches to have been destroyed, but they could see with their own eyes that the barbed wire in front of the German trenches hadn't been destroyed. This was because the week-long bombardment first of all had run out of shells, then used the wrong type of shells. High-explosive shells were supposed to destroy the barbed wire, but a lot of shrapnel shells were used which simply rained balls of lead down on to the ground. Well, this didn't destroy the barbed wire. A patrol the night before had gone out into no man's land and had reported that the German wire had not been destroyed. This report was just brushed aside – it was contrary to the optimism that was expected – so the 'Pals' knew that the German wire hadn't been destroyed.*

At home in Accrington, mothers and wives awaited news of their menfolk. It was very slow in coming and, as Bill Turner relates, eventually they learned the truth from an unexpected source:

*A viaduct straddles Accrington, and one evening during the latter part of the first week a trainload of wounded men stopped on the viaduct and someone from the train shouted down to ask where they were. One of a group of women replied, 'Accrington,' and he said, 'Accrington? Your lot's been wiped out.' And away the train went, leaving them with that message. One understands the feeling that that gave. Women were going down to the newspaper office, but the newspaper had no knowledge of what was going on. A week or two after that, the official telegrams started coming.*

By the end of the day the British held a three-mile-wide portion of the German position, to a depth of a mile, and just three of the thirteen target villages, but it had been achieved at the cost of nearly eight casualties for every one German. Haig blithely commented that the casualties could not be considered severe in view of the numbers engaged. Yet 50 per cent casualties were so rare in military history that they usually represented a defeat as decisive as the French had suffered at Waterloo.

The Battle of the Somme went on for a further 140 days, and yet of the 141 days that the battle raged we remember just one – 1 July 1916 – a day of horror without parallel, on which the nation suffered a psychological blow that left scars which have never healed. Martin Middlebrook concludes that the blunder was due to an overreliance on technology:

*Looking at 20,000 men dead on the first day of the Somme, that's a disaster. But all because of overreliance, overconfidence on the technology actually doing a sound job. In the end, looking at Rawlinson's grand plan, it's completely based on an overreliance on shelling, on artillery, and that was its great mistake, surely?*

# THE BOMBER DREAM
# AND THE BUTT REPORT
✂

Probably the two most remarkable German victories of the Second World War occurred in the mind of the British people. In September 1939 Britain succumbed to a kind of mass hysteria brought on by the myth of the bomber. In Stanley Baldwin's infamous phrase, 'The bomber will always get through'. Without adequate intelligence of what kind of bomber force Hitler had – in fact, his tactical bombers were not designed for civilian bombing at all – the British government prepared the civilian population of London for little less than the apocalypse. Casualties would be so enormous that public swimming-baths must be prepared to receive all the corpses. And, on such a note, Britain went to war, as Max Hastings relates:

> On the first day of the war, when a false air-raid alarm was issued, many people believed that a great German air armada was going to appear over London and London would disappear in a pall of smoke. It was that bad. People had a completely Armageddonistic picture, and they hadn't done what anybody who was a serious strategist of land power or sea power would have done and actually measured what the technology of that time and in the quantities in which it was available was likely to be able to achieve.

Britain's doting dog-lovers hysterically massacred their pets to save them from the horrors that the 'sausage-eaters' would rain down on them from the skies. Finally, the bomber got as far into the English psyche as to threaten English cricket. The doyen of cricket writers, Neville Cardus, recorded the moment that the threat became a reality for most Britons. It was on the day that Hitler invaded Poland and Cardus was in the Long Room at Lords. A game was in progress though there were few spectators to watch it. An impeccably dressed member of Lords, with spats and rolled umbrella, stood next to Cardus watching the play. Observing protocol they did not exchange words as they had not been formally introduced. Suddenly two workmen entered the Long Room in green aprons and carrying a bag. They took down the bust of W.G. Grace, put it in the bag and departed. Cardus's companion watched their every move, then he turned to him. 'Did you see that, sir?' he asked. Cardus replied that he had. 'That means war,' he said. No formal declaration was necessary between governments. It had all been said or unsaid, in that single moment. The Germans had moved into Poland behind the bowler's arm.

The problem was that the legacy of the abattoir that had been the Western Front lay heavy on the service chiefs in the interwar years. Senior officers of the RAF had all flown over the trenches in the First World War; indeed, some of them were ex-infantry and had served in the trenches before transferring to the Flying Corps. Massacres like that of 1 July 1916 on the Somme had convinced them that Britain needed a new way forward in warfare. There must be an easier and cheaper – in terms of lives lost – method of destroying a modern, industrialized enemy. A state like Germany or Russia, with an army numbered in millions, could suffer enormous casualties on the battlefield before suffering defeat. If, however, damage was inflicted on the industrial heartland so that the capacity to wage war was reduced, victory could be achieved without the dreadful blood-letting that had occurred during the First World War.

Thus, the prime objective of the Royal Air Force in the interwar period was to develop a Bomber Command that could attack accurately the German industrial capacity, communications and vital war factories, reducing both military casualties on the battlefield and civilian casualties from the Royal Navy's economic blockade. As a result, there developed a belief that the airmen could deliver solutions to wars, that they could deliver victories, without paying the terrible price that was inherent in head-on confrontations on the battlefield between armies.

Even in 1917 and 1918, bombing of cities by heavy bombers had seemed an easy option. With anti-aircraft defences minimal, even low-technology bombers, slow and with no capacity to defend themselves, seemed destined to dominate the war of the future. The doctrine developed that the bomber would always get through. This was because the fighter plane was the poor relation in the interwar period, its job to protect its own bombers. During the 1930s, however, the tremendous increase in aircraft speed offered a means of fighters combating the threat from the bomber.

The faith in the supremacy of the bomber persuaded politicians to believe that the technology of precision bombing could win a war almost independently of the use of ground troops. This was a dream based on inadequate intelligence work. No bomber force existed in the 1930s – the truth is that none exists now – that had this level of technological expertise. In fact, the Germans did not even share the dream, developing the *Luftwaffe* for army support rather than independent campaigning. The fear that Britain had in 1939 of a massed German bombing raid on London, killing hundreds of thousands in a matter of a week, was merely the reverse side of their own bomber dream and had more to do with H. G. Wells and *The Shape of Things to Come*.

At the start of the war in 1939 the RAF saw its role as conducting daytime, precision raids on naval and military targets, with civilian casualties being kept to a minimum. This, however, was the 'phoney war'. Technological developments in anti-aircraft defences made the low-tech bomber totally vulnerable to hi-tech fighters like the Me109. Losses in Bomber Command were so severe that Britain was forced into night-time bombing to reduce the casualty rate. And so the 'bomber dream' was tarnished. As Martin Middlebrook relates:

*In those early raids they quickly and painfully found that in broad daylight German fighters made mincemeat of the bombers. First of all, even the relatively primitive German radar detected the bombers well offshore. Up went the Messerschmitt 109s, and the RAF suffered terrible casualties. In one of the most serious raids, on 18 December 1939, they lost twelve out of twenty-four Wellingtons dispatched against the German fleet when they hadn't even needed to fly over Germany. Also, as a secondary consideration, not one of the bombs that all those bombers had dropped caused significant damage to the German fleet. Barnes Wallis, the great scientist who invented the dam-busting bomb whom I interviewed some years ago, said he'd found it fantastic that in all the years before the war the RAF had done no scientific research at all on the effect of high explosives on large structures. They did all that by trial and error under the pressure of war itself.*

For eighteen months Britain continued to send her bombers into Germany, navigating by dead reckoning and dropping their bombs by the same rough and ready method. Frank Metcalfe, a bomber pilot with the RAF in those early days, describes how difficult bombing targets at night could be:

*It was 5 November 1940 and we were tasked to bomb a railway marshalling yard at Hamm in the Ruhr, an enormous place where*

◁ In the early days of the war British Whitley bombers were used mainly for dropping anti-war leaflets on Germany. Slow and unable to defend themselves they were part of the lie that comprised the Bomber Dream.

_they were collecting tanks and things like that. We got off the ground. It was as black as the inside of a cow; it was raining, snowing, hailing, absolutely dreadful. I had great difficulty keeping the aeroplane going, and we set off for the Ruhr, which was about two hours away. Eventually, an aircraft battery opened up on me, and I went and dropped my bombs on it and a lot more joined in and we got well and truly plastered, so I set off home. But I had no idea where we were, and my navigator hadn't a clue; we hadn't seen anything since we left Britain. The wind was nearly ninety miles an hour, blowing us further away, so by the time we'd flown two hours we were 180 miles further on than we ought to have been and had to come back against that headwind. To cut a long story short, we landed in the North Sea – I haven't a clue where – out of fuel. I expect we'd lost a bit with the ack-ack fire. We ditched. My gunner was killed. My navigator got me into a dinghy, and I was pretty well knocked out. We were picked up heaven knows how long later by HMS Viga, a British destroyer, who picked us out of a minefield, and as she went out blew her stern off. Not the happiest day of my life, you understand, but that was not untypical._

Evidence began to accumulate that the bombs were not hitting their targets, and the decision was made to investigate the effectiveness of bombing sorties. The results, produced by civil servant D. M. Butt, shattered the dream of the bomber. As Martin Middlebrook relates:

_The crews were coming back, and on their return they would be interviewed by one of the airfield intelligence officers, who would ask: 'Did you find the target?' And the crew would probably say: 'Yes, pretty sure we found the target.' The tail gunner would say: 'I saw the bombs go down, and we saw big explosions and then there was a fire. We're pretty sure we hit the right target.' And that was it, the intelligence officers had heard what they wanted to hear, that the targets were being hit. All the reports on one station were then correlated and forwarded to the group headquarters, where intelligence officers then correlated all the reports from the stations in their group, and sent them to Bomber Command. Bomber Command intelligence officers correlated all the reports and produced an overall report for the night's operations, pretty optimistic, and handed it on to the Air Ministry, who in turn gave it to their public relations department, who issued it to the press and the radio. So you heard on the radio, as I heard as a boy, that last night our bombers attacked targets in Germany. Two bombers were lost, but many targets were hit, etc., and it all seemed to be going very well. Casualties were not severe, the German night fighter force hardly existed at this time,_

_and it wasn't until later, well into 1941, after the campaign had been going for fifteen months, that doubts began to creep in, and the doubts came back through neutrals: the Americans were neutral, so were the Swedes and the Swiss, and friendly people in Germany, they were all reporting that the bombing damage was nothing like as effective as the RAF made out._

_Something was happening technically at that time which allowed the truth to be established. Among the various technical devices being made available for Bomber Command was something called the bombing camera. It was housed in the bomb-bay of a bomber. The pilot was ordered to fly straight and level after he'd dropped his bomb-load for ten or twelve seconds while the camera turned over and exposed a number of plates. Eventually, one of those plates would show his bomb bursting on the ground. The War Cabinet was the body that started to say, 'Is Bomber Command doing as well as it's saying it's doing?', and it appointed a Mr Butt, a member of the War Cabinet secretariat, and the RAF was ordered to make available to him all the bombing photographs that had been taken during the last five or six months, and he did the famous Butt bombing survey._

_These are the results of the Butt report: he examined 600 photographs in which the crews had claimed to have bombed the target, during the moon period in France and Germany. He found that only one in four of those was within five miles of the target; in non-moon periods only one in fifteen was within five miles of the target, and in Germany the figure was only one in twenty within five miles of the target. In the Ruhr area, where most of German industry was, because of the haze there were even fewer within so many miles of the target._

_It came as a very bitter shock to Winston Churchill and the politicians to perceive that, despite this extraordinary vision of the potential of air power which the air marshals had sold, the Germans were barely aware of what target the RAF had intended to attack because so few of their bombers had got anywhere near it. They'd ended up dropping bombs all over Germany._

Faced with the inability to strike its specific military targets, Britain had to choose between accepting that she could not defeat Germany because she could inflict no damage whatsoever on the German war effort, or to resort to a form of warfare – previously anathema to British politicians – of concentrated, if indiscriminate, destruction of Germany's basic war material – her people. The destruction of civilian morale had, in the First World War, been carried out by the Royal Navy's blockade. Statistics for civilian casualties from starvation and disease resulting from the blockade were not easily available. However, it is against this form of economic/social warfare that Bomber Command's new bombing campaign must be seen, as Max Hastings shows:

The pursuit of the Bomber Dream was eventually to lead to civilian bombings and the destruction of German cities such as Dresden.

▷ Air Chief Marshal Sir Arthur 'Bomber' Harris. He took the logic of area bombing to its extreme and won few friends for a policy that was little more than terror bombing.

*Whatever view one takes about the morality of bombing later in the war, almost every historian of the Second World War has concluded that in 1940 and 1941 it was absolutely understandable that Britain resorted to bombing Germany. The only means that Britain possessed, having lost her army and with the fleet vulnerable to German air power, to carry the war to Germany was by bombing. If we didn't bomb Germany, then we had very little choice but to admit we never had any hope of winning.*

Churchill might have preferred to charge with the 21st Lancers, as at Omdurman, to deliver the *coup de grâce* to Hitler's black flag legions. Montgomery might have preferred to out-think, out-plan and out-manoeuvre Rommel or Rundstedt in some great war game, Cunningham to outfight the German fleet in a new Jutland, or Douglas Bader to cleanse the skies of bandits with avenging wings of Spitfires and Hurricanes. Instead, 'Bomber' Harris chose to kill Germans, in their houses or in their factories, at work or at rest, because he, no romantic, would fight the war he could fight. And so began area bombing, as Max Hastings describes:

*Bomber Command would launch a campaign of so-called area bombing designed to attack whole industrial areas of Germany and, to use the extraordinary phrase they used in the paperwork of that time, 'to dehouse' a sufficient number of German industrial workers, to demoralize the population to the point where they were no longer capable of producing armaments. If they hit factories as a by-product, that was fine; if they killed civilians along the way, then that was the way it was. But the officially stated target was to drive from their homes and to render presumably demoralized and miserable and hopeless a sufficient proportion of the German industrial*

*civilian population to bring Germany to its knees. If that sounds a fantastic idea to us now, it appeared the only realistic policy for the RAF in the spring of 1942, given its resources. The policy documents of the period state that to dehouse the German industrial population was what the RAF was now to make its principal objective of war.*

The Bomber Dream was now a nightmare. What had begun as a means by which technology could save lives was now on the road to Dresden, Hiroshima and Nagasaki.

# AGENT ORANGE
⚜

Military technology is often designed to reduce the disadvantages of a particular environment. Aerial observation, through balloon or reconnaissance aircraft, was an enormous step forward, and yet, in heavily forested or deeply overgrown jungle areas, even this advantage had its limitations. Concealment, and with it the consequent military advantage of surprise, often gave the weaker or more primitive force a means of reducing a technological shortfall on their part. Night, smoke, mist, foliage and an assortment of meteorological conditions come free of charge to the low-tech armies of the world. In Vietnam during the 1960s, the Americans faced all the problems of fighting a low-tech enemy in an environment that suited it and lessened the advantages normally possessed by the more advanced Western power.

By 1966 the Americans conceived of a technology to help their troops in the Vietnam jungle: weedkiller. Used in domestic gardens, it was mass-produced and became known as Agent Orange. Huge quantities were dropped to destroy the jungles of Vietnam, to expose enemy troops and to make conventional bombing of targets easier. Jack McManus took part in Operation Ranch Hand, which was the codename given to America's herbicidal warfare. McManus helped load Agent Orange into the C–123K aircraft that were used for the spraying of larger areas. He had to wade into the herbicide to release the valve that allowed the liquid to be dispersed. Here, Jack McManus explains the advantages of using Agent Orange:

> *We used defoliants to spray jungles and crops to destroy hiding-places for the enemy and to destroy crops that the enemy was using for subsistence. The logic of that was that the environment was a heavily jungled area, and the jungle gave the enemy protection and hiding-places to ambush*

The US troops on the ground in Vietnam were to become victims of an unexpected form of 'friendly fire' – Agent Orange.

▷ Admiral Elmo Zumwald, commander of the American Navy during the Vietnam War. Admiral Zumwald authorized the use of Agent Orange in the Mekong Delta. His son, who was serving with the US forces there, contracted cancer and died as a result.
◁ American bombers dropping herbicides on Vietnam forests. The effects of Agent Orange on both American troops and Vietnamese civilians was deadly and long lasting.

*American troops. Our purpose of defoliating was to take away that tactical advantage they had of being able to hide, then close in and kill our troops.*

There is no doubting the military advantages that initially flowed from Operation Ranch Hand. However, unknown to McManus, and indeed to most of the American military services, production of the herbicide produced carcinogenic dioxins. The fact that Agent Orange would harm both friendly and enemy soldiers who encountered it was conveniently overlooked. When the American military discovered that laboratory animals had developed cancer in tests when exposed to Agent Orange, they stopped its use in Vietnam in the late 1960s. But it was already far too late. Agent Orange had become a form of 'friendly fire'.

Jack McManus found that as a result of working with Agent Orange his health was virtually destroyed. He was diagnosed as having the highest dioxin levels of anyone in the United States. As he said:

*Quite frankly, the first time I was informed what the level of the dioxin in my body was it didn't have any significance to me because I didn't know what it was being measured against. They just sent a letter and said this is the amount you have, and it didn't have any real significance. When one of the Ranch Hand medical studies was published, it talked about the levels of dioxin in the Ranch Hand group and in a control group. A high of 1,300 and 1,100 were the high numbers, the two highest individuals, going down to very minuscule numbers on the control group, in those people who hadn't been exposed.*

Orders were also given to spray the perimeters of military compounds. Larry Lay worked on one such compound. Asked what Agent Orange was like, Larry replied:

*You ever put talcum powder on? It may have been wet when they dumped it out of the back of the plane, but once it got into the atmosphere, once it settled to the ground, it was just like an orange powder, like talcum powder. And it got over everything. And you breathed it, tasted it, ate it, and got a bad taste. We didn't really know that it was Agent Orange at the time, but in a matter of a few hours all the foliage surrounding the compound was brown and dead.*

Since he returned from Vietnam, Larry Lay's life has been a nightmare. His daughter was born with spina bifida. As well as being seldom free from illness himself, the three children he fathered have all been affected by Agent Orange. However, Larry's situation has become desperate as the government has refused to acknowledge that his problems stem from his exposure to the herbicide.

*It must have affected my genes, especially with Stacy having spina bifida. My second child is two years younger than Stacy, and he's got about thirty of these non-malignant tumours and needs about eight more cut out of him. The government won't look at him either. My third child is going stone deaf from nerve damage. So I don't know how Agent Orange couldn't have affected me, to have three out of four children with some kind of genetic defect. I've got emphysema, half a lung, crippling arthritis, artificial knee joints, a heart murmur and a bad heart valve. They gave my daughter a 100 per cent service connection to Agent Orange but won't give me anything. I don't understand how the government can say that she's got it and pay her. If I gave it to her, they ought to pay me too, and that's the way some other vets feel. And they're not admitting to a lot of the cancers some of the guys have got.*

Admiral Elmo Zumwald commanded the US Navy during the Vietnam conflict. He authorized the use of Agent Orange to defoliate the jungle on the river banks his craft were patrolling in the Mekong Delta.

*The Pentagon had assured all the commanders that it was non-carcinogenic to humans, no ill effects. The Army had been using it for three years and had noted some skin problems, but they thought of a minor nature. And we now know that the chemical companies knew themselves of the carcinogenic nature, but none of the military at that time did. And we therefore thought that it was a marvellous solution to a very serious problem.*

Admiral Zumwald's son, who served on the 'Swift Boats' in the Mekong Delta under his father's command, died of cancer in the 1980s. The admiral blames Agent Orange – which he ordered to be sprayed – for his son's death.

*In 1984 Elmo went in for a routine biopsy to see whether his non-Hodgkin's was still dormant and instead found that, in addition to non-Hodgkin's lymphoma, he had Hodgkin's disease, one of what the doctors tell us is a very, very scanty number of cases of people who have had both at the same time. That made his battle even more difficult. He continued to fight courageously to look into every form of treatment. In 1986, three years after his initial diagnosis, it became clear that the chemotherapy and radiation were not going to kill the non-Hodgkin's lymphoma. He then became terminal.*

A study was commissioned by the American Air Force into the effects of herbicides, but for years those suffering from the effects of the herbicide could gain no compensation for their medical conditions. As Senator Thomas Daschle relates:

*I would say in a word: intransigence. The government was extremely disconnected, there was no real desire to be responsive, they had heard all these things before, they thought it was a myth, they thought that veterans were making this up, they thought that if there was a health problem that it couldn't possibly be related. The drug companies, the chemical companies were a very aggressive force in opposition.*

Vital information was suppressed to avoid paying the affected veterans and their families the compensation they were entitled to, as Larry Lay relates:

*There was clear evidence found by the researchers, found by people within the burrows of the Pentagon that showed without any question there is a definite link between birth defects and exposure to Agent Orange. Yet that information was suppressed, that information was held from us in spite of every effort that we made to try to have it released.*

While researching the effects of Agent Orange, Admiral Zumwald 'learned, first, that the studies done by chemical corporations of the human effects of dioxin were fraudulent, in my judgement. They had been manipulated.' The final report by the Air Force stated that there was no link between Agent Orange and birth defects. However, the original draft had told a very different story. Words had been altered. Where it had been stated that the results of the study were of great concern, the words 'very reassuring' had been introduced. Finally, in the early 1990s, the American government accepted thirteen diseases associated with exposure to Agent Orange. The thirteen included the cancers that killed Admiral Zumwald's son. Admiral Zumwald explains the cover-up that took place:

*During the course of my nine months of work for the Secretary of Veterans' Affairs, one of the things that I discovered was that the studies done by chemical corporations had been manipulated in such a way as to give negative results. For example, in one specific study, workers who had been exposed to Agent Orange were, some of them, placed in the so-called control group so that there were more elevated cancers in the control group. This helped to mask the elevation of the rest of the workers in the group that was being studied. In my report I said that if one disregarded the fraudulently done studies, which had always been used to question the accuracy of the very good Swedish scientific studies, and instead relied on the non-manipulated studies, I believed there were some twenty-eight health effects that were the result of exposure to Agent Orange. Incidentally, we now have thirteen such health effects that are compensated, and if I live we'll get the additional fifteen.*

Arnold Schecter, Professor of Environmental Science at the University of Texas, sums up the effects of Agent Orange both on the Americans who used it as an ecological weapon and on the Vietnamese, who suffered in silence from both an ally and an enemy who could not resist the Siren call of the latest military technology:

*There were approximately three million Americans serving in Vietnam and perhaps several hundred thousand Vietnamese in the area sprayed by Agent Orange. We know that some veterans and some Vietnamese had Agent Orange sprayed on them, so they could have been breathing it in, they may have got it on their skin and absorbed it, or they may have eaten foods that were contaminated. The health effects on the Vietnamese have been described primarily as being an increase in cancer, especially liver cancer, and malformed children.*

# REFERENCES

21      J. S.A. Hayward, *Stalingrad: An Examination of Hitler's Decision to Airlift.*

39      J.D. Potter *Fiasco* (p.111).

39–40  J.D. Potter, *Fiasco* (p.120).

41      J.D. Potter, *Fiasco* (p.201).

43      H. Herwig, 'The Dynamics of Necessity' in A. Millett etc, *Military Effectiveness* Vol 1 (p.88).

45      Barbara Tuchman, *August 1914* (p.171).

46      Holger Herwig, 'The Dynamics of Necessity' in A. Millett etc, *Military Effectiveness* Vol 1 (p.93).

75      V. Nebrida, 'The Balangiga Massacre', PHGLA.

77      Quoted in Geoffrey Regan, *Guinness Book of Military Blunders* (p.69).

77      Quoted in Geoffrey Regan, *Someone had Blundered* (p.270).

77–8    L. Allen, *Singapore 1941–2* (p.53).

80      H.P. Willmott, *Empires in the Balance* (p.105).

83      L. Allen, *Singapore 1941–2* (pp.197–8).

84      L. Allen, *Singapore 1941–2* (p.200).

102     Norman Dixon, *On the Psychology of Military Incompetence* (p.108).

102     Norman Dixon, *On the Psychology of Military Incompetence* (p.166).

103     Norman Dixon, *On the Psychology of Military Incompetence* (p.240).

124     Quoted in Mark Adkins, *Urgent Fury* (p.322).

129–30  Quoted in Mark Adkins, *Urgent Fury* (p.160-1).

131     Quoted in Mark Adkins, *Urgent Fury* (p.208).

131     Quoted in Mark Adkins, *Urgent Fury* (p.355).

132     Quoted in Mark Adkins, *Urgent Fury* (p.291).

132     Mark Adkins, *Urgent Fury* (p.340).

141     Quoted in Geoffrey Regan, *Saladin and the Fall of Jerusalem* (p.111).

# FURTHER READING

Adkins, Mark, *Urgent Fury*, London, 1989.

Allen, L., *Singapore 1941–2*, London, 1977.

Barker, A.J., *Townshend of Kut*, London, 1967.

Barnett, Corelli, *The Desert Generals*, London, 1960.

Cervi, E., *The Hollow Legions*, London, 1972.

Charmley, John, *Churchill's Grand Alliance*, London, 1996.

Clark, A., *The Donkeys*, London, 1961.

Divine, David, *The Blunt Sword*, London, 1964.

Dixon, Norman, *On the Psychology of Military Incompetence*, London, 1976.

Ellis, J., *The Sharp End of War*, London, 1980.

Ellis, J., *Brute Force*, London, 1990.

Elphick, Peter, *The Pregnable Fortress*, London, 1995.

Farwell, Byron, *The Great Boer War*, 1977.

Ferguson, Niall, *The Pity of War*, London, 1998.

Hamilton, Nigel, *Monty: The Making of a General*, London, 1981.

Hamilton, Nigel, *The Master of the Battlefield*, London, 1983.

Hamilton, Nigel, *The Field Marshal*, London, 1985.

Hastings, Max & Jenkins S., *The Battle for the Falklands*, London, 1983.

Hastings, Max, *Bomber Command*, London, 1979.

Holmes, Richard, *Firing Line*, London, 1987.

Hough, Richard, *Admirals in Collision*, London, 1959.

Knight, Ian, *The Zulus*, London, 1989.

Knight, Ian, *Brave Men's Blood: The Epic of the Zulu War*, London, 1990.

Knight, Ian, *Zulu: Isandhlwana and Rorke's Drift*, London, 1992.

L'Etang, Hugh, *The Pathology of Leadership*, London, 1969.

L'Etang, Hugh, *Fit to Lead*, London, 1980.

Lyons, M.C. and Jackson D.E.P., *Saladin: The Politics of the Holy War*, Cambridge, 1982.

Mack Smith, Denis, *Mussolini*, London, 1982.

Macrory, Patrick, *Signal Catastrophe*, London, 1966.

Middlebrook, Martin, *The First Day of the Somme*, London, 1971.

Middlebrook, Martin, *Arnhem*, London, 1994.

Morris, Donald, *The Washing of the Spears*, London, 1966.

Nicolle, David, *Hattin 1187*, London, 1993.

Potter, J.D., *Fiasco*, London, 1970.

Powell, Geoffrey, *Buller. A Scapegoat?* London, 1997.

Regan, Geoffrey, *Someone Had Blundered*, London, 1987.

Regan, Geoffrey, *Saladin and the Fall of Jerusalem*, London, 1987.

Regan, Geoffrey, *The Guinness Book of Military Blunders*, London, 1991.

Regan, Geoffrey, *The Guinness Book of Naval Blunders*, London, 1992.

Regan, Geoffrey, *The Guinness Book of More Military Blunders*, London, 1992.

Regan, Geoffrey, *Snafu*, New York, 1993.

Regan, Geoffrey, *Backfire*, London, 1995.

Regan, Geoffrey, *The Guinness Book of Air Force Blunders*, London, 1996.

Regan, Geoffrey, *Lionhearts*, London, 1998.

Riley-Smith, Jonathan, *The Feudal Nobility and the Kingdom of Jerusalem*, Conn., 1973.

Ryan, Cornelius, *A Bridge Too Far*, London, 1974.

Strachan, Hew, *European Armies and the Conduct of War*, London, 1983.

Symons, J., *Buller's Campaigns*, London, 1974.

Thompson, Julian, *No Picnic*, London, 1985.

Tuchman, Barbara, *August 1914*, London, 1962.

Turner, E.S., *Gallant Gentlemen, a Portrait of the British Officer*, London, 1956.

Willmott, H.P., *Empires in the Balance*, London, 1982.

# INDEX

# PICTURE CREDITS

While every effort has been made to trace copyright holders for photographs and illustrations featured in this book, the publishers will be glad to make proper acknowledgements in future editions in the event that any regrettable omissions have occurred at the time of going to press.

**Associated Press:** 30*top*, 159.
**Bridgeman Art Library:** 14/5 (Spion Kop, 1900 [chromolitho by Neuman], Africana Museum, Johannesburg, South Africa), 106 (Field Marshal Montgomery by John Worsley [b. 1919], Imperial War Museum, London, UK).
**British Museum:** 142.
**Corbis:** 21 (Bettmann), 24 (Museum of Flight), 30*bottom* (AFP), 40 (Museum of Flight), 77 (Bettmann), 105, 108 (Bettmann), 121 (Bettmann), 130, 134 (Hulton-Deutsch Collection), 174/5 (Bettmann), 176 (Hulton-Deutsch Collection), 178/9 (Bettman).
**David Nicolle:** 143.
**E.T. Archive:** 20, 22 (Imperial War Museum), 70/1 (National Army Museum), 110/1 (Parachute Regiment), 114, 138 (Uffizi Gallery).
**Hulton Getty:** 16, 28*top*, 33, 36, 37, 38, 79, 81, 84*bottom*, 90/1, 136, 168.
**Imperial War Museum:** 35, 48, 95, 101, 145, 146, 148.
**Mary Evans Picture Library:** 11(La France de Bordeaux), 18 (Vanity Fair), 26 (Black & White), 27 (Le Petit Journal), 45 (Illustrated London News), 46 (Die Grosse Zeit), 47 (Die Grosse Zeit), 61 (Tenniel), 66, 68 (The Graphic), 74 (Le Petit Parisien), 75 (Journal des Voyages), 118, 119 (Li Hua), 123 Illustrazione del Popolo), 139 (John Fulleylove), 151 (La Baionnette), 166 (La Baionnette), 167 (The Golden Horseshoe).
**PA News:** 31, 97, 99, 100, 172, 181.
**Popperfoto:** 23, 28*bottom*, 39, 43, 44, 52, 55, 56, 58/9, 65, 82, 84*top*, 86, 87, 88, 92, 107, 117, 120, 125, 129, 135, 153, 156, 158, 162/3, 164, 180.
**Punch Limited:** 115.
**Commander Mark Cheyne:** 63.
**Telegraph Colour Library:** 127, 128, 154/5.

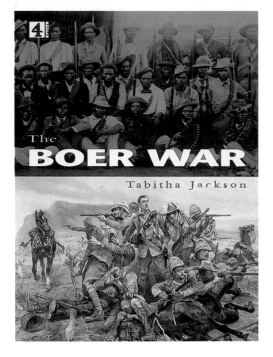

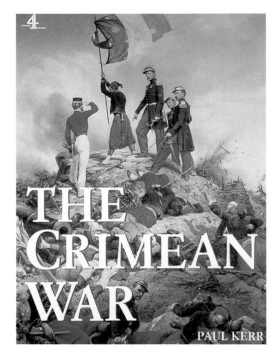

# THE BOER WAR

Tabitha Jackson
0 7522 1702 X
Hardback, 192 pages, £18.99

# THE CRIMEAN WAR

Paul Kerr
0 7522 1184 6
Paperback, 192 pages, £12.99

When Britain went to war with the Boers in October 1899, everyone was confident that it would be an easy victory and 'our boys will be home by Christmas.' But the Anglo-Boer War was neither glorious nor swift. It not only irreparably damaged the British Empire but led to the establishment of apartheid in South Africa.

The war eventually lasted nearly three years. During these years ordinary soldiers and civilians suffered appalling atrocities and were the victims of disease, siege and terror as the whole country was drawn into the conflict. When the Boers finally surrendered, the English signed a pact betraying the black South Africans, who had fought alongside them, as a concession to their defeated enemies.

This is a portrait of a war through the eyes of ordinary soldiers and civilians, bringing it to life through powerful and emotive testimonies. It includes previously unpublished letters and diaries written by British, Canadian and Australian soldiers and, for the first time, accounts by black South Africans about their experiences during the war.

*The Boer War* is illustrated throughout with archive photographs – many previously unseen – extracts from letters and diaries, and maps showing the extent of the war.

The Crimean War (1853–56) raged for three years between Russian on one side and Turkey, France, Britain and later Sardinia, on the other. It transformed the balance of power and the political complexion of a continent – indeed it was the crucible in which modern Europe was formed.

In many ways a war of innovation, it was the first to use railways, steamships, and the telegraph. Significantly for posterity, it was also the first war to be reported by a professional correspondent, *The Times*' William Howard Russell, the first to be photographed, and the first to which professional war artists were assigned.

*The Crimean War* uniquely combines an extraordinary visual history of this conflict with oral accounts, revealed for the first time in a remarkable number of eye-witness statements. These appear in the form of the letters and diaries of soldiers and sailors, doctors and nurses, artists and reporters, local inhabitants and tourists, and are drawn from all sides of the conflict.

This intimate and spectacularly illustrated history, reveals the Crimean War as it has never before been seen.

BOOKS

# A selected list of books available from Channel 4 Books.

The prices shown below are correct at time of going to press. However, Channel 4 Books reserve the right to show new retail prices on covers which may differ from those previously advertised.

| | | |
|---|---|---|
| The Boer War | Tabitha Jackson | £18.99 |
| The Crimean War | Paul Kerr | £12.99 |
| Shell Shock | Wendy Holden | £14.99 |
| Station X | Michael Smith | £14.99 |
| Classic Aircraft | Brian Johnson | £18.99 |
| Classic British Cars | Brian Johnson and Jeff Daniels | £18.99 |

All these titles can be ordered from your local bookshop or simply by ringing our 24-hour hotline on 01624 844444, email **bookshop@enterprise.net**, fax 01624 837033 or fill in this form and post it to B.S.B.P. Limited, PO Box 29, Douglas, Isle of Man IM99 1BQ. Please make all cheques payable to Channel 4 Books or complete your credit/debit card details.

Name . . . . . . . . . . . . . . . . . . . . . . . . . . . . . . . . . . . . . . . .

Address . . . . . . . . . . . . . . . . . . . . . . . . . . . . . . . . . . . . . .

. . . . . . . . . . . . . . . . . . . . . . . . . . . . . . . . . . . . . . . . . . . .

. . . . . . . . . . . . . . . . . . . Postcode . . . . . . . . . . . . . . . . .

Card Number:

☐☐☐☐ ☐☐☐☐ ☐☐☐☐ ☐☐☐☐

Card Name (please tick one):

Visa ☐ American Express ☐ Mastercard ☐ Switch ☐

Expiry date . . . . . / . . . . .     Issue number (Switch) . . . . . . .

Signature . . . . . . . . . . . . . . . . . . . . . . . . . . . . . . . . . . . . .

POSTAGE AND PACKING FREE FOR ALL ADDRESSES IN THE UK

www.panmacmillan.com          www.channel4.com